Out of Obscurity into the Light

An Account of Missionary Minister,

Gerrit Kuijt, Pioneer Among the Papuans

by

W. B. Kranendonk & A.F. van Toor

Translation and adaption from the original
Dutch Al 't heidendom zijn lof getuigen
under the guidance
of

Miep Kuijt-Bos

Out of Obscurity into the Light
An Account of Missionary Minister, Gerrit Kuijt, Pioneer among the Papuans

ISBN 978-1-628-13-012-6

Published in association with the literacy agency of
Old Paths Gospel Press
PO Box 318
Choteau, MT 59422
Email: **providence-books@3rivers.net**

Original Book Al 't heidendom zijn lof getuigen
W.B. Kranendonk and A.F. van Toor Published
2003 Den Hertog B.V. Houten
ISBN 90 331 1694 4

Editor: Elizabeth Collins Oman
Design & Layout: John Breeze

Printed and bound in the United States of America

Dedication

I dedicate this book to my five children, Klazina, Wim, Gert, Wilhelmina and Lia.

You were as much a part of the work in "Irian Jaya" as your parents were. The Papuan children were your playmates. You learned their languages and explored their world.

However, you paid a price. From the time you were six years old, you went to boarding school and came home only twice a year. Even when you were home during school holidays, we, your parents, still had to go on with the daily needs of the work.

Yet, wherever you were, you were always in our thoughts, prayers and in our hearts.

I want to thank each one of you for your support and for the love you had for us your parents and for the love you still have for me today.

Dad loved and I love each one of you dearly.

May the Lord bless each one of you richly.

Mom

Miep Kuijt-Bos

Foreword

by Miep Kuijt-Bos

It is my wish that this edition of the original book:*Al 't Heidendom Zijn Lof Getuigen* written by W. B. Kranendonk and A. F. Van Toor will be to God's honour and glory and for the extension of His Kingdom. This edition is the same story as in the original book but with some modifications.

It is my hope that you, the reader, will be inspired by this story and will have that same desire and a Godly call to bring the Good Message to all. As it says in Isaiah, "Blessed are the feet that bring good tidings over the mountains."

Please realize that the environment influenced how the people lived and dressed at that time. There were no materials to make anything besides what they were wearing. To this day it amazes me that they even discovered from what and how to make twine. They did what they could with the very little available to them. We found them to be a people with high moral standards and, even though this might sound strange to you given their lack of clothing, a people with modesty. The Lord gave us a great love for these people and they are still loved today by my family and me.

Over the years the Lord blessed the work abundantly. People were reached with the Good News, that mankind can be saved by believing in God and in His Son Jesus Christ, who came into this world to save sinners. The Lord who called us also gave us the strength to do His will.

It was beautiful to see how people changed after receiving Christ—the joy radiating from their faces, free from the evil spirits. Now some of them are teachers, pastors, medical helpers and some have earned a university degree. It is hard to believe how we found them in Pass Valley in 1963 and again in later years in other valleys and where they are now, by the Grace of God.

To Him is all the Power, Glory and Honor!

W. Kuijt-Bos
Chilliwack, BC Canada
August 2013

Foreword

by the Original Authors

The Papuan people have become so dear to my heart. Oh, how I wish I would be able to keep them from the powers of unbelief and satanic forces. My desire is to tell them of the Lord's work and how He poured out His dear Spirit. I also would like to tell them of the Redeemer of the world.

Thus Gerrit Kuijt expressed his life-long desire to proclaim the Word of God. As a missionary minister, but also as an individual, he felt an urge to proclaim the name of the Savior in places where it had never been mentioned before. He had the same desire as Paul to go there "where Christ was not named." (Rom. 15:20) Rev. Kuijt lived among the people of Papua and had a strong bond of love with them.

This book is not intended to be a historical account of the mission work of the Netherlands Reformed Congregations in New Guinea. Nor is it is an anthropological study or a chronological, detailed account of the acts of one individual. Rather, this story outlines the life of Rev. Gerrit Kuijt, while showing how God's ruling hand builds His Church in a wonderful way, regardless of the sin-stained work of man.

Also this mission work was done by people: all were individuals with good intentions, yet each had their own (sometimes difficult) character. At times, tempers would flare and there would be fierce reactions. At the same time, there was a touching sympathy and a cordial commendation of each other to the throne of grace.

On the Mission Day of the Reformed Congregations in June 2002, Rev. Meeuwse warned against distorting or elevating our human efforts and against falsifying history. He remarked, "In God's Word we do not read of perfect missionaries. Even Paul and Barnabas quarreled about a man of whom Paul later wrote that he was profitable to him for the ministry. How is that possible? God's Word is honest and does not glorify man when it describes how the Gospel is spread throughout the world. For man, there is a road full of affliction and trials, but with God's faithful care and His steadfast providence, His Word is spread. Mission work is God's work. It would not be edifying to boast of man's work; this would lead to discouragement and grief. In contrast, glorifying God's work brings humbleness, wonder, and a quiet trust. It is this that keeps us from focusing on all kinds of facts and innumerable things that man has done. Although it is good to report honestly, we want to focus especially on what God has done."

Thus, on this mission day, Rev. Meeuwse did not treat his audience to a mere accounting of the facts. He said, "Do you know what your attitude will be then? You will think, 'Was my name mentioned? After all, I have worked there, too. I have been in Irian Jaya. Will my family members be mentioned honorably and by name? Are we going to be honored?' Is this how we should listen? Or should we rather have a longing in our hearts to hear something of our King? Should we be longing to hear something of God's sovereign work of grace and the formation of His bridal Church of Jews and Gentiles? Should we be longing to hear how it was God's good pleasure to use the mission work of the Reformed Congregations, which is just a small instrument in His hands? What really matters is to remember the works of God and to praise Him."

A word of thanks is needed for those who helped create this book. Gert Hogendoorn, Dr. Chr. Fahner, Rev. C.G. Vreugdenhil, and C. Janse have contributed much (historical) information, the one in the form of a Masters' thesis, and the others with different publications on the mission work in Irian Jaya. The mission board trusted us greatly by giving us access to their archives. Finally, the widow of Rev. Kuijt, Mrs. M. Kuijt-Bos, spent much time giving us information and verifying the information others provided. Without all this help and support—also from those whose names have not been mentioned here—this book would not have been published.

It is our sincere hope that while reading this piece of human history, the reader may recognize God's dealings. God's ways are at times mysterious ways, yet they will certainly lead to the glory of His great Name—in Holland, North America, and Papua, in the hearts of people from different races, before His throne... and here on Earth.

Nunspeet/Apeldoorn, October 2002   W.B. Kranendonk/ A.F. van Toor

Table of Contents

Chapter 1

What's Impossible for Man . . .

Doctor Hueting rushes through the streets of Katwijk. The family doctor is on his way to the City Hall on the outskirts of the village. As he hurries up the stairs of the building, he takes little notice of the two stone lions on either side of the stairs that guard the entrance. At the counter he is greeted as a familiar visitor. "Good morning, Doctor. Did you have another busy night?"

"No, it was not too bad. I was at Gerrit Kuijt's residence. Klasina, Gerrit's wife, had a healthy baby boy at 8:30 pm; he is to be named Gerrit after his father."

The registrar completes the birth certificate dated May 22, 1933 and asks two clerks, Van Neerbos and Gerretsen to sign as witnesses. Gerrit Kuijt Jr. is now an official resident of Katwijk.

The Katwijk City Hall, officially opened on
September 21, 1932, by Princess Juliana

It was not unusual to see Doctor Hueting give notice about the birth of a child at the town hall. This happened when the father was absent and the mother was recovering from the birth; the family doctor was expected to notify the authorities. In Katwijk, it was very common for children to be born while their fathers were away at sea. "Absent due to occupation," was recorded in the registry. The men of Katwijk earned their livelihood as fishermen and could be away for weeks at a time on the North Sea. They often fished as far away as the Orkney Islands above Scotland.

Gerrit Kuijt's occupation as a merchant marine required that he travel the world leaving his family for half a year or more at a time. His work provided a good income, resulting in Gerrit owning a large three-story home at Thirteen Secrataris Varkenvisserstraat, a stone's throw away from the sea. Behind the house was a cottage, which was common in Katwijk. During the summer months the house was rented out to vacationers while the family resided in the cottage.

Klasina rests comfortably among the soft cushions of her bed. Her heart is filled with thankfulness for the child received from the Lord. She can honestly say this child was petitioned from the Almighty God. Klasina was thirty-one years old when she married Gerrit, who was five years older.

She had so wanted to have children. Unfortunately, she had had two previous miscarriages. Yes, they owned a large home but it had been missing the pitter-patter of little feet and the joyful laughter of children. This had driven Klasina to seek "Him, with Whom all things are possible that are impossible with man." Earnestly and unceasingly, she pleaded with the Lord to give her a child and if it were a son that he might spend his life in the Lord's service. And the Lord answered her prayers.

While holding the little one in her arms Klasina recalls a conversation with Gerrit. Together they had discussed the possibility of the baby being a boy. The custom in Katwijk is that he should be named Willem after Opa Kuijt. But Gerrit decided to go against this tradition. Not Willem, but Gerrit would be his name. Who knows if there will be more children?

Gerrit is intuitively correct; little Gerrit remains their only child. He is a child of much joy who, at times, will fill their lives with concerns.

Klasina's life had not been without its difficulties. She had very dear parents. Father Van der Plas, more commonly known as Cowper, sold his fish in Leiden. When he returned home at the end of the day it was noticeable from a distance whether he had had a successful day. The more his cap was slanted the better his sales had been. Mother Van der Plas was known as a God-fearing woman. However, the opportunity to speak confidently about His Glory was often taken from her as she suffered from the cruel attacks of Satan. Doubt and strife were her portion in life.

Father Van der Plas with his fish cart

At the same time, Mother Van der Plas was ahead of her time by providing the opportunity for Klasina to take lessons on the lute. Klasina was a good student and wanted to continue her studies to become a nurse. However, this did not happen.

Her mother became ill and from then on the doctor was a regular visitor at the Van der Plas's. As time went by, the doctor became more and more concerned. "Klasina," he finally said, "forget about becoming a nurse. Right now you must take care of your mother." Klasina did not hesitate to take on this responsibility although she realized that from then on, her life would take an entirely different direction. Until her mother's death several years later, Klasina lovingly looked after her.

Opa and Oma Kuijt, parents of Gerrit Sr.

Father and Mother Van der Plas, parents of Klasina

Klasina Van der Plas and Gerrit Kuijt Sr.

It is June 4, 1933. As the preacher climbs the steps of the pulpit of the Nederlands Hervormde Kerk of Katwijk, the chiming of the church bells ceases and the magnificent pipe organ music stops. Klasina sits at the front of the church. Her thoughts drift away to her husband, who is not present for the baptism of his son. "Absent due to occupation." The words of the age-old baptism form are read:

> *Conceived and born in sin; washing away of sins possible through the blood of Jesus Christ; new obedience; a seal of the covenant; righteousness of faith; the command of Jesus: let the children come unto me.*

In Klasina's heart a prayer rises to her God above to help her raise the little one in the fear of the Lord; that He will place His hands of grace upon little Gerrit. Softly, but with determination, she answers "yes" as the water is poured over his head.

Little Gerrit is Klasina's precious treasure. The upbringing of their son rests mostly on her shoulders. She surrounds him with all her love and care, and Gerrit grows up healthy. When the child goes out to play, Klasina first bends her knees in prayer. It can be so dangerous on the streets of Katwijk with all those automobiles!

Opa and Oma Kuijt live in a little house beside the Old Church. Gerrit is frequently found with Opa Kuijt, who is also known as *Ronkel*. Opa loves animals; behind his house he has a variety of livestock, including goats.

Opa Kuijt and Gerrit Jr.

6

When Gerrit is six years old, his mother enrolls him in the Christian Elementary School. Young Gerrit is unaware of the political unrest that threatens the world. The German invasion of Austria and Poland was only news for adults. Yet the sorrows of war would not pass him by. When the Germans invade the Netherlands, the naval fleet has already been evacuated to England in 1939, and Gerrit Sr. is already away at sea. Little Gerrit will see his father again until after the war.

Gerrit as a student in elementary school

Grade 5 of the Christian Elementary School, July 7 1944
Gerrit is the first left in the back row.

In the sixth grade Gerrit is placed in a preparatory class where Mr. Van Rooijen tutors students after regular school hours to prepare them for high school. While he is in school, his friends enjoy playing soccer with the leather ball Gerrit received from his father.

Gerrit has no doubt. about what he wants to do when he grows up. "I am going to become a missionary," he tells his friends. It is not common for a boy to become a missionary but in Gerrit's case it is no surprise. When he and his friends go to play in the sand dunes he takes along his Bible, and before Gerrit is ready to play, he first reads God's Word; and prays, surrounded by his friends.

For mission work, you have to give up something. Gerrit sacrifices his stamp collection, which astounds everyone as he is an avid collector and really values his collection. When his mother asks him what he would like for his birthday—a new bike or a watch—he replies, "Oh mother, do not give me either one. Please give the money to the mission fund."

"Moving?" Gerrit looks at his mother in utter astonishment. "Why? We have a lovely home. Why must we move?"

Mother Klasina explains that the Germans have ordered that a large section of their street must be demolished. The invaders are fortifying their defences along the coastline to prevent a possible invasion by the Allied Forces. Everything must be cleared away so the Germans have an unobstructed field of fire.

Mother gets help from family and friends to pack the house and young Gerrit pitches in like a real man. After all he must take his father's place. Only the necessities are taken along when mother and Gerrit evacuate to Drenthe, a province in Northern Holland, where they will stay until the end of the war. When twelve-year-old Gerrit eventually returns to Katwijk, there are many changes. Homes have been destroyed and not much is left of the Varkenvisserstraat.

In anticipation of Gerrit Sr's. return, the family now lives at 336 Varkenvisserstraat. There is great joy when father finally returns to Holland. It is the end of 1945 when the remaining fleet returns to the harbour in Rotterdam. However, none of the marines are permitted to return to their homes. Instead Klasina and Gerrit Jr. are invited to Rotterdam to visit Gerrit Sr.. After their visit, the ships set sail again, this time transporting troops to and from Indonesia.

A year and a half later his father returns. He has been diagnosed with tuberculosis, contracted from the troops which were being shipped to and from Indonesia. Gerrit is forbidden to visit his father in the hospital. He is too young and could easily be infected by the contagious disease. This falls on deaf ears. "Father's in the hospital and I am not allowed to see him?" Gerrit repeatedly sneaks into his father's room and quietly sits beside his bed.

Young Gerrit is pale, tires easily, and is gradually losing weight. "It must be all the hard work he is putting into his studies," assumes his mother. Gerrit has to write his final exams that year. But then Gerrit loses his appetite, starts to cough and experiences chest pains. His mother becomes alarmed when she notices that he has developed a slight fever and he perspires at night.

The night before Gerrit is diagnosed with tuberculosis, the Lord makes it clear to him that he will become a missionary. He will bring the Word of God to places where it has never been brought before. Far-away peoples will hear of the only Name given under heaven.

There, in the quietness of his bedroom, Gerrit tells his mother of his longing to go to the mission field. The Lord has called him so it will happen! When his exams are completed he wants to enrol at the Bible College in Doorn under the leadership of Dr. Bardelmeijer. Gerrit makes plans, convinced that he is following the will of the Lord, although these plans seem impossible. However, the Lord, Who is true and faithful to His Word, will make Gerrit go through deep waters. The following morning the doctor confirms his mother's dreaded suspicions; Gerrit contracted tuberculosis while visiting his father.

Both Gerrit Sr. and Gerrit Jr. are able to take their treatment at home. For six months, Klasina has two patients to care for. They both must rest and take their medication. Gerrit has to swallow thirty to forty tablets daily. After six months, he can get out of bed and walk for a few minutes each day and he gradually increases the length of time for his exercise. Slowly he becomes more active but still requires lots of rest to regain his strength. During this time, the Lord works powerfully in his soul. Gerrit has a strong desire for God's Word and His Righteousness. Later he writes: "I could not go to God's house because of the tuberculosis and was envious of those who walked past our house on Sundays and during the week to go to church to listen to the Word of God.

After a year, Gerrit seems to have recovered but, understandably, his studies have suffered. His high-school teachers decide that Gerrit must postpone his final exams but Gerrit is determined to give it a try anyway... and he passes!

The Netherlands Bible Institute "De Koppel" in Doorn

Great is the disappointment, however, when in 1947 Gerrit once again is diagnosed with tuberculosis. This time the doctors decide he must be admitted to a sanatorium and start treatments all over again. Gerrit remains calm and still believes he will go to the mission field and proclaim Christ. "Shall God's promises fail?"

His recuperation is slow but finally the time comes when Gerrit is allowed to return home to complete his recovery. At long last he can register at the Bible Institute in Doorn, better known as the Bible and Mission College. This Institute is located in a large villa on the Buurtweg (Buurt Road). The owner of the building is Guus Kessler, the son of an English millionaire. Guus did not wish to follow his father's footsteps as one of the directors of the Shell Oil Company but instead became a missionary. The young Kessler brought the Gospel to the Huancayo, Peru's poverty-stricken people. Following Christ's example, he chose to be poor on account of the riches of the Gospel.

It is 1949 and again mother Klasina can be found on her knees. Her son Gerrit is sick. Her prayer is short, "Oh Lord, be merciful to him." The doctor is uncertain about what is causing the illness but advises her to keep the boy's tummy warm. The condition worsens rapidly and the doctor sends Gerrit to the Katwijkse Gasthuis, a seniors' home, which is temporarily turned into a hospital, for further observation. It quickly becomes apparent that Gerrit has a ruptured appendix.

Anxious days follow for Klasina, days in which she once again, as after his birth, gives him to the Lord. "Lord use him in Thy service and use his life to the extension of Thy kingdom." However, the situation gets worse until the doctor uses a recently discovered medicine called penicillin. The fever disappears and Gerrit quickly recovers.

The new home at the corner of de Parklaan

After the war, Gerrit Sr. received government compensation for the loss of their home on the Varkenvisserstraat. Although the amount received was nowhere near the true value of the house, he managed to get enough funds together to build a beautiful new home at the corner of Parklaan and Laan van Nieuw-Zuid. Gerrit Sr. supervised the construction himself.

Young Gerrit can regularly be found at the construction site, with his hands in his pockets, carefully observing the construction process while asking the builders about the construction details. It is here that Gerrit inadvertently receives his first carpentry lesson which will be of benefit later in his life.

Gerrit builds a special friendship with one of the carpenters named Brouwer. They not only discuss the intricacies of woodwork but also spiritual matters such as the tabernacle of our bodies that will one day be broken down and how the Lord builds Himself a house in heaven not made by hands which will be occupied by His children. The fact that the carpenter is a member of the Netherlands Reformed Congregation ("NRC") does not hinder their conversations. Regularly, you can find Gerrit at the Brouwer's residence discussing the divine ways of the Lord. During their conversations, the names of old scholars and of Rev. G. H. Kersten were often mentioned.

Gerrit decides to visit the NRC in Katwijk. With a desirous heart he listens to the reading services which are a blessing to his hungry soul. Every Sunday he takes his place at the back of the little church. Unseen, so he thinks, but Elder Bos has noticed the young man. The Bos family is very hospitable opening their doors to visitors including military personnel from the airbase at Valkenburg and nurses of the Dr. Willem Van de Bergh Stichting (an institution for mentally challenged adults and children). Father Bos asks his children if they know the young man with the dark curly hair and the dark-rimmed glasses. No, they do not know him. "Is he perhaps a teacher?" Father Bos says, "Why not ask him over for a cup of coffee?"

The following Sunday, fourteen-year-old Miep Bos approaches the young Gerrit as they leave the church, "The man who just read the sermon is my father and he would like to invite you over for a cup of coffee." Gerrit, who is friendly and outgoing, has no qualms about joining the family for coffee. He tells them that he is a student at the Bible College in Doorn; he has a longing to become a missionary which he earnestly believes will happen.

Gerrit inquires whether the NRC has any plans in regard to mission work. He tells them that he wrote a letter to Rev. Verhagen in Gouda to ask these questions but never received an answer. Mr. Bos discovers that Gerrit had the wrong address. Rev. Verhagen is no longer living at 32 Vredebest.

Gerrit writes another letter. This time he addresses it to Rev. Bel, a member of the Mission Board ("MB").

> *Reverend, I have many questions; I would appreciate an opportunity to meet with you or another pastor from your*

denomination. Can you please name a time and a place where we can meet and I will be there, God willing!

Rev. Bel agrees to have a meeting and in the summer of 1955, Gerrit travels to The Hague where they meet at the home of Rev. Bel's son. A cordial conversation takes place where Gerrit declares his soul's earnest longing and Rev. Bel promises to present his case to the MB.

Reverend Bel,
a member of the MB

September 19, 1955; still no reply. Gerrit decides to write another letter:

> *I am not writing this letter to annoy you but only as a reminder. You know that I am not a member of the NRC and under normal circumstances I cannot make an appeal to be heard. Now my only prayer is that God Himself will speak and exceptions can be made. As I know that He directs all things, I do not have to be concerned that anyone, including myself, can stand in His way.*
>
> *This is just a short note, Reverend. Please remember me: do not forget me as Joseph was forgotten when he was in prison.*

Gerrit continues his studies at Doorn even though he is not physically strong and his lungs have scars from the tuberculosis. Determined and believing in the promise of God that He will use him in His service, he continues on. And then tuberculosis strikes a third time. All his hopes seem to be dashed! Gerrit is admitted to the Zonnegloren Sanatorium in Soest. There he wrestles with God. In June of 1956, Gerrit shares his struggles with Rev. Bel.

> *Have I been a hypocrite? Reverend, I must again go through deep waters. Have I after all deceived myself and has God then not called me? You wrote about calling and conversion and is this God's way to prevent me from going? This I can tell you, I do not want to place the mantel of the prophet upon myself nor do I wish to put myself in the position of a missionary. I have to surrender myself to the will of God who knows best.*

> *I wish I could have met with the Curatorium and the delegates but unfortunately at this time it is not possible. You may know that my heart weeps and I cannot understand why this is happening again. At the Bible School which I attend they tried to take care of me for a while; earnest prayers are sent up for my recovery. But so far these have not been answered.*

> *Now I have to wait patiently. Psalm 77. Past mercies lead me to rely upon the help of God Most High.*

Gerrit spends quite a while in the sanatorium. The doctors place his name on the list for surgery. But the Lord intervenes. While brushing his teeth one evening, Gerrit is surprised when he runs his tongue along his teeth and feels small grains of calcium. He calls for the nurse, presuming that he is going to have a lung hemorrhage. But the nurse shrugs it off. "Come on, Kuijt, get real! Grains of calcium. Impossible!"

At the same moment, foaming blood gushes out of Gerrit's mouth. He feels like he is choking as he can hardly breathe. As soon as the bleeding stops, the nurses set him straight up in bed using pillows for support and watch him anxiously. But Gerrit feels so much better, he puts the pillows on the floor, lies down and goes to sleep.

The following day, x-rays are taken of his lungs. They show that the spot on the left side is calcified and on the right side (where he previously had a scar from his earlier bout with tuberculosis) a miracle has taken place.

Fellow students visiting Gerrit in the Sanitorium while he is being treated for TB

A nurse at Zonnegloren Sanatorium tells Gerrit that Rev. K. De Gier held a mission service in The Hague. The minister called on young people who feel a personal desire to go to the mission field. This sparks hope in Gerrit's heart. Will mission work actually become a reality in the NRC? What progress has been made? Are there already people who are being trained for work for the mission field? Has a mission field been designated where work will commence? He decides to write another letter to Rev. Bel. He refers to their earlier conversation held two years ago.

> *Since that time several events have taken place in my life. I had to endure more physical suffering which brought me into the depths of despair. Even in the days when my future is still a mystery, my thoughts unwittingly wander to your congregations. I*

15

cannot forget you, even when all seems to be hopeless. I am still convinced about my calling for the mission field. Through all the suffering it has become more apparent. We will see how it will come to pass.

I would like to inform you that, at present, I am a candidate of the Livingstone Memorial Mission, an American mission society, which also has a branch in The Netherlands. However, as time goes by it becomes clear to me that I will not go out for this mission.

(Gerrit officially belongs to the Hervormde Church and yet realizes that he will be sent out by the NRC even though this denomination does not have any definite plans to send out missionaries.)

There are plenty of other Mission Societies but none appeal to me like your congregations do. I hope that I am not too zealous but that I may follow the Lord's glorious ways. He will undoubtedly open a way. It is very possible that I, just like Moses, will have to go into the desert.

In the past, I asked several doctors whether it is possible that a change can take place in such an old scar. They said, 'That will not happen. The scar is dormant so don't you worry about it.' However, the Lord, by means of this bleeding (which in itself was traumatic) has reduced the scar to the size of the tip of my little finger.

My personal physician congratulated me but I gave God the honour. The situation now is better than ever before.

As a result of these circumstances I believe that an opportunity will be provided for me to become a missionary. There are still so many thousands of people who have not heard of the only Name.

Chapter 2

"I Have Always Known it "

Rev. Bel keeps his promise and informs the Mission Board about the young man from Katwijk who is so persistent and sincere in his request for an opportunity to meet. In August of 1956 the congregation of Rotterdam-Centre is designated as the Mission Church, but because there is a shortage of ministers in the NRC, the church has not yet received the go-ahead to place a call for a missionary minister. Since the church is already investigating possibilities to start mission work, the MB agrees to meet Gerrit. Collaboration with the Free Presbyterian Church of Scotland (FPC) which in the past has been unsuccessful might now be a possibility. The FPC has plans to send a Dutch male nurse to Zimbabwe. Perhaps if the NRC pays the nurse's salary this might be an opportunity for the two churches to work together. Of course a fundamental agreement has to be put in place. According to Rev. Rijksen, "The NRC would like to have a finger in the pie." However, this opportunity fails to materialize as the FPC rejects all efforts of working together.

Members of the

MB

Rev. H. Rijksen

Rev. Verhagen

On March 25, 1958, the MB gathers in Gouda. Rev. Kieboom is unable to attend as he is getting ready to immigrate to America. Present are Rev. Bel, H. Rijksen, and Verhagen. After having a confidential discussion, they call Gerrit Kuijt into the meeting. Gerrit explains how his mother pleaded with the Lord before his birth—if the child was a boy that God would use him in His Kingdom—and how he, from a young age, has had a love for mission work. He continues by revealing his deep impressions of death and eternity and he tells of his personal strife and struggle; how Satan tries to influence his thoughts so that Gerrit believes he has committed the "unpardonable" sin against the Holy Ghost.

Gerrit also speaks about the trials he experienced with tuberculosis which was a thorn in his side. At the same time he shares with them of the comfort and assurance that the Lord will provide a way to open doors that appear to be closed.

The MB is unable to make any promises to the young man. He is not a member of the NRC and even if he were a member, he must first receive a recommendation from the consistory of Katwijk. Even then he will still have to wait and see if the Curatorium (Board of Church Governors) will accept him. This is how Gerrit returns home. Yet he waits patiently, trusting that God will take care of the situation.

It is only three days later, on March 28, 1958, that Gerrit appears before the five consistory members of Katwijk to be questioned about his "knowledge of the divine truths of God." Another member of the Confession of Faith Class is Kees Bos, who will later become his brother-in-law.

Whether Gerrit attends catechism classes is unknown. It is interesting to note that in the church records of February 17, 1958, one month before Gerrit's evaluation, attention is called to a 'Van der Plas' and a 'Kuijt', how they faithfully attend the reading services. The consistory decides to pay these two a visit at a suitable time.

On Easter Monday, April 7, 1958, Gerrit Kuijt and Kees Bos stand in front of the church to make their public Confession of Faith. Rev. C. Molenaar begins by asking them questions from the original church doctrine written in the 1600's by Voetius, one of the early church fathers:

"Do you acknowledge... ?" "Do you believe... ?" "Do you promise... ?" Gerrit Kuijt makes his affirmation with a strong "yes" by which he officially becomes a member of the NRC.

Then the congregation stands and sings:

God will Himself confirm it with His blessing,
And on the roll of nations He will count
All these as born on Zion's holy mount
In many tongues one God, one faith confessing,

Gerrit thinks to himself, "All nations —Jews and gentiles —and not only in the Netherlands but also gentiles in far-away countries." Gerrit is convinced of this. "Does God Himself not say this in His Word?"

Gerrit becomes a good friend of the Bos family. He regularly stops by for a cup of coffee, especially on Wednesday afternoons after daughter Miep has her cooking lessons. She often brings home samples of her baking and once teasingly says to him, "Today there is nothing for you as I have just enough for the six of us." But Mother Bos intervenes. She has a soft spot for this young man and takes his side.

Meanwhile, while Gerrit acquires a broader education, mission work always is at the back of his mind. He is interested in the medical field and is enrolled in a carpentry course and anthropology classes.

It is at least a month after his Confession of Faith when Gerrit once again visits the Katwijk Consistory. He is there to request a recommendation to be heard by the Curatorium in Rotterdam. The Moderator, Rev. Molenaar is ill so Rev. de Gier from The Hague was there to take his place along with Elders Van Egmond and Van Hove from Leiden.

With sincere interest they listen as Gerrit tells them how the Lord has drawn him out of the darkness to His Wonderful Light and has placed in his heart a love for mission work and that he would especially like to be sent out in accordance to church orders.

The consistory decides to recommend Gerrit to be accepted as a missionary. They have reservations about Gerrit's health. Is it realistic to send this young man who has a history of tuberculosis to work in tropical conditions? The consistory decides to write a letter to the Sanatorium Zonnegloren in Soest to get a medical opinion. Several days later, the consistory receives a reply from Dr. J. A. W. Berghauser Pont, Director and Medical Specialist, who advises them he has no authority to provide any information without prior approval from Mr. Kuijt.

Father and Mother Bos play an important role in Gerrit's life

Sunday night with Gerrit at the organ - Miep and Uncle Sam singing along

The MB who is responsible for sending missionaries overseas is also concerned about the physical condition of Gerrit Kuijt. On June 4, 1958, Rev. Rijksen informs the MB that he has received a letter from the consistory in Katwijk advising them that they have provided a letter of recommendation for G. Kuijt to become a missionary. Rev. Rijksen, Chairman of the MB, reminds them that Kuijt has had tuberculosis and at one time even vomited blood. He insists that Gerrit obtain a doctor's certificate stating that he is physically capable of working in the tropics.

The doctor takes a deep breath and with a thoughtful look says, "From a medical point of view I should not let you go Kuijt. But I am afraid that if I do not you will get sick from despair.

In June of 1958, in the tiny waiting room of the Theological School on the Boezemsingel, you can feel the tension in the air. Eight people are waiting for a turn to give their testimony to the Curatorium. Gerrit Kuijt waits patiently. Against the wall are bookcases and hanging above them are pictures of Rev. Brakel as well as other men who played an important role in the history of the NRC. The man ahead of him, Cor Harinck from Kloetinge, is accepted to start his studies and it should be noted he originally did not come from a church background.

When Gerrit enters the meeting room he is directed to a place at the head of the table. He is given an opportunity to explain the reasons why he wishes to become a missionary. Once again, he relates how the Lord had spoken in his life and given him convictions of death and eternity and how God revealed His grace, seeking him out in the distress of his soul. He tells them of his call to bring the Gospel where it has never been proclaimed before. He vividly describes his love for mission work his hopes and dreams for so many people who are created with eternal souls.

Gerrit has to wait in the hallway again. Finally he is invited back into the room where the Chairman of the MB informs him that he has been accepted to begin his studies to become a minister. This goes beyond what the consistory of Katwijk stated in its recommendation. This decision marks a new era for the NRC. After Kuijt successfully completes his theological studies, a long awaited desire can be realized—the start of his mission work.

Meanwhile, Elder Bos from Katwijk (Miep's father), who accompanies Gerrit to Rotterdam, nervously walks up and down the Boezemsingel (boulevard along the water's edge). In his heart a prayer ascends to God if He will yet perform a miracle.

At the front of the building a balcony door opens and a voice from one of the curators calls out, "Bos, he has been accepted!" Elder Bos is filled with thankfulness. As they return to the train station he asked, "Isn't this a miracle to you, Gerrit?" "Not really!" Gerrit replied, "I have always known it. The Lord is true to His Word."

Elder Bos supported Gerrit by having him read the Scripture in church

Elder Bos does his best to support the young man. He has Gerrit collecting the offerings in the Katwijk church. This gives Gerrit a seat in the bench reserved for deacons. He even permits Gerrit to do the scripture reading from the lectern, "to make him more comfortable for the future," said Bos.

When Gerrit Kuijt reports for his first day at the Theological School in Rotterdam it is as though he is entering a different world. His classmates are W. Suijker and C. Harinck.. G. Mouw, who had been accepted with the others, has to wait at least one more year. Objections were received that he had not been a member of the NRC for a full year. Although Gerrit has not been a member for a year either, this requirement apparently does not apply to him.

Kuijt and Harinck seem out of place. Harick is originally not from the NRC and he and Kuijt soon realize there are many things they must become familiar with. It takes quite a while before Kuijt starts wearing a black suit. A change from a coloured to a black tie takes even longer. To wear a black hat is absolutely out of the question for now! Harinck has his light-coloured coat dyed black but Kuijt refuses to do that. A black coat is only bought when his light-coloured one wears out.

They both have great respect for their fellow students. Huisman and Schipaanboord are jovial fellows and it will not be hard to get along with them. They are not so sure about Wisse who uses different vocabulary. Kuijt is not the only one who needs to get used to his class mates; they also need to get used to him. Gerrit is jovial and cordial; speaks frankly about his faith, his knowledge of Christ and the forgiveness of sins. Sometimes he is not understood by his fellow students and there are times he does not understand them either.

from L to R Students C. Harinck, G. Kuijt, W. Suijker, L. Huisman, A. L. Kok & G. Schipaanboord

Relationships among the students at the theological school, however, are warm and friendly. They have to study very hard but there is always time for a little joke or a witty remark. However, there are certain jokes that Kuijt does not participate in. When the students try to trick Rev. L. Rijksen into believing that he has already dealt with a certain chapter, Kuijt will not play along.

There are occasions when the other students tease Gerrit about his certainty of his calling. When Rev. Zijderveld discusses other mission fields that he is personally interested in, Gerrit invariably replies, "They are not an option for me for I am being sent to people who have not yet heard the Gospel." Fellow student Wisse does not understand his fervent passion for mission work and, according to him, Kuijt will never succeed.

At lunch, one of the students is expected to serve the soup, which is often done by Schipaanboord. The student usually scoops extra meat into Gerrit's bowl. The other students agree. "We have to fatten him up. That way the natives will have something to eat when they cook him in their pot." Good advice flows freely. "Gerrit, be sure your hair is not too long or it will be too easy for them to scalp you." The other students also kid Gerrit about his bachelorhood. Sometimes when one of them returns from a preaching engagement he suggests, "Gerrit, you should go and preach there for I saw a nice decent wife for you." Even Rev. L. Rijksen found this a topic to joke with Gerrit about.

Kuijt and Harinck develop a solid friendship. During their break one can often see them walking and conversing with each other. Kuijt's relationship with Rev. Rijksen is also a very special one. Rijksen acts as his mentor but at the same time is like a father to the young man. Regularly he protects Kuijt and tries to nurture him in a friendly manner. "Kuijt, this will not do," or "This is not how God instructs His people."

His teacher, Mr. Van Bochove, is also sympathetic towards Gerrit. He respects the fact that such a young man is prepared to sacrifice his life to work among the gentiles. Gerrit also has a good relationship with Rev. J. W. Kersten, who does not find it necessary to verbalize everything strictly according to the NRC language.

He accepts Kuijt for his chiliastic sympathies (the doctrine that Christ will reign upon Earth for a thousand years). Did he not have similar feeling from reading books written by the Puritans?

There is also time for recreation

Gerrit and fellow students on a trip to evangelize

Many conversations take place between teacher and student as they travel together from Rotterdam to Scheveningen. The conversations make the trip enjoyable. From Scheveningen to Katwijk is a short bus ride. When Rev. J. W. Kersten suddenly dies of a heart attack, Gerrit is shaken and deep sorrow fills his heart. "Why, Oh God, why?"

After Rev. Kersten's death, Rev. De Gier becomes the new instructor. The latter completely rejects Kuijt's ideas with respect to eschatology, yet the two men truly like each other. Kuijt regularly gets rides with Rev. De Gier from Rotterdam to The Hague.

Kuijt has no difficulties with his studies. He had already completed his program at The Bible Institute in Doorn, where the focus was more on evangelism and mission work. Now he has to acquire the necessary theological knowledge. But he regularly wonders about the use of all this knowledge for the mission field. "What can I do among the gentiles with all this information about infra and supralapsarianism or the difference between two and three covenant teachings?"

Two of Gerrit's instructors: Rev. J. W. Kersten (left) & Rev. L. Rijksen

Kuijt also has more to learn about the NRC language. He was not born and raised in the NRC and you can tell by his style of prayer. Rev. Rijksen asks the other students to lend Gerrit a hand. They are to encourage him and not let him struggle on his own. "Try to make him familiar with expressions that are common within our circles," says Rijksen. When Gerrit preaches his first trial sermon Rev. Rijksen says, "You need to utilize our language a bit more." Gerrit pulls out his note book and jots down notes. He completely understood what Rev. Rijksen means about the importance of speaking the "people's language" in order to be accepted. He improves with practice and the congregations accept him as he is.

Kuijt is a practical person but above all a missionary through and through. His studies at the Bible Institute in Doorn have left their influence on him. He has many questions about infant baptism and the End of Time. When discussions are held about mission work and the coming of God's Kingdom, the discussion frequently ends in a debate about chiliasm. Kuijt is never short of relevant texts and passages of scripture on the subject. Rev. Rijksen eventually puts an end to such discussions and advises Kuijt to leave those issues alone.

Student G. Kuijt (far left, standing) with his fellow students and instructors

But topics such as dogma or the building up of the church do not have Kuijt's immediate interest. He would like to leave school and begin his mission work. It is an inner drive, not an uncontrolled desire for adventure or freedom. In his prayers he never forgets to include "the uninformed gentiles who have never heard anything of the Gospel." In his program of studies very limited attention is given to the fact that Kuijt is to be sent out to do mission work. Rev. Kersten reviewed a few mission books with him but Rev. Rijksen is of the opinion that Kuijt will become a minister in the NRC. Therefore, he must have the same education as the other students.

Tension mounts as the students prepare to present their first sermon. In the Boezemsingel Church, which seats over two thousand people, sit the professors, the fellow students, and a few audience members, but the rest of the pews are empty. Preparation for the sermon is difficult; presenting the sermon even more difficult; the criticism afterwards - the worst! "You can't go into the congregations like that." "You can't go up on the pulpit like this." "It just does not make sense." "It sounds like a Sunday school story." The teachers probably mean well but all the students, including Kuijt, are disheartened. Discouraged by the comments, Kuijt wonders where to go from here. "Maybe I am not a fit for the NRC after all." The Board of Directors shares his concerns.

Thankfully things improve. Kuijt acquires more confidence in preaching the Word of God. While bringing the Word of God to the different congregations he often preaches from the Book of Acts of the Apostles in which mission work is prominent. He convinces the congregations of the urgency and responsibility of getting out the message of God's word to the gentiles. Kuijt is encouraged.

Returning to school after his speaking appointments he frequently declares, "Go ahead and criticize me but the people in that church heartily support me." Indeed, within the congregations there is a rapid acceptance and trust for Kuijt's ministry. And what if his choice of words and his expressions are somewhat different at times? The listeners have no problems with this. Missionary Kuijt is allowed to be different.

In his third and fourth year of theological studies, Kuijt is regularly absent in order to prepare himself more specifically for his future mission work. He needs to take courses and training in The Netherlands and abroad. In England he attends the Wycliffe Bible Translators Institute and for his medical certification he goes to the Royal London Homeopathic Institute. There he is taught midwifery, dentistry and the treatment of tropical diseases.

However, the emphasis remains on his theological studies and preaching in the NRC.

Student Kuijt at the Theological School in Rotterdam

Chapter 3

Show Us Thy Way

The MB has a tough decision to make. Many different locations have been carefully considered including West Africa and various Portuguese territories in East Africa. On behalf of the NRC in the United States of America, they also investigate the possibility of going to Algeria. However, this is not feasible as Algeria is at war.

Student Kuijt is convinced that his final destination will be Dutch New Guinea

For student Kuijt the location is not a problem. He is convinced that Dutch New Guinea (today known as Papua) will be his destination. The Lord has revealed this to him. However, the MB still needs to be convinced. After much deliberation, they agree in principle to designate New Guinea as their future mission field.

In December 1959, the MB accepts the decision. They will contact Rev. Korneman of the Christian and Missionary Alliance (C&MA). Student Kuijt is required to contact the Tropical Institute in Amsterdam, the Royal London Homeopathic Institute and the Institute of Linguistics in England. Rev. L. Rijksen promises that the theological school will help fast-track Kuijt's studies.

Rev. G. Hegeman, a friend of Kuijt, visits Katwijk

The MB delegates: H. Rijksen, Vergunst, Hegeman and Zijderveld contact the Dutch authorities to discuss the possibility of starting mission work in the Indonesian archipelago. Even though the region is volatile due to political unrest, the MB does not want to back out of their initial decision. If the Lord Himself does not cut off this opportunity, neither will the MB.

The MB does not intend to send missionary Kuijt to New Guinea by himself. Diny Sonneveld, a nurse, will carry out the medical work and Dick ten Voorde, a teacher, will be in charge of the literacy program. The three are aware of the increasing political tension in Dutch New Guinea. However, they decide not to back down and request to be sent out.

In the weekly NRC countrywide church newspaper *De Saambinder* an article appears stating that the *King of the Church* commands mission work. It goes on to say that Kuijt will first live and work in Sorong with Rev. Woldendorp. Nurse Sonneveld will initially work at a leprosy hospital in Mili while Dick ten Voorde and his wife will be working at a training center for village teachers in Ifar. This will help them prepare for the time when together they will open a mission station in an undeveloped region.

The MB is disconcerted because, among the many positive responses received from all over the Netherlands, they have also received a less-than-positive letter. The consistory of the NRC in the City of Zeist expressed grave concerns about plans to commence missionary work in Dutch New Guinea. The missionaries will have their hands full learning to speak and document the language of the region. The consistory wonders whether the number of people that can be reached in such an area is large enough. In other words, "Is it really worth the money and effort?" Furthermore, the consistory points out that, "in our congregations we have an elaborate system of dogmatics" and there is a question as to whether there is a place for this kind of thought in the world of the Papuans, the indigenous people of New Guinea.

This last argument does not sit well with the MB. "An elaborate system of a dogmatic religion? No, the teaching we confess is sound biblical doctrine." This will have to be made clear to the consistory of Zeist because the expression they use is an affront to the NRC.

According to Rev. H. Rijksen, "It is true that there are many different languages spoken in Dutch New Guinea but the linguistic experts would rather talk about dialectic differences." In view of this, the consistory of Zeist is given an appropriate response.

The MB does not want to proceed too hastily. They establish an advisory committee comprised of three young scholars, Van Leijenhorst, De Jong and Verweij, who will research all aspects concerning the establishment of a mission field.

They also deliberate over the "fruits of the work." If the Lord grants it, Papuans will be converted and perhaps a church can be established. However, what kind of a church will it be? For sure, such a church will not have the same character as a church in Holland. No, the church that will be created in New Guinea must have distinctive Papuan characteristics. There must be communication with the existing

Evangelical Christian Church of Papua (ECK). On the other hand, the mission must remain independent and have no affiliation with other churches.

With a grim face, Rev. Zijderveld places a letter on the table. He has received a letter from Mr. Van Steenis whose brother-in-law, Lodewijkx, lives in New Guinea. Lodewijkx writes that "it is ill advised to start mission work now as the country is experiencing some political upheaval." Again the MB discusses whether the choice of Dutch New Guinea is the right one.

Kuijt as a medical student in England

In England, Kuijt is unaware of all these trepidations. Elated, he writes to the delegates of the MB that he has been able to acquire some medical equipment consisting of syringes, a sterilizing unit and four delivery forceps. "If you were to purchase these brand new it would cost at least thirty pounds but I purchased these for six pounds! I could not pass up such an outstanding opportunity but if you think it is too much money, please feel free to take it off my expenses." He also learned that there is used medical equipment available at Simavi in the Netherlands and the

MB should look into this. "Who knows what you may acquire there for a reasonable price?" Kuijt further suggests that he should attend a jungle-training camp for three months in the Australian part of New Guinea (east side); followed by three months of practical work in Dutch New Guinea (west side); and finally a linguistic course back in Australian New Guinea. Subsequently, by March of 1962 he will be ready to be sent out. At that time a final decision can be made by the MB as to whether Dutch New Guinea will become the designated mission field.

The MB does not like Kuijt's proposals and wants him to first take linguistics and then take his ecclesiastical exams. By doing so, he will at least have completed his theological training and preparations can begin for him to be sent out. A request of Rev. Hegeman that Kuijt first spend six months in North America is not granted.

Hilkemeyer, an engineer who is a representative from the Dutch Government in Dutch New Guinea, looks around; he is used to many things but he has never before addressed a group of clergymen. He understands the intention of them and enthusiastically speaks of the island in the Indonesian archipelago which he loves so much. He describes its magnificent natural surroundings, its pristine beaches, the jungles and a culture reminiscent of the Stone Age. He talks at length about the natives who have never been in contact with white people and who, in comparison to Western Europe, have gone through a very different development.

The government official says that mission work by the NRC is worth pursuing; however, it must be done in conjunction with the ECK (the church that resulted from mission work done by the Nederlandse Hervormde Kerk (NHK). Together with ECK, the NRC can look for a region where a work can be started: for example, the mountainous region around the Baliem Valley situated in the centre of the island.

Hilkemeyer points out that working together with the Mission Institute of Oegstgeest is essential. He finally recommends that Kuijt should spend some time working at an ECK mission post. By doing so, he will be able to acclimatize; gain knowledge of the tropics, become familiar with working in difficult conditions and have an opportunity to observe the native people and their culture.

After the government official left, the ministers quickly come to an agreement. Rev. Rijksen and Vergunst will visit the mission centre in

Oegstgeest. While there, Rijksen and Vergunst speak with two mission experts, Rev. Mackay and Dr. Locher, who respond positively. "Of course, Dutch New Guinea is a vast island where many thousands of people live in the jungles. The command of the Lord is clear: 'Go and teach all nations, baptizing them in the name of the Father, Son and Holy Ghost.'"

There will be plenty of work for the NRC. Mackay and Locher recommend that Kuijt first works with an experienced missionary. Rev. Woldendorp of Sorong is the most appropriate person. Kuijt will be able to make orientation trips through the region with him. And so it is decided.

Gradually, plans for the mission start to come together. First, the Board of Governors will examine student Kuijt. If the results are satisfactory, the MB will have further discussions with Kuijt regarding his special calling, his ability and his qualifications for mission work. Once that is completed, student Kuijt can then be declared eligible to be called by the sending church.

Since Kuijt is no longer receiving any income from the theological school, the MB decides to provide him with a monthly allowance of three hundred guilders. However, any amount received for speaking in the various congregations will be deducted from this allowance.

Many matters need to be arranged, including matters of a practical nature and matters of policy. When Kuijt puts in a request to purchase a tape recorder, the MB first needs to think about it and then discuss the necessity of the tape recorder with Rev. Woldendorp. A broad discussion ensues on the subject of who will officiate at Kuijt's installation on February 15th, 1961.

The MB decides that Rev. Vergunst will perform the ordination service and Rev. Rijksen will provide the sending out sermon after which candidate Kuijt will preach a short inaugural sermon. Rev. Elshout prepares policies that include a financial agreement as well as guidelines that must be adhered to by the Missionary Servant of the Word. It is not only about salary but about clothing for the tropics, transportation costs, a schedule and duration of furloughs and future emeritus compensation. A clause is even included concerning dereliction of duty. Student Kuijt, still in England and busy with his studies, has not been involved in any of these decisions. From under the cover of a tent in the Chigwell area, Kuijt regularly corresponds with Rev. Elshout to let him know how he is doing.

We have had three weeks of linguistics with reasonable good results. The course load is heavy and takes up the entire day. The wake-up call comes at 6:00 am with lights out at 10:30 pm. Kuijt writes about the main subjects: how to proceed with a system for writing and pronunciation, problems in translation on the field, and how to work out the grammar. All subjects are difficult and very time consuming.

It is not without tension that student Kuijt entered the hall where the Board of Governors and the MB are gathered. He has completed his exams and has been thoroughly questioned on dogmatic exegesis, hermeneutics and church history as well as missiology, social history and other subjects pertaining to mission service. Kuijt is warmly addressed, "This student is outstanding in the way he gave himself whole heartily to his studies at the Theological School in Rotterdam including the other specialized courses completed in Amsterdam, Oegstgeest and England."

The congregation of Rotterdam-Centre calls candidate Kuijt

The Board of Governors as well as the MB unanimously declare Kuijt's candidacy for ministry in the congregations and as a missionary to the gentiles.

That same evening the consistory of Rotterdam-Centre gathers. The congregation places a call to candidate Kuijt to be sent out from their congregation to distant peoples.

On February 3, 1961, the MB expresses a certain degree of discomfort with respect to candidate Kuijt being single. It is noted that Kuijt will soon be sent out to Dutch New Guinea with a young female nurse. The delegates wish to deal honestly and frankly with the situation. Although all members are convinced of the advisability of marriage, they cannot come up with a ready-made solution for the problem. Finally, they decide that they can do nothing else but suggest to Kuijt to "look for a suitable partner."

But history is written by the Lord Himself. People, including the MB, can envision all kinds of scenarios but the Lord is in control.

Miep Bos has known Kuijt since she was fourteen years old. She is presently studying to become a home economics teacher. It was one of her former teachers who encouraged her to pursue this area. "Miep, you are such a good seamstress. Wouldn't you like to become a teacher in that field?" Every day Miep travels to The Hague to attend classes at a school located near the Laan van Meerdervoort.

Gerrit Kuijt? Miep thinks he is a very nice young man and sometimes she notices his interest in her; however, Miep is practical. "Do not fall in love with that young man because he is going to the mission field. Leave your family and follow him?" Miep has no desire to do this. Besides, you must have a calling to become a missionary and Miep does not have this. Gerrit is a nice fellow but that is all! It has to stay that way. Even though she assists him in procuring the gear required for the mission field, this does not mean a thing.

However, when Grié Miep's older sister gets married on November 16, 1961, Miep asks her friend Gerrit to be her escort to the wedding. Later on Gerrit was heard to say, "When I have made a decision I like to act upon it." Shortly after the wedding he asks Miep to marry him.

A few weeks later Gerrit says, "I would like us to get married before I leave." Miep is taken by surprise. How is all this going to work out? At home, an apprehensive Miep seeks advice from her mother. While washing windows, she starts the conversation by saying, "Mother, Gerrit wants us to get married before he leaves." Instead of her mother being upset and saying, "It is not possible," she is quiet for a moment and calmly replies, "I can understand that." With this, Miep's fears are put to rest.

Sometime later, Gerrit suggests, "It seems to me that it would be better for you to stay here after we are married." "But, Gerrit that means I will have to complete my degree as a married woman." "Why not?" answers Gerrit. "I know our destination. It is Dutch New Guinea. Once there, a mission field must be found and it will be easier for me to move around when I am by myself. Your parents will take good care of you and as soon as you are finished with your education you can join me."

Miep Bos

On January 3, 1962 Rev. Elshout receives a short note in the mail, "I hereby wish to announce some important news. On January 18th, 1962 I plan to marry Miss Bos from Katwijk aan Zee. This will come as a complete surprise for most of you and to be honest it is kind of a surprise for me too. I have never been concerned about getting married but I realize all things work together for the good of those who love God. I will be sending you an invitation shortly."

Proposed, engaged and married all within six weeks. Indeed spontaneity at its best!

GERRIT KUIJT
Theol. kandidaat

en

WILHELMINA BOS

hebben de eer u, mede namens wederzijdse ouders, kennis te geven van hun voorgenomen huwelijk, waarvan de voltrekking D.V. zal plaats hebben op donderdag 18 januari a.s., des namiddags 2 uur, ten raadhuize te Katwijk.

De kerkelijke bevestiging heeft plaats in de Ned. Herv. Kerk (Oude Kerk), Boulevard, te Katwijk aan Zee, des namiddags 2.45 uur, door de weleerw. heer Ds. L. Rijksen van Rotterdam (West).

Katwijk aan Zee, 3 januari 1962
Parklaan 1
Remisestraat 45

Receptie: na de huwelijksbevestiging, van 5—6.30 uur in Hotel „Noordzee".

Toekomstig adres: tijdelijk Boulevard, Katwijk aan Zee.

The wedding invitation of G. Kuijt and W. Bos

Miep is nervous whereas Gerrit sits calmly next to her. Diny Sonneveld and Mr. and Mrs. ten Voorde have gone into the other room. Miep's thoughts are like a whirlwind. "In a little while we will be called in and then they will question me about my calling but I do not have a calling! Lord, help me. I don't know what I am supposed to say." Gerrit glances at her and thinks, "Everything will work out." When he looks at his future wife again, she looks at ease. The Lord revealed to her that her calling is to follow her husband. This is a biblical and wonderful command!

Gerrit is called into the meeting and nineteen-year-old Miep remains behind. Eventually Miep is also called in. She knows most of the pastors because when they preach in Katwijk they stay with the Bos family.

Rev Rijksen advises her that they wish her to accompany Gerrit after their wedding. "I will gladly go with Gerrit, Reverend but I must first finish my studies." she promptly replies. (This is what they both had agreed on.)

"But Miep," says Rev. H. Rijksen, "If you get married and do not accompany him, rumours will start among the people."

"Well," answers Miep without hesitation, "then we won't get married yet."

The ministers glance at each other and then look to Gerrit. Now what? Gerrit burst into laughter, puts his hands up in the air saying, "Ha! See, I told you so."

The ice is broken. At the end of the meeting, Rev. Vergunst walks Miep to the door and says, "Miep, you must promise me that you will go as soon as possible."

"Reverend, this I promise. As soon as I am finished with my education, I will go."

The white Hervomde church on the Katwijk Boulevard

The white Hervormde Church on the Katwijk Boulevard is filled to capacity when the bridal party enters. Ministers, fellow students, family and friends fill the pews. Rev. L. Rijksen (from Rotterdam-West) approaches the pulpit. At 6:00 pm that evening, a reception at the

Noordzee Hotel gives everyone an opportunity to congratulate the young couple and share in their joy.

On January 18, 1962, nearly twenty-nine years after the registration of Gerrit Kuijt's birth, an official entry is recorded at the Registry documenting the marriage of Gerrit Kuijt to Wilhelmina Bos.

Wedding picture of Gerrit and Miep

Rev. L. Rijksen brings the couple into the church

Chapter 4

They Shall Declare My Glory

On February 15, 1962, a day that will remain etched in the memory of many, the Ahoy Hall in Rotterdam fills up with churchgoers. This is an unusual sight. In the enormous building where otherwise exhibitions, mass meetings and farm fairs are held, church people are now trying to find a seat. Thousands of chairs have been set up; at the front of the hall stands an improvised pulpit. This is where the service of ordination and investiture of candidate Kuijt will take place.

The Ahoy Hall in Rotterdam

The organ music is hardly noticeable because of the high ceilings in the hall. Elder A. Van Bochove announces the first stanza of Psalm 97 (Psalter 423) to be sung:

> *Jehovah reigns as King,*
> *To Him all homage bring;*
> *Ye islands, earth, and ocean,*
> *Break forth in glad devotion . . .*

Majestically the singing of two thousand five hundred people fill the space. Candidate Kuijt feels so insignificant. He who so firmly believed that he was going to be a missionary and now, here he is, ready to be sent out to gentile nations—people who also have a soul for eternity but are unfamiliar with the Word of God. They are living in darkness bound to idol worship and fear. Even worse is that idol worship does not bring honour to the God of Heaven and Earth. It is, therefore, an accursed worship.

Wholeheartedly, Kuijt joins in on the fourth verse:

Confounded be all they; Who in their folly pray
To gods of man's creation; And boast of vain salvation
Jehovah, Him we laud, For He alone is God.
Come, all ye gods, draw near, And worship Him with fear,
By His dominion awed.

Originally, it was not the intention to hold the ordination service in the Ahoy Hall. Does the NRC in Rotterdam-Central not have their own church on the Boesemslinge? Would it not be splendid to ordain candidate Kuijt as minister of the divine Word in their church? However, candidate Kuijt is not the property of Rotterdam and they cannot monopolize him. Many NRC churchgoers from across the Netherlands feel a special bond with the young man from Katwijk who is so friendly and congenial but also so earnest in his preaching. They all wish to share in this service. Furthermore, this sending out concerns the entire NRC. It is the first time in their church's history that they are sending out a missionary minister together with several other mission workers. In past years, love and support for the mission has grown among the church people and generous donations have been made. Many want to be present at this auspicious occasion —the installation of Kuijt!

Soon it becomes apparent to the Rotterdam consistory that their own church building will not be able to seat everyone. They look into the possibility of renting the Hervormde Koninginnekerk (Queens Church) which is located only a hundred metres from the Boezemsingel church. The audience will be able to listen to the services on loud speakers. Cars and buses can park at the cattle market square only 200 metres away. However, when it becomes clear that attendance will be so great that the combined church facilities are still too small, the consistory, after consulting with the MB, decides to rent the Ahoy-Hall.

Just before the service, a knock on the door of the makeshift consistory room is heard. Hesitantly, a member of the Boskoop consistory enters. He delivers an amount of 1,000 guilders to be used for mission work and the expansion of God's Kingdom. After the service, Rev. Hage will present 250 guilders on behalf of an anonymous donor (a woman) from the Walcheren congregation to the treasurer of the MB. These donations are tokens of love directed to the mission work and gratitude that the Lord has provided a missionary minister to them.

Hervormde Koninginnekerk, Rotterdam

Rev. A. Vergunst, Secretary of the MB, did the ordination of Candidate G. Kuijt

Rev. A. Vergunst has chosen a text from the Old Testament, Isaiah Chapter 66, verse 19.

And I will set a sign among them, and I will send those that escape of them unto the nations, to Tarshish, Pul, and Lud, that draw the bow, to Tubal, and Javan, to the isles afar off, that have not heard my fame, neither have seen my glory; and they shall declare my glory among the Gentiles.

It is one of the last verses found in Isaiah. The prophet provides a summary of all his prophecies with one central purpose—the Glory of God. That is also the theme of his sermon. He has three focal points: the mark of this glory, the messengers of this glory, and the radiance of this glory.

In his prophecies, Isaiah speaks to the people of Israel that the Lord is a God of judgement. This is necessary because the people of Israel put their trust in the temple ordinances and having possession of the temple. The Israelites rely on their own merits. However, God is Holy! God cannot have communion with sin or with a sinner unless his justice is satisfied. As proof of this, but also as a sign, the Lord will allow the temple to be destroyed, and the Israelites to be carried off to Babel. Despite the severity of this judgement, it is still a sign of the Lord's Glory.

However, Isaiah may continue his prophecies in which he foretells the rebuilding of the temple and the return from Babel. This is another sign—a sign that the Lord in His righteous anger will still remember them in His mercy. The God of judgement is also the God of grace, who, on behalf of the Mediator, Christ Jesus, grants grace to dead and hell-bound sinners. No one can stand before the God of judgement because the human race is lost in Adam's fall (sin) and in his or her own sin. The destruction of the temple is a symbol of this, but by the God of all grace and to the honor of His Compassion, sinners are saved - saved through redemption and faith in the Lord Jesus Christ. The rebuilt temple shall be a sign of this.

Without knowledge of God as the God of judgement, there cannot be true knowledge of Him as the God of all grace.

Therefore, the glory of God has to be proclaimed and the sign of the cross must be proclaimed not only as a sign of judgement but also as a sign of grace.

This preaching will not be in vain for those who have come to know Jesus as their personal Saviour and in so doing will escape the final judgement. They in turn will speak about the glory of God not only to the Jews but also to the heathens who never heard His voice before. Like Isaiah, they are driven by their love for God and their neighbour to urge others to believe and repent. The Lord by the Holy Spirit shall use this preaching to the praise of His own glory. They shall worship the Triune God with all honour and praise for their salvation.

Wall mural of the Prophet Isaiah, found in Italian Undine

Miep Kuijt glances at her husband whose face radiates pure joy. To be found worthy to bring the Gospel and to declare that it is possible for everyone to receive forgiveness for all their sins by the Lord. With and through Him we can find rest and peace. How privileged they both are!

When Rev. Vergunst reads the Form for Ordination, warmth fills Miep's soul. "He who has promised, is faithful and true." With full assurance Kuijt answers the following questions:

"I ask thee, whether thou feels in thy heart that thou art lawfully called of God's Church, and therefore of God himself, to this holy ministry?"

"Yes, truly with my whole heart."

"Whether thou dost believe the books of the Old and New Testament to be the only Word of God and the perfect doctrine unto salvation, and dost reject all doctrines repugnant thereto?"

"Yes, truly with all my heart and understanding."

"Whether thou dost promise faithfully to discharge your office, according to the same doctrine as above described and to adorn it with a godly life?"

"Yes, truly with my whole heart!"

One by one, the Mission delegates place their right hand on the head of Kuijt who is kneeling. Each one offers a benediction.

Gerrit Kuijt, the boy who knew with certainty that one day he was going to be in the Lord's service, is now confirmed to be a Minister of God's Word; a Shepherd and Teacher, even though his flock will not be in this city or even in this country. As the congregation of Rotterdam, personal and mission friends sing the blessing of Psalm 134, many are unable to control their emotions. As the service of the afternoon concludes, singing resounds throughout the Ahoy complex again:

God will Himself confirm them with His blessing,
And on the roll of nations He will count
All these as born on Zion's holy mount,
In many tongues one God, one faith confessing.

It was apparent, even before the afternoon service commenced, that it had been a wise decision to rent the Ahoy Hall. This became even more obvious by the evening when approximately 4,000 people filled the Hall to witness the sending out of the three mission workers. What a historical moment.

It is a rare occurrence, to have a minister preach his inaugural sermon at the same time as he is sent out for mission service. Rev. Kuijt ascends the pulpit and announces the first Psalm 99 (Psalter 432), which correlates to the afternoon's service:

God, who rules in state Is in Zion great, He excels in worth
All, that dwell on earth. Honor and acclaim His exalted Name,
All ye high and lowly, He alone is holy,
At His footstool bow….

The voice of the Elder resounds through the loudspeakers as he reads the following verses out of the Bible:

"I will make mention of Rahab and Babylon to them that know me: behold Philistia, and Tyre, with Ethiopia; this man was born there. And of Zion it shall be said, This and that man was born in her; and the highest himself shall establish her." (Psalm 87)

The chosen text is from Luke 1:37, which in simple words expresses what the newly installed preacher has experienced in his own life, "For with God nothing shall be impossible."

"God's promises can never fail," begins Rev. Kuijt. "God's promises speak of the coming of Christ to obtain salvation for sinners. These promises also speak of God's applying work of this salvation. From man's side, it is impossible to be saved. This is due to the lost state into which we have fallen. But, what is impossible with man, is possible with God. This message must be proclaimed to God's honour, and our salvation. Not only is it necessary to know this personally, but we must also share this knowledge with others. This is not only possible but it shall happen. In mission work, nothing is impossible with God. To know this gives us courage to go to New Guinea and to begin mission work, even though the circumstances are difficult."

"But," Rev. Kuijt asks his audience, "Shall we wait for a better time to begin? If Paul had waited for better times he would never have started his work. But Paul received a mandate to go and... "God led in safety through the flood... and turned the sea to solid ground." (Psalm 66) God's ways are always through impossibilities; so that none can boast save in God alone."

Several times Rev. Kuijt implores his audience to carry the mission work in prayer. "For all things must come from Him who has promised to be with His Church until the end of world. This knowledge and assurance of God's omnipotence gives peace to go forth in the power of the Lord."

For a moment, Gerrit Kuijt reflects back to the time when he was a boy. As a young lad, Gerrit poured out his heart to his mother, who brought everything in prayer before the throne of grace, who prior to his birth had already consecrated him for the service of the Lord.

Gerrit thanks his mother with all his heart in the presence of the four thousand people. He also thanks his father, his young wife Miep, his parents-in-law to whom he owes so much, and the relatives, friends, and others who have, humanly speaking, contributed in one way or another to him becoming a missionary. Above all he speaks humble words of thanksgiving to his Divine Sender.

The last Psalm to be sung (Psalm 108) reflects what is in his heart.

I'll sing Thy glory to the nations,
Thy praise among their populations.

The Chairman of the MB, Rev. H. Rijksen, now addresses the gathering from Luke 14:23: "And the Lord said unto the servant, Go out into the highways and hedges, and compel them to come in, that my house may be filled."

Rev. Rijksen explains first the historical background of this text.

"The Great Supper is to be interpreted, as a symbol of the Kingdom of God's Grace here on earth and as the entrance hall of the Kingdom of God in Heaven. The great Host, the Lord, first sends His servants into the city to invite the most prominent people (the Jews). These prominent people have received invitations before but they are not interested in participating. They bluntly refuse to come.

"The Host, with holy indignation for this humiliation, now sends his servants into the streets of the city to invite the lower-class people, the publicans and sinners. They come… yet there is still room. As the host wishes to have a full house, he again sends his servants out but this time to invite the Jews who live outside the city and the homeless ones (the gentiles) from the highways and alleys to sit and eat at the table of the King."

Rev. H. Rijksen points to the sequence of the Host's instructions.

"First, tell them, then bring them and finally compel them to come. That is also the task of missionaries; a task given to them by God that requires patience and perseverance. It may even take years before there is any visible fruit.

"The circumstances in which our missionary team is being sent out do not look very bright. In spite of the circumstances, the command remains the same, 'Go out to be witnesses of Christ.' This witnessing will not happen without opposition and setbacks, but it is Israel's God who gives strength to carry on."

Rev. Rijksen addresses the necessity of supporting the mission team and their work through prayers. He thanks the local Mission Committee and especially Mr. Polder, who were instrumental in making sure that this service could take place, both from a logistical and a financial aspect.

Mr. Polder, who was a great supporter of the NRC Mission

Rev H. Rijksen directs his final words to the missionary team, Rev. Kuijt, Dick ten Voorde the young teacher, and nurse Diny Sonneveld. One by one, he asks them if they are prepared to do their utmost, no matter where the future may lead them. Each one earnestly replies, "Yes." Their answers are given as a promise and a pledge before the countenance of the Lord.

Several other speakers say a few words. Rev. L. Rijksen, Rev. Kuijt's teacher, speaks on behalf of the NRC. Rev. Perdok speaks on behalf of the Council of Missions congratulating the NRC and the missionary team as now mission work can actively commence.

Around 10:00 pm, Rev. H. Rijksen closes the service with a prayer of thanksgiving. "There are so many reasons to thank the Lord for everything He has provided. Nevertheless, even greater is the necessity to pray for a blessing from Him Who is called the Lord of the Harvest."

The deep sound of a horn announcing the departure of the M.S. Oranje, can be heard throughout the entire harbour of Amsterdam. Steam clouds rise up out of the enormous smokestacks. Near the gangplank, last minute photographs are taken of the missionary team.

Miep Kuijt is accompanying her husband as far as Italy and will then return to Holland on her own. The rest of the team shall sail on to Singapore and from there they will fly to New Guinea.

The ocean vessel passenger ship MS Oranje

Last photo before departure.
L/R: Diny Sonneveld, Ada ten Voorde,
Dick ten Voorde, Rev. G. Kuijt & Miep Kuijt-Bos.

Many friends and acquaintances are standing on the wharf waving good-bye. Rev. L. Rijksen, along with Kuijt's colleagues, has travelled to Amsterdam to say farewell. Rev. Kuijt enjoys the moment and cheerfully shakes hands with everyone. "Brothers," he says, "I still have extra tickets with which you can travel along as far as Ijmuiden." (Ijmuiden is the last Dutch harbour before you enter the North Sea.)

Eagerly, the students look at the tickets in Kuijt's hand but Rev. Rijksen is unyielding; they must return to Rotterdam to continue their studies.

Upon their return to Rotterdam, the teacher realizes one of his students is missing. Student Karens has stayed behind. He could not resist the temptation to sail on one of those huge passenger ships. When he returns to Rotterdam, he hears from the other students that Rev. Rijksen is very upset with him. However, student Karens knows that Rev. Rijksen's disposition on Monday will be very lenient if he had preached well on Sunday. Therefore, Karens first inquires, and then phones Rev. Rijksen to offer his apologies. Sure enough, Rev. Rijksen had a good Sunday.

Chapter 5

Land of Exorcists and Soothsayers

Shaped like a wounded, dying black grouse and locked between the South Pacific Ocean and the Arafura Sea is the enormous island of New Guinea. New Guinea is the world's second largest island after Greenland. If you want to travel from the east to the west of New Guinea you must count on at least twenty-four hundred kilometres of difficult terrain. The distance from the north to the south coast is less than seven hundred kilometres; however, this stretch is virtually impossible to cross because of the rugged mountains.

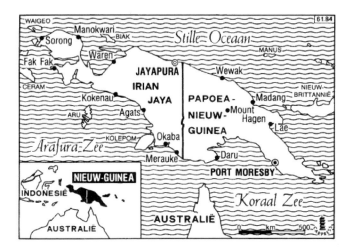

To the north of Australia is the large island of New Guinea

The border from north to south is as straight as an arrow and divides the island in two. To the east is the Australian part of New Guinea (now Papua New Guinea) and to the west is Dutch New Guinea, later also known as Irian Barat, Irian Jaya and now Papua.

However, nature does not respect the boundaries drawn by man. The mountain ranges jut five thousand metres into the sky, and some are blanketed in snow year round. In the 1950's the western portion of the island had a population of approximately 800,000 people. There are many tribes; some live hidden within the jungles and coastal marshes. Hundreds of languages are spoken, many of which are related to one another. Among the tribes, the rivalries for territory, domestic animals or wives often result in fierce fighting. Head hunting is retaliated. The call for revenge always wins over the desire for peace.

Wherever a different civilization sets foot on the island it leaves traces on both the cultural and religious life of the Papuans. The old lifestyle is influenced and the traditional spirit worship is brought into discussion.

In 1512, Portuguese sailors spotted the island from a distance but dared not land. In 1526, Jorge Meneses, the first Portuguese governor of the Moluccas, accidentally landed on Waigeo, a small island near the Vogelkop (Bird's Head). He was on his way to Ternate on the Moluccas islands to purchase cloves. The wind, however, forced him to the east and he landed on the island which he named "*Ilha dos Papuas,*" or "Papua" after the Malaysian word for 'papuwah' which means curly hair.

*In the 19th century, explorers dared to travel up the various
rivers where they were not always welcomed*

"Raja Papua, the king of these people is immensely rich in gold and slaves and lives in the middle of the island," wrote the explorer, Antonio Pigafetta. Pigafetta had only heard of this by way of mouth. The story really does not make sense, but interest in this mysterious island was awakened.

Reports from Pigafetta meant that both Portuguese and Spanish explorers wanted to be the first to discover this "Golden Island." In 1545, the Spaniard De Retes claimed the island for the Spanish throne.

But the Dutch also wanted a piece of the action. As dogs waiting to steal the bone from their opponents, Dutch Republic ships circled the island in 1606. Sailors were at the railing of their vessel, *Het Duyfke*, shading their eyes with their hands while peering at the coast. Mercator the cartographer is correct. In this place there must be an enormous island, Nueva Guinea. They anchored their ship in the Digul Bay to look for the gold. The sailors' hopes were quickly dashed, however, for there was no gold to be found. They conclude that the stories about this island are nonsense. The men of the United East-Indies Company think the same when Commander Jan Carstenz reports from his voyage along the south coast of New Guinea. The officials smile mockingly, "Read that again! SNOW?" Indeed SNOW is written in his journal. "Snow this close to the equator!" Normally, Commander Carstenz was well aware of everything that went on but the officials thought he must have been drunk when he wrote this! However, just in case he is right, he deserves to have the snow-capped mountains named after him (which in fact happened).

Considerable time went by before the United East Indies Company finalized its first commercial contract in New Guinea. A treaty with the Sultan of Tidore stipulated that the territory was forbidden to all Europeans except, of course, the Dutch. It was impossible to monitor this treaty, however, and the English also tried to establish their power on the island. Eventually, all interest in the island waned. It would take almost one hundred years before explorers showed interest in the island again with the trade of myrtle tree bark. This soft, juicy tree bark was in great demand owing to its fragrance, which was placed in pillows or finely ground and then mixed with tobacco. But this business never really took off. Neither did the trading of turtles, birds of paradise or amber.

The snow-capped peaks of the Carstenz Mountains

New Guinea remained an insignificant island among the Indonesian archipelago, in contrast, for example, to the Moluccas, which the Dutch government was in control of. In New Guinea there was not much more than a government post with a few "exiled" officials.

The island remained an intriguing destination for scientists, however. Biologists and geologists found an ecologically pure and untouched territory to do their research. In the beginning of the 20th century, numerous expeditions took place in New Guinea and gradually the region was mapped.

In March 1942, the American General Douglas MacArthur looked solemnly over the railing of his torpedo boat. He had waged a heroic but hopeless battle and had to pull back from the war zone. The Commander-in-Chief of the Far East acknowledged defeat to the Japanese. He was being evacuated from the settlement of Corregidor in the Philippines. This distressed MacArthur, for now the Asian archipelago was going to be lost. If the Americans had been able to keep control of these islands, they would have been able to close off the connecting sea route back to Japan and could have cut off communication between Japan and the Japanese-occupied Indonesian settlements where most of Japan's raw materials came from.

The Commander-in-Chief looked towards the islands. "I shall return," he promised, "then I will drive the Japanese flag off all these islands."

After a relatively speedy advance of the Japanese into New Guinea, the Australian troops stopped the Japanese and foot by foot regained the occupied territory. Thousands of Japanese and Australian troops were killed in battle. Then, as promised, General MacArthur returned. In October 1944, the Americans launched a large-scale landing operation on Leyte, near the centre of the Philippine archipelago. The battle at Leyte ended in an overwhelming Allied victory with the sinking of three Japanese battle ships and the destruction of ten cruisers, nine fighter planes and a submarine. The backbone of the Japanese fleet was broken.

The official signing of the peace treaty, whereby the Japanese surrendered the South Pacific, took place on the American battleship "Missouri". General MacArthur signed on behalf of the allies.

After this battle MacArthur started to conquer the Indonesian islands Rioe-kioe, Bonin and Vulkaan Islands from his base in the Philippines. The Japanese desperately defended themselves but MacArthur's unique strategy called "island hopping" was successful. The battle for Hollandia (now known as Jayapura) enters the history books as a model of military strategy.

After World War II, the Dutch return to Indonesia. But now there is an anti-colonial atmosphere. The country no longer wants to be controlled by a Western European power. In a very short time, the Independence Movement grows into a national outcry: *Merdeka*! (Freedom!) On August 17, 1945 Sukarno and Hatta declare independence although it will take until 1949 before this is acknowledged by The Netherlands. The Republic of Indonesia is established. New Guinea is not included.

The battle of Hollandia by the allies, led by MacArthur

President Sukarno

Sukarno continues to claim New Guinea. With haste, the Netherlands establish government stations in the interior of the island. A financial and economic base is established with the development of lumber mills, the extraction of oil, the trade of crocodile skins, nutmeg, mace, and copra (the first layer on the outside of the coconut). Gigantic Dutch subsidies support these initiatives. Indonesia does not like these developments. Pres. Sukarno feels New Guinea belongs to Indonesia and his people supported him in this. "The Indonesian flag must fly from Sabang to Merauke, from the most western place to the border of Australian New Guinea."

Finally, the United States of America steps in. In order to avoid the country being driven even more into the arms of communist Russia, they support Indonesia. On August 15, 1962, a treaty is signed in New York affirming that New Guinea belongs to Indonesia.

Johan C. Geissler.
He and Carl W. Ottow are
considered to have been the first
missionaries in New Guinea

The first mission work in New Guinea dates back to the second half of the nineteenth century. Carl W. Ottow and Johan C. Geissler first settled on the west side of New Guinea in 1855 but their efforts amounts figuratively to "ploughing on rocks." In the first twenty-five years of mission work in New Guinea more Protestant missionaries died than gentiles were saved.

In 1862 the Utrecht Mission Society sends its first mission students, including J. L. van Hassell, to the northwest of New Guinea. Several years later, the Missionaries open their first little church.

To attract the natives to their services, they lure them with luxury items such as syrah and gambir which the natives chew along with tobacco. The missionaries also regularly buy slaves (mostly children) who were stolen from other tribes. This provides them with servants and in this way these children were saved from a life of misery, thereby receiving a Christian upbringing. This is labelled as "disguised slavery" writes the Utrecht Mission Society in 1909. However, "the end justifies the means."

The missionaries also try to influence the surrounding area by opposing the gentile customs and instituting Sunday as the day of rest. Where trust from the inlanders is gained, the people listened to the missionaries. More than once the missionaries succeed in saving shipwrecked Europeans out of the hands of the natives and prevent tribes from raiding one another.

However, all this only touched the Papuans outwardly, not their heart. The natives are willing to be courteous towards the missionaries in order to earn their favor. Therefore, they changed their lifestyle to some degree. But an extended period of absence from the missionaries is enough for the natives to revert to their old ways. When epidemics break out or other calamities happen, it is attributed to evil or unsatisfied spirits; then the notion awakens that the *Adat* is violated.

There is resistance towards the mission work, especially from the witch doctors and *konoors* (soothsayers) who claim to have magical powers. The konoors actually believe to be in possession of spirits and see all kinds of visions. They influence the people by telling them the spirits have spoken. Who dares to contradict?

A smallpox epidemic takes place in 1904-1905. There is no relief against the disease even though the natives bring sacrifices to their holy places. But the vaccinations the missionaries give do help. The spirits in the Dorehbaai on Numfoor and Biak lose their battle against Western medicine.

There is no room for the Gospel. But there was room for *raaks,* murdering, capturing of slaves, and head hunting to settle old feuds. At these times the position of the missionaries is perilous.

In order to have some protection, they appeal to the Dutch government to establish a government post in New Guinea. The administration of their area is currently handled by the Commissioner of

Ternate, which is too far away. Help always arrives too late from Ternate and it is difficult to keep law and order. A good start is made when a commissioner is appointed in 1898.

Nature is magnificent in its beauty

This is no place for missionaries. The tropical climate in general is very unhealthy, especially the *haze* (vapours) from the jungles and the marshlands along the coast. Who can tolerate to live for such a long time in isolation and who can live with the constant feeling of being in danger by the Papuans or live in fear of the snakes that can unexpectedly sink their poisonous teeth into your body? The pioneers especially have a hard time coping. They had no knowledge of the country, the people or their language, and they have to fend for themselves. As a result, they experience all sorts of horrendous hardships. Many mission workers succumb to the climate and the hard physical labour.

The missionaries have no chance. There are chances for the foreign traders who, without hesitation, succeed in swindling the natives resulting in them being wary of strangers. The Utrecht Mission Society even decides to send a Christian salesman *(tokohouder, or* shopkeeper*)* to give the natives an opportunity to purchase their goods at a fair price. Credit is not extended, the Sunday is to be honoured, and no alcohol is to be sold. This endeavour has little success.

Still the Utrecht Mission Society perseveres. By bringing together small groups of Christians they establish hearth fires in the hope that later they can influence the others. They believe that a breakthrough will come. Then requests will come from all directions for *Goeroes* (preachers and teachers). On the island Roon, where initially no fruits were seen, a powerful awakening to the Gospel takes place. On New Year's Eve, 1907, the natives voluntarily throw their *korwaars* (idols) into the sea in order to begin the New Year without idols.

In the spring of 1908, F. J. F. van Hasselt undertakes an expedition through the Geelvink Bay. Wherever he goes, he encounters interest for the Gospel and is asked to send Goeroes.

Even from the island of Biak (a notorious place for pirates) no less than seventy-two idols are placed before the feet of the missionary. Also at the old posts, there is a movement like it has never happened before and goes from village to village. This movement places a great responsibility on the mission. "If the work does not commence immediately in every aspect, we will miss the opportunity to gather in the harvest which is waiting for Christ."

Evangelist John van Balen has made a deep impression on the people. He has received a dream and henceforth speaks to the natives about a golden ladder which they must climb in order to receive eternal life and which they may not climb if they do not repent from their idolatry and turn to the Lord.

The Second World War deeply affects the mission work. All foreign missionaries are interned by the Japanese on the island of Ambon. The Japanese forbid religious instruction; Bibles, hymnals, and all Christian literature have to be burned. However, in most areas the local evangelists continue preaching. Among the foreign missionaries while being interned there are many who lose or their own life or their wife or children. When the war is over, church life slowly restores. Vacancies are difficult to fill. The local people have insufficient schooling. In 1951, the NHK takes over responsibility for the mission work in New Guinea.

The need arises to establish a theological seminary for local pastors. The school starts in 1954 in Serui with the thought that the mission needs to make itself superfluous. The church in Papua must be led by pastors and office bearers from among the Papuan people. It takes until 1956 before the first independent church, the *Gereja Kristen Injili* (GKI, or ECK), is established in New Guinea. The NHK continues via the Mission in Oegstgeest to participate in the work of the ECK.

Headquarters for the mission of the NHK in the Netherlands

In 1955, the *Tweede Kamer* (Second House of the Dutch Parliament), under pressure from the *Katholieke Volks Party* (KVP) the Catholic People's Party accepts a motion that Catholic and Protestant missions in New Guinea can work wherever they want to. From this moment on the boundaries where the Protestant missions are in the north and the Roman Catholic missions in the south, fade. The Roman Catholic missions move northward and the Protestants extend their activities into the Baliem Valley. It is very important to the missions on the island that the government opens a post in Wamena located in the Baliem Valley. At the request of the ECK, the *Rheinische Missions Gesellschaft* (RMG) in Barmen, Germany provides two missionaries to work in the interior: Pastors Paul G. Aring and Siegfried Zöllner. Their first post is opened in Angguruk in the Yalimo district, a five-day walk from Wamena in a southeast direction.

To open the Angguruk area, a strip is built. The first Mission Aviation Fellowship (MAF) aircraft lands on September 23, 1961. The work in

63

Wamena (Baliem Valley) extends to the northeast and in 1962 Kurrima is opened. The tribal people (Yalis) have war problem alliances and traditional enemies. Rumours about cannibalism are true. In July 1963, eleven people from the main mission station and surrounding area are killed and eaten by the natives.

In addition, other mission organizations establish themselves in various areas of the interior. The Christian and Missionary Alliance (CAMA) mission settles in the Pyramid area. Three other Protestant organizatíons: the Unevangelized Field Mission (UFM), the Regions Beyond Missionary Union (RBMU) and the Asia Pacific Christian Mission (APCM), unite to form an independent church nammed *Gereja Injili Irian Jaya* (GIIJ).

Since 1956 the Australian Baptist Missionary Society and the Mission of the *Gereformeerde Kerken Vrijgemaakt* (Article 31 Reformed Churches) have been active in the Upper Digul area. There are supporting organizations such as the Mission Aviation Fellowship (MAF) and The Missions Fellowhip (TMF).

There is a certain amount of co-operation among most mission organizations and respect among the missionaries. The island is divided into sections with no one allowed to encroach on the others mission station or area.

The ECK has little contact with the Roman Catholic mission, but respects their presence. The Faith Missions unite to create the TMF the ECK and the Roman Catholics do not join because of irreconcilable differences in Theology.

The period of 1960 to 1970 is a decade of church planting in valleys and villages. The work among the Danis in the Baliem Valley and surrounding areas progresses with extreme difficulties. It is not until after 1970 that there is a breakthrough.

Chapter 6

Learning Dependence in the Jungle

"Java, Sumatra, Borneo, Celebes, Flores, Sumba, Sumbawa, Timor..." The teacher taps his cane on the blackboard as he points out each island on the map. When he is satisfied that the children have memorized the Indonesian Islands he asks, "Which one of you knows where the M.S. Oranje is expected to be now?"

The M.S. Oranje has become a common subject in the classroom. It is not so much about the passenger ship itself but about the mission team on board. The teacher's cane slides from Amsterdam to Ijmuiden, up the North Sea in the direction of the Channel. Each time the cane stops, the children call out the name of the place: the Channel, Mediterranean Sea, Strait of Messina, Crete, Port Said, the Red Sea, Gulf of Aden, Indian Ocean, Ceylon, along the north point of Sumatra to Singapore.

The teacher nods in agreement and continues to talk about the dangers the mission team will face and the obstacles that must be overcome. But he makes it clear that it is for a good cause; the Word must go forth.

> *The weather until now has been exceptional. We have been on the Mediterranean the past several days. I most often think about Paul, the great apostle to the gentiles, who made many voyages in the same area where we are sailing at the moment. On Paul's voyages the sailors were dependent on the wind which was needed to fill their sails.*

> *I am sure that God's people in those days were more dependent on and in need of the Lord. Paul likely never experienced sailing on a ship that travelled through the waters at a speed of twenty-two nautical miles per hour (approximately forty kilometres per hour).*

Mrs. Kuijt disembarks in Italy to travel back to the Netherlands by train. The M.S. Oranje continues its voyage on the Mediterranean Sea in the direction of Port Said. It will be fourteen months before the newlyweds embrace each other again.

Missionary Kuijt on board the MS Oranje

On the ship Rev. Kuijt is never bored. There is always something interesting to see or someone to talk to. The missionary in him cannot be denied and freely he witnesses to whoever wants to listen to the Gospel, the rich message for poor lost sinners.

> *Yesterday as we were passing through the Strait of Messina, between the boot of Italy and Sicily, I unexpectedly got into a conversation with two members of the ship's orchestra. I pointed out the necessity of true repentance to them. They listened attentively, especially the accordionist who entrusted to me that he would gladly exchange his sailing career for a regular job on land. Who can tell what good may come out of this contact? Even here on this ship is a mission task.*

After the ship arrives in Singapore, the mission team flies on to Bangkok and the same day continues on to Biak. Here the members of the group temporarily part ways, each going to their own destination to prepare themselves for their future work. Diny Sonneveld goes to Wasior, Dick and Ada ten Voorde to Hollandia, and Rev. Kuijt to Sorong.

The counsel for the NHK church in the Netherlands has made arrangements ahead of time for a welcoming reception. Pastors were notified and are waiting to receive them. When Kuijt makes a stop in Manokwari, he is greeted by Rev. Gijsbers and at the next stop in Sorong Rev. Woldendorp welcomes him.

The orientation starts immediately. Rev. Woldendorp introduces Kuijt to several schools in the area, which are fruits of their mission work. The students, especially the girls, sing beautifully.

This morning I was planning to record their music but the Papuan lady teacher became sick, so the program was cancelled.

Rev. Kuijt is impressed by all the work that is being done by the ECK in the Vogelkop (the Bird's Head).

Together with Rev. Woldendorp, Kuijt visits Rev. Osok in Kalasamen. Both decide to attend a worship service at a local church. The building is a simple structure with a corrugated aluminum roof; there are a few wooden benches but the listeners prefer to sit on the ground. At the front there is a flute orchestra and a Malaccan teacher leads the service in the Malayan language. At first glance the service does not appear to be anything special but at second glance you notice that the people are not the usual church goers. In this village, isolated from the outside world, there is a population of some two hundred and sixty men, women, and children suffering from leprosy. They are outcasts from their society and each has their own story to tell. Perhaps they've left behind a husband, wife or children. When the white spots became visible they were forced to leave everything behind. The curse of "unclean" took over their lives but at the hospice they find kindness and love from two Swiss nurses who are not hampered by fear of this disease. They also do not stop their work because of the political unrest or the fighting that takes place around them

The work of compassion must go on. Kuijt cannot hide his admiration for these heroines. "Bravo!" he enthusiastically writes. "There is so much work being done by men and women of which we are unaware..."

The initial introduction with the reality of mission work does not discourage Rev. Kuijt. Together with Rev. Woldendorp he makes a tour through the Klabra district south of Sorong. All his experiences are recorded in detail for the home front.

As far as I am concerned, I am not disheartened by the perils we will encounter in the future nor the difficulties faced with nature. Of course that does not mean that dangers do not exist. I have already experienced some of them. However, this does not discourage me.

A visit with a coastal Papuan family

A prauw of a Government representative in the north of New Guinea

The helicopter landed about fifty metres from the house where I am staying. This flight was offered to us by the NNGPM (Netherlands New Guinea Petroleum Company) who also provided lodging fit for a king in their guest house at Klamono, their oil headquarters. It is really too bad that the oil industry is declining; New Guinea would have benefited from the industry. For example they donated the local hospital and also the church building for the Dutch-speaking community.

The flight went according to plan; it was a bit windy, as the machine was open on both sides. Being in the air we got a beautiful view of the endless jungle of New Guinea. Here and there a river slithers like a snake through the jungle and we saw the approximately fifty kilometre long road from Sorong to Klamono that has also been built by the NNGPM. The following day we went by boat to Bagun, which took approximately five hours. On both sides of the river is the impenetrable jungle. Now and then a Jaarvogel (wreathed hornbill) flew out and we heard the screaming of the cockatoos.

Wreathed hornbill

Here and there we came across a sleeping young crocodile that had not yet figured out that they must at least go down when they hear a motorboat approaching. This trip is again paid for by the NNGPM. The leader in Klamono, who I only know by his first name, Tuan Max (Mister Max) is an Ambonese Christian who supports the church and shows in this way his love for his Christian brothers and sisters.

We were warmly received in Bagun. The local guru *(teacher) greeted us on the little landing, which I very carefully eyed whether it would hold my weight. In general, Papuans are small in stature and their homes and platforms are built accordingly.*

Later, on that same journey, several rotting tree trunks collapsed under my weight. Once I fell through a set of stairs. On another occasion I almost plummeted through the floor of a pole dwelling with the result that some repair work had to be done that same evening. After a short period of rest, Rev. Woldendorp was eager to continue on in the direction of Wanurian, where the local government is managed by a Papuan official. Thankfully we were able to find several men and boys who were willing to carry our gear.

You must understand that we not only had our necessary clothing but also enough food for ten days plus contact articles.

As soon as we stepped outside the village, we entered the jungle. A narrow footpath led the way in the direction of Wanurian. To me, everything seemed the same and I could not distinguish a footpath. Besides that, I needed all my attention 'to keep my soul alive', to use a biblical expression. Soft tropical rain began to fall; it did not bother me too much as I had on my raincoat but the raincoat did not prevent me from getting soaked from perspiration. I don't believe that I have ever sweated so much in my life as I did on that trek. You know that I wear glasses; everyone who wears glasses will agree how annoying it is when rain spatters on your lenses. Plus the condensation on the inside of my lenses! But we had to keep going, could not rest for even a moment, except when I slid off a tree trunk and had to scramble up out of the mud. "Do not stop," I told myself, because whenever I did slow down I felt the body of a Papuan carrier in my back forcing me to hurry up. Boy! Can those Papuans trek and that all on their bare feet! Shoes are a hindrance for them.

After an hour and forty-five minutes we arrived at a village where we would stay for the remainder of that day. I thanked the Lord sincerely for His goodness that He allowed me to make it safely through the jungle. Then I noticed that some bloodsuckers had attached themselves to my legs.. Touching them with a burning cigarette is the best way to get them to release their hold. Several times while trekking, I called on the Most High to help me through. Without His help I would have never made it. Sometimes, I prayed, 'Lord, guide my foot to the right spot as I am exhausted' In the jungles of New Guinea you learn how dependent you are on Him.

What Kuijt describes as quite a harrowing experience, Rev. Woldendorp merely brushes off as a leisurely trip. Here is what he wrote:

We returned from a ten-day trek through the swamps of the Klabra region in the southwest of the Vogelkop. We have been working in that area for about ten years and have a small number of confessing Christians. The area is under government control and it cannot be compared with the interior. This tour was easier as we could stay at the homes of the evangelists and they took care of our cooking and laundry. Travel here is relatively safe. The trek was typical for this region. First we took the NNPGM helicopter to Klamona and stayed in their guest-house, which means first-class lodging. The next day we went by motor boat to the kampong of Bagun; then trekking through the mud and swamp of sago trees. From there on we used canoes followed by another day of trekking. The last few days we travelled again by motor boat and helicopter.

Rev. Woldendorp is very impressed with Rev. Kuijt. "He is proving to be an excellent travelling companion who shows an enormous interest in the local people, with whom he eagerly made contact. He has adjusted himself to each situation without a problem and is not easily discouraged."

In the meantime, the MB is concerned about the political situation, but Rev. Kuijt shrugs off their concerns.

Honestly, I am as relaxed as can be. Perhaps Rev. L. Rijksen was right in what he said to me. "You overestimate yourself and you underestimate the reality." But the Lord reigns.

The Indonesian government has assured everyone that when the administration of New Guinea is transferred, the safety of the churches and the Dutch will be guaranteed. Missionaries will be able to continue their work without hindrance.

When Rev. Osok attends a Synod of the ECK, he has a letter from Rev. Kuijt in which he asks the Synod for help in selecting a mission field. The Synod advises him to go to the Baliem Valley as there are still areas where the Word of God has never been heard. Rev. Aring in Wamena also agrees.

The MB heartily approves but wants ten Voorde to be included in the expeditions as they feel that two heads are better than one. When one is discouraged the other can encourage him. Rev. Aring can also provide valuable assistance In the meantime Nurse Sonneveld will continue to work in Wasior.

But, before the expedition can proceed into the interior, some difficulties must be overcome. To name one Rev. Kuijt needs to receive official permission to be able to go into the interior because of his past history with tuberculosis.

The Lord is testing my faith again. As you know the interior is declared a quarantined area. This means they are extremely careful not to import contagious diseases which are foreign to the region, such as leprosy and tuberculosis. To make a long story short, my case is being evaluated. I had all the necessary medical documents with me from the doctors in Holland and these have been sent via the hospital in Sorong to Hollandia. Just this morning the doctor in Sorong received a message from Hollandia requesting more information; they even want to know what medicines I have taken. There is a possibility that before being granted permission to go into the interior, I must take some more medicine. Oh well, I will hear about this in Hollandia. However, let all of us together earnestly ask the Lord to show us His plan whether to go to the Baliem Valley or not.

And indeed Rev. Kuijt receives permission to go into the interior.

After consulting with ECK and CAMA, an area is designated where they can look for a suitable mission site. It will not be the Baliem Valley. Angguruk will become the home base, which is located southeast of Wamena, where Wim Vriend has settled and is prepared to give his support.

A native from the interior   *An important person from the interior*

Although there are times of joy and peace there are also times of disappointment and discouragement. In a letter to Rev. L. Rijksen, Kuijt writes that he will soon die. He is at peace with that thought. Rev. Vergunst reprimands him gently in a letter, about this assuming that he, like Elijah, is sitting under his juniper tree. He wrote, "I hope that in the meantime the Lord has made things a bit easier for you and that you will have a long life that is consecrated to God and His service." Kuijt replies that he, in all seriousness, believes that next year the Lord will take him home.

> *Please do not think that I am writing out of discouragement or that life is too hard for me. I am cheerful and plan to labour until the night falls for me. I only say this, so whatever happens does not come to you without warning.*

> *Isolation is very difficult for anyone especially when you are alone—it plays havoc with one's mind.*

View from the air while surveying.
Without MAF, mission work would have been impossible in most places.

Endless miles of broccoli-like canopy stretch out below them. The glitter of streams can be seen and the sunlight creates rainbows on the waterfalls. On board the Cessna is Rev Kuijt and Aring. The engine drones on. These valleys are home to people who have never been in contact with the outside world. The humming of the big bird in the sky frightens them and they disappear into the forest. In some of the villages below are only a handful of huts. The only signs of life are the occasional plume of smoke.

The question is, "What tribes live here and are these tribes hostile?" If they are hostile to one another, new carriers will have to be hired in each tribal area. In general, Papuans will not cross into each other's territory; it could cost them their lives. So it might take weeks before friendships can be cultivated with a tribe and before the trek can be continued.

Plans have to be made for the undertaking; food and gear must be purchased for at least a three-month period. Of course, we cannot take everything along. The items that will be carried on the trail are packed in aluminum containers and the items that will be dropped from the plane at a later date must be packed into large burlap bags and carefully padded on the inside with thick layers of long grass. All the bags are sewn shut and numbered. When a request for a drop is made to MAF they only take the numbers which are asked for.

After several months of preparations, Rev. Kuijt leaves Angguruk and heads to "The Valley of the Seventy (huts)."

Chapter 7

In Spite of a Setback

It gradually becomes apparent to the MB that there is a strained relationship between the various members of the mission team. Even before the team left Holland, there had already been a disagreement among the team members. The MB resolved the issue through mediation and hoped that once the team arrives in New Guinea, things would work out. Then the team would have to depend upon one another and would be forced to work together.

But relationships do not improve and the situation becomes worse. Missionary Kuijt has a strong desire to start his work and does not let this deter him. Gerrit had already suggested before being sent out that it would be better not to send everyone out at once. He envisions the future as follows: it is best to first locate a place to work and then build some accommodations before sending out the rest of the team. This is one of the reasons why his wife stayed behind in the Netherlands.

The MB emphatically insists on having Dick ten Voorde involved with the search for a mission field. This does not happen. Rev. Kuijt later explained that unfortunately there were not enough places to sleep. Rev. Rigters had a different opinion,

> *Rev. Kuijt desires to wander as a Paul and seeks the freedom to go where he wishes. He sees himself as a pioneer who does not want to be hindered.*

To try and restore the situation, the MB asked ten Voorde to terminate his work at Ifar and join Rev. Kuijt as an evangelist. Kuijt and ten Voorde can support and strengthen each other. It does not change anything.

During this time political tensions in Hollandia (capital city) were increasing and, in some instances, the situation became panicky. Foreigners are getting ready to expatriate and people from other organizations are leaving the country. The MB leaves the decision whether to stay or leave up to the team. For the time being they decide to remain. However, ten Voorde dreads leaving his wife behind in Hollandia, while he goes into the interior for considerable lengths of time. In the meantime they realize that an airstrip will take several months or even up to a year or more to build. Mission worker, Dr. Willem H. Vriend from Angguruk speaks from experience when he says; "If within two years you succeed in building a basic station with a landing strip and some primitive dwellings, you may speak of a blessed progress of the work..."

"As long as Rev. Kuijt and ten Voorde are in the interior building a strip, there will be no need for nurse Sonneveld. And Ada ten Voorde will have to wait in Hollandia or even in the Netherlands. Should Kuijt decide to trek into the interior alone, ten Voorde will be unemployed."

Missionary Dr. Willem Vriend has settled in Angguruk

It is a very low point in the history of the mission. On May 11, 1962, Rev. Kuijt writes, "In Ifar they are very happy with ten Voorde. He does an excellent job and Rev. Middag said that our churches can send another twenty of such teachers." Also from Yalimo the request comes to "send that ten Voorde along." However, the MB realizes they are dealing with a situation that is beyond repair. Even mediation from Rev. Rigters cannot resolve the situation. The ten Voordes as well as Diny Sonneveld return to the Netherlands arriving at Schiphol on September 9, 1962.

How do they explain such a conflict within the mission team to the congregations?

Rev. Vergunst writes to Rev. Rigters.

> *For years we have pleaded about the necessity of mission work in our circles. We are thankful to God that the realization finally took hold, that the whole world is our mission field and we only bring shame upon ourselves by living in segregation. The support of our people is overwhelming and we are constantly amazed by the tokens of love and the gifts for the work. Our youth is enthused that we have our own missionaries. Their enthusiasm is heart-warming. People read about missions and attend mission evenings; in short we rejoice about this movement. When this situation becomes public, it will be disastrous. We are a very small organization and there is such an emotional bond with the mission team. Everyone speaks about them and there is much prayer for them.*
>
> *You will understand that we are saddened by the situation. However, this setback does not happen outside God's decree! We believe that God's work will always be tested. We assume these setbacks to happen in a certain way but now it comes from a totally different direction.*

The announcement to the congregations is very low-key. The *Saambinder* (a church magazine) reports:

> *Due to developments that are closely connected to the work of our mission team in New Guinea, we deeply regret to inform you that Mr. and Mrs. ten Voorde and Miss Sonneveld have returned to the Netherlands. For the time being Rev. Kuijt will remain in New Guinea. We have instructed him to continue the*

work.

It is decided not to release the ten Voordes and nurse Sonneveld but to look for another mission field for them. In consultation with Rev. MacKay from Oegstgeest, another possibility is found in Nigeria. A few months later they are sent out to begin their work in Igede. Here their abilities and talents unfold and their labours are still visible to this day.

Pioneer Kuijt carries on alone in New Guinea. Many mission workers, dignitaries and business people left the island to return to the Netherlands or move to the Australian side of New Guinea. Hollandia looks like a ghost town. Many homes are empty.

From across the street a man approaches the missionary. "Hey Gerrit, when are you leaving?"

"I am going on Tuesday," he answers.

"Tuesday? How can that be, no plane is leaving on Tuesday."

"That is not what I mean! I am going into the interior."

The man stares at him in astonishment. Everyone is leaving and he plans to go into the interior? But Kuijt cannot leave. He has not yet had a chance to start mission work in a place where the Gospel has not already been proclaimed.

After a short stay in Angguruk, the pioneer sets out again to Yalimo, "where the sun rises" (thus to the east). He is on his way to the "Valley of the Seventy" (one of the villages has 70 huts). Rev. Zöllner accompanies him for a while. It will be a difficult trek as mountains more than two thousand metres high must be crossed. The young twelve-year-old guide, Malik, accompanies Kuijt and promises to stay with him. Five coastal Papuans: Frederik Paraibabo, Junus Jochu, Zeth Faidiban, Adi Awon and Jacob Reba carry the gear.

> *At first it appeared that many of the local people were eager to help carry the necessary baggage. Everything was ready to go but after all nobody, not even one person, was willing to help us. The men stood at a distance watching what was happening but refused to lift a finger. It was 8:00, 9:00 and then 10:00 o'clock and still no one came forward. The gear stood on the Angguruk airstrip for all to see. Even promises of an axe or other payment were of no avail.*

Kuijt decides to leave with Zöllner, the five coastal Papuans and Malik. The goods are cut back to a bare minimum but even the most essential items—a battery, pick axes, bush knives, radio, tents, and food—prove to be a heavy load.

A narrow path runs through the jungle. It winds up the hill and then unexpectedly goes perilously straight down the mountainside. Sweat pours down Kuijt's head. After several hours the path ends by the Obarek, a river that is impossible to wade across. The bridge consists of three small trunks, which are high above the swirling river. "I must be honest and tell you I was afraid to cross."

Rev. Zöllner in Angguruk

Rev. Zöllner goes first. On hands and feet he carefully crawls inch by inch to the other side. The small tree trunks bends dangerously under his weight. Kuijt follows, and prays, wondering whether his life is going to end here. "With God's help I made it."

The climb continues to Heliaki, a kampong (village) on a mountain.

> *Sometimes we had to bush-whack our way with axes. Our clothes were drenched with sweat and you could literally wring them out.*

Gasping, Kuijt sinks to the ground. He is exhausted and cannot keep up. Malik sees this and, without hesitation, picks up Kuijt's gear as well and continues up the mountain.

The reception in Heliaki is friendly. The missionary approaches the village *Kepala* (chief) who greets him: "*Bannesum.*" Apparently, news has spread through the jungle about *Bannesum* (the bearded one). The group spends the night in the village; the next morning the journey continues.

After five exhausting days they arrive in Wasaldak. With a sigh of relief Kuijt lowers himself to the ground, "Let's rest for just a moment." Here several villages are close together with a total of about three hundred huts, which means approximately three thousand people. These people have never been in contact with white people or with the Gospel.

One of their typical bridges

The preliminary strip site that was selected by MAF from the air is several days further on. The mountain ridge that needs to be crossed in order to get there is more daunting than all the others. In addition, the battery is dead and radio contact is impossible. Because of this, the missionary decides to stay in Wasaldak. Kuijt believes that it might be possible to build an airstrip there. Dr. Vriend provides his input. He acquired his experience in mission work through trial and error. He has learned that you have to know the local traditions so you can understand their behaviour. He believes it is irresponsible for Kuijt to go by himself. It is definitely not a walk in the park. Much will be required—physical strength—probably more than his health can endure. Plus there are many dangers.

Rev. Kuijt with a group of locals from Kosarek

The preliminary strip site that was selected by MAF from the air is involved in such a trek. The Yalimo area is not yet under government control. There is no support to fall back on. The various tribes are hostile toward one another, but with their spies they know exactly what is going on with each other. It is one thing for a troop of armed police patrols to go through the areas of the different tribes but it's quite another for a small group of unescorted missionaries.

Vriend's opinion is that when Kuijt starts, there is no turning back.

A problem arises when the radio breaks down. Then

someone has to walk back to the home base to get it repaired. But a white person must stay behind to give the coastal boys emotional and spiritual support. The white man needs to have another European with him as a partner and a comrade on whom he can rely. In isolation, tensions can run high. Suppose Kuijt is successful in reaching the place that MAF suggested as a strip site. Then the locals must be persuaded to help. That can only happen if they know why they are working.

A strip is an attractive undertaking as the natives have already heard about the advantages of having one. This motivates the men to work. But you do not want to think about the possibility that after all the planning and work that you might have to stop the building of the air strip as it is not feasible. How can you explain this to the locals? There is a chance of being in serious danger if they find out that you are now planning to build an air strip in their enemy's territory. All of a sudden it is the enemy, not them, who is going to reap the desired benefits of the strip.

But to build an airstrip takes a great deal of time. The area where Rev. Kuijt is going is sparsely populated so it will be difficult to find sufficient workers.

The picture painted by Dr. Vriend is extremely pessimistic. It is not that Vriend doesn't want to help. He is more than willing to make the necessary arrangements to have supplies dropped from Angguruk. Vriend is not even sure he will remain in Angguruk. The times are uncertain and he might be needed somewhere else. Then Rev. Zöllner will be left behind by himself.

Of course I know that ultimately God is in control, but that does not take away our responsibility to investigate all the options. My urgent advice is: "Do not make this exploratory trek, it is not possible."

When he understands that Kuijt has already departed, his advice is,

Keep going. Now it is all or nothing. But before October 1, 1962, there must be a second man in Hollandia, even if he has to come from the Netherlands.

Thus end the comments from Dr. Vriend.

In the pale light of a candle under an improvised tent the young preacher writes on a note pad;

> *Pray that the natives will help build the strip. Sometimes they work, sometimes they don't. It is my constant plea that the Lord will incline their hearts to work willingly under the guidance of the five coastal boys. I admire them.*

He knows that his departure out of Angguruk is a topic of discussion by the ECK.

> *But if God has not called me to work here, He will cause my work to be in vain. Then I hope He will shortly disclose this to me. Until now, He has helped me wonderfully. The adversaries are many: the political circumstances, the departure of the team, Rev. Rigters who believes that I do not have the stamina to persevere. But the Lord renewed my strength time and time again. I think I have found a possible site for an airstrip centered between several larger villages. The strip site designated by MAF is another two or three days trek from here. I can honestly say that I am of good courage. This is not a letter of complaint; I am a little uncomfortable in my tent but otherwise I am fine.*

> *Thankfully, we had a food drop today. It was high time. Since Friday we survived on sweet potatoes that the people provided for us. The population is very friendly and is not even armed which is a blessing. The language is different than the one in Angguruk but my little guide, Malik understands them.*

Dr. Vriend provided Rev. Kuijt with instructions on how to take the measurements for the strip. The slope should preferably not be more than ten percent and definitely no more than fifteen percent. With the help of a garden hose and some dropped tools the area is measured as accurately as possible. One section is grassland and the other is forest. Large boulders will have to be removed, trees chopped down and roots pulled out. In the meantime, a few of the coastal Papuans returned to Angguruk to pick up a portable generator. The trek took a long time as it was impossible to wade across a fast-flowing river. The locals refuse to help but finally, after a great deal of hard work, the coastal Papuans successfully build a makeshift bridge and the crossing is successful.

Dr. Vriend is not happy. The boys tell him that the incline is about ten percent; he has a hard time believing them. If that were true, would MAF not have discovered this location from the air before? However, he has little choice but to give the generator that he values so much to the boys. Jacob returned to Angguruk but information about the strip measurements is also sketchy. In the meantime Kuijt cannot just sit and wait for approval and so he continues with the work.

While being alone Kuijt's thoughts go back to what all has transpired since his arrival in New Guinea.

It becomes clearer to me that the Lord will stand up and will shut the mouths of the liars. With the help of the Lord my being in Irian will not be stopped not even by the devil. God's work proceeds. I want to put a stop to all our squabbles, or as Jesus said, "No one who sets his hands to the plough will look back" and with the words of Paul, "Forgetting what lies behind, and reaching out to that which lies before me."

I experience full cooperation from the natives, who are friendly and enthusiastic about helping with the strip. You should hear them: "wah, wah, wah!" (Hello) You should see the old as well as the young at work. I am deeply moved and thank the Lord from the bottom of my heart for such cooperation. We are in the midst of fourteen villages which have many inhabitants. I sure hope that the MAF will give their approval and that we will not have to discontinue the work.

He asks the MB for five sweaters for the coastal Papuans as in the evening the mountain air is considerably cooler. After hearing about the request the Kievit firm gladly provides them.

Standing in front of his tent, the missionary can see the village of Kosarek. To the left are the villages of Minè, Hombukè, Silekasi and Wasaldak, which has about forty huts. To the right he sees Wasa, which has seventy huts, Uldam, Normat, and Tapla. To get from one village to another you have to walk for at least a day because the villages are strategically located on mountain ridges. This large valley is itself divided into several smaller valleys.

Sometimes Kuijt hears the singing of the dancers. That means there is a pig feast. The Papuans rub their skin with pig fat and adorn themselves with feathers and shells, with pig bones through their noses and bamboo in their ears. In ecstasy they sing and dance until they drop. "How long will it take before they will no longer sing to the spirits, but to the living God?" Several times Rev. Kuijt has been invited for a community meal. A meal of sweet potatoes and a steamed pig is prepared in a cooking pit as a token of friendship.

Frederik has not been feeling well for weeks. He complains of stomach pains and pains in his chest and back. Finally he decides to return to Angguruk. Thus a valuable aide is lost to the missionary.

> *Fred has carried heavy burdens for us and I think his name deserves a place in the historical records of the mission.*

The work progresses slowly. A large quantity of ground must be moved with primitive tools. There is still no approval from MAF to build the landing strip. The wheelbarrows dropped from an airplane are heavily damaged. After being hammered back into a somewhat reasonable shape, the tires still need to be inflated. However, they do not have a pump.

> *The strip will be sloping downhill. As we need to fill a steep slope we must remove a layer of about three metres of dirt mixed with rocks over a width of twenty metres. We hit boulders that will have to be dug out. But the Lord gives aid. Because our field is sloped, each heavy rainfall sends torrents of soil and rock into the lower part of the strip where the fill is needed.*

The generator stops working after only one week. Via radio, Dr. Vriend tries to give some instructions on how to fix it but it appears that the manufacturer's directions do not correlate. When the fuel tap is accidentally stripped, the generator is completely out of commission.

As long as there is daylight the group works on the airstrip; this leaves little or no time for Kuijt to work on the language. He receives a great deal of support from the four remaining coastal Papuans. Kuijt hopes that one of them will be inclined to the service of the Lord and can be trained as an evangelist. However, little is noticeable of any missionary zeal among them. On the contrary; Jacob has already indicated he will return home as soon as the strip is finished.

The MB received the following note:

> *Many thanks for the sweater that was sent to me from the*

mission delegates in Holland.

I received it yesterday in a drop from the sky in small airplane. His name is Cessna.

Not only did I get a sweater, but also a present from mother Rev Kuijt, which included a large tin of delicious chocolates and also six red hankies.

Here are we, four coast Papuan boys, and Rev. G. Kuijt.

Actually we are five coast Papuan boys but one has returned to Hollandia.

Sender: carpenter Junus H. Jochu

Kuijt takes Junus' note that was written on the wrapping of a cereal package with him when he returns to Angguruk. From there Kuijt will go on to Hollandia for his medical checkup. He has already been in the jungle for three months. The doctor in Hollandia is satisfied, although he is concerned about Kuijt's weight. He lost fifteen kilograms yet he is allowed to stay away for half a year with the stipulation that he faithfully takes his medication.

The missionary writes to the MB that he has met a minister in Hollandia who works for the NCRV radio station who did an interview with him. It will be broadcast in the middle of January, 1963 under the title *First Digging and Then Preaching.*

Rev. Teuscher advised me to inform you about this and to ask the NCRV when the broadcast will air. Interested people will then be able to listen.

Later the Board discussed the involvement of Rev. Kuijt with radio programs and newspaper interviews. "This is a personal issue" the Board decides, "and it does not concern us."

Hollandia has changed drastically in a short time. There are virtually no Dutch people left and it has become a deserted city. The transfer of leadership will take place on May 1st, 1963 and the question is: "Will the Indonesian government provide visas?"

This immediately prompts Kuijt into action. He has already been separated from his wife for ten months. He writes a letter to his wife asking if there is any way that she can come sooner. Maybe she can take her final examinations earlier? Rev. Rigters agrees with his action.

When the missionary flies back into Angguruk just before Christmas he has a new radio with him;

> *A beautiful all-transistor instrument which means that we can use the batteries much longer.*

From the army he gets three extra batteries and a tent. The batteries will be charged in Angguruk and the army tent will have to be air-dropped. Upon Kuijt's arrival in Angguruk a helper excitedly meets him.

"Has Pendeta Kuijt already heard what happened?"

"Heard what?"

"Near the camp of Kosarek, someone has been killed and eaten! Now a war has erupted between some tribes."

The trail from Angguruk to Kosarek has become familiar; first the steep climb and then the Obarek River. With its swift-flowing currents and whirlpools, the river is impossible to cross. The shortest route is to cross a tributary of the main river but this is also a gruelling route. First they have to climb over slippery rocks and then hop from boulder to boulder. On his back Rev. Kuijt carries his radio packed in an aluminum container. He is walking unevenly because he lost the heel off one of his shoes. Malik accompanies him and is also carrying quite a load. Suddenly the missionary feels his foot slip out from under him. He plummets down the hill for about ten metres, bouncing and crashing. Immediately Malik clambers after him and puts his arm around the Pendeta who is dazed and motionless—his shoulder, arm, chest—everything hurts. Tears fill his eyes, not because of the pain but because he receives so much care, attention and love from Malik, his faithful guide. Now, more than ever, he feels that this young man is a gift from God. With the boy's help he struggles up the embankment and they proceed slowly and carefully on their trek. It takes them three days but finally they arrive at their destination, Kosarek.

Unfortunately, there are some problems. The boys have argued among themselves about which of them is the leader (there is nothing new under the sun). Rev. Kuijt feels it should be Zeth. However, this is not so easy to accept by the others and a lot of talking needs to take place before this is settled.

However this is not the only disappointment. The missionary took a level with him so the slope can now be measured more accurately. The boys stretch the water hose tight while Rev. Kuijt holds the level. "Adri, go a little higher. A little more." Quickly Rev. Kuijt calculates the angle of the strip. No, this cannot be! Once more the measurements are taken and again the same results: twenty-seven percent! According to MAF a ten percent grade is okay, at the most fifteen. Kuijt had made allowances for a few extra percent but this really is too much. Do they have to dig down more? To level off the slope to eighteen percent would be impossible; they would have to build a dike about two hundred metres long and eleven metres high.

Swift and treacherous river

Rev. Kuijt's tent. This picture shows the isolation. His only regular contact with the outside world is via the two-way radio.

After some time he calls the boys and tells them the result of his calculations. In disbelief they look at him. Do they have to quit? Just yesterday they had more than one hundred people at work here. Kuijt tells them plainly and honestly. "On this site in Kosarek it just will not work." He must go to the original strip site on the other side of the mountain. Jacob and Adri tell him that they will not go along. It is too much for them. First the trek to get there, and then trying to make contact with the Nipsan people. No,this will not be successful. Are not the people over the mountains the arch enemies of the people in the Valley of the Seventy?

The following day Rev. Kuijt decides to inform Angguruk via the radio. Perhaps they have some advice. But Angguruk is not able to help. The matter is brought to the MAF. Is it possible to make the strip any shorter say 300 metres? It would take a year-and-a-half to finish it but then they could at least land smaller airplanes with lighter loads. Hank Worthington of the MAF checks this suggestion out as he flies over the site. A few days later the inevitable answer from MAF is that the strip site is no good and it is useless to continue.

It is January 10, 1963. Kuijt is in the grass hut that the boys have built for him. Everything is utterly primitive: a few rough handmade shelves filled with axes and nails, knives, plastic rope, rice, sugar, and tinned food. The radio receiver is standing on an improvised little table. The walls are made from wood and the roof is of long grass and leaves. With the light from a small kerosene lamp, Rev. Kuijt informs the MB by writing that the strip cannot be completed as the slope is much too steep.

You and I will probably ask ourselves whether all efforts have been in vain. I am convinced that the answer is "no". With all the villages we have made close friendships. The people trust us and show their affection by giving us food and their manpower.

Rev. Rigters, on behalf of ECK, suggests giving Rev. Kuijt a place in Ponteng. To push on to Nipsan will again open a world of difficulties and setbacks. In Ponteng under ECK, he can start mission work. A strip also has to be built there. It is not too far from Angguruk and, if necessary, help can be obtained from Dr. Vriend.

The MB is confronted with a difficult decision. On the one hand there is a proposal to have Rev. Kuijt work in the ECK which would mean no independent mission work for the NRC. But to expose Rev. Kuijt again to such difficult conditions, especially with his wife arriving shortly, is something else. The MB decides to accept the proposal of the ECK and refuse to give Kuijt permission to go to Nipsan. ECK will keep working in the Wasaldak Kosarek area.

A feeling of disappointment remains with the MB. Could all these obstacles have been avoided? Were all these setbacks a result of the behaviour of brother Kuijt? Was he influenced too much by his emotions? In a long letter the German Rev. Aring endorses Rev. Kuijt.

> *From the very beginning I had a close bond of brotherly fellowship with him and I know that his coming here to work in New Guinea has resulted in rumours both good and bad even before his arrival on the Island. Gerrit, like all missionaries who commence a new work, have to make decisive decisions based on their best knowledge while being all alone and living in isolation. This being the case, for sure some mistakes took place. It is only natural. But we can never blame Gerrit for this or hold it against him taking into consideration the circumstances wherein he started.*

The minister continues that Kuijt not only has been working as a strip builder but much more as a witness for his Lord. By grace he has been able to make contact with the natives and learn some of their language, which forms a basis for future work. Aring has the highest regard for Kuijt and values his work in New Guinea. He also receives support from Rev. Woldendorp:

> *I understood that Rev. Aring gave a positive report about our colleague Kuijt. That is good. I must say that I also have a deep admiration for him that he can so unselfishly set aside his own interests. He lives in a little tent without any comforts in utterly primitive circumstances. He clearly has charisma for this pioneer work. What he needs is a practical person beside him. Of course we can always find some negative points but these do not outweigh the positive ones!*

Rev. Aring doubts whether Ponteng is the right place for Kuijt. But there are still other possibilities. He can trek further to the place Nipsan that has been approved from the air by MAF for a strip. Alternatively, he can temporarily go to Wamena to keep the ECK mission work going on there in the valley.

Now a period of uncertainty and confusion sets in. Opposing views and advice follow each other in rapid succession. One message says, "Immediately depart for Nipsan and build a strip there." But in Nipsan a tribal war is going on, which has already cost several Papuans their life. The Nipsanners are not known to be a peace-loving people. Other places are mentioned; Oksibil, a region near the Australian New Guinea border, the Lere-project on the north coast and the Geelvink Bay.

Rev. Aring considers the work of Rev. Kuijt to be very important

Rev. Kuijt keeps the delegates informed of all these possibilities. They can no longer comprehend the situation. As soon as they get used to one idea, there are three new suggestions on the table.

Then the question arises about who the NRC should be affiliated with. Must the contact with ECK continue or should they join the Faith Missions? If so, should it be CAMA, the UFM, TEAM, or the RBMU? Or is contact with the mission of the Canadian Reformed (Article 31) Churches (who are working in the south of New Guinea) a better option?

The letter exchange between Rev. Kuijt and the MB is characterized by confusion and misunderstanding. Accusations go back and forth. The one accuses the other of horizontal thinking. "Where is your faith?" The answer is "Let us be thinking horizontally". "Really I would like to know." "Where is your common sense?"

No matter how stern the tone of the letters is at times, they close with best wishes and heartfelt blessings: "Kuijt, we do not forget you, dear brother, be assured of that."

Because it takes weeks for letters to arrive, unexpected situations can occur. For example, suppose Kuijt writes a strong letter while sitting in front of his tent in Kosarek. To get it to the Netherlands, first it is brought to Angguruk by one of the boys, which takes a few days before the letter arrives and there it must wait to be flown out by MAF to Hollandia. When the letter finally arrives in Rotterdam after about four to six weeks it lies on the pile of mail until the next MB meeting. Then a curt reply is written and sent back. When Kuijt finally receives the reply, his initial feeling of upset has long since gone. Because the circumstances are constantly changing and plans keep altering, the return reply again gives new cause for irritation that has long since passed.

It also happens that the delegates have to deal with more than one letter at one time—upset ones and friendly ones. Afterwards both sides send their apologies. Communicating from such a distance proves to be very difficult. Kuijt writes,

> *I understand your difficult situation. The situation here is sometimes very confusing and that causes you to become very frustrated. Aring has said to me, "Stay calm, wait and see how things unfold." But if I follow this advice, then you send me letters asking why I am not writing. And when I try to write as detailed as possible, you cannot make head nor tail of it.*

Meanwhile, Rev. Kuijt remains in Kosarek, where he builds a house and plants a garden; exactly as Dr. Vriend advised.

> *Try to keep good relationships with the indigenous people of the Valley of the Seventy. They must be very disappointed and certainly cannot understand why the strip is not good enough. Their hope of getting a strip and all the advantages, have now disappeared into thin air and they for sure begrudge their rivals a strip. To keep them happy you can build a house. Later an evangelist can live in it.*

And indeed, Lukas Kimuo, a *guru agama* later moved in. Kimuo was trained at ODO to become a village teacher. He also holds a certificate that entitles him to preach. His salary is paid for by the NRC mission.

Roof of leaves and grass for Rev. Kuijt's new residence

Chapter 8

Reunited

Absorbed in thought, Mrs. Kuijt is ensconced in a corner of her compartment. The cadence of the train makes her drowsy. Miep Kuijt-Bos. She officially has that name and it makes her happy and thankful. At the same time sadness tugs at her heart. The name Kuijt-Bos is the only thing she has for the time being. The man who belongs to the name has left. They have been married for six short weeks and they will not see each other again for a long time. It is true that they both agreed to this. For her it is to finish her education and for Gerrit it is to establish a base in the jungle and make a home for his wife. Now her husband is somewhere on the Mediterranean Sea while she is on her way back to The Netherlands. The distance between them will become even greater when she is in Katwijk and he is in New Guinea; it is hard to imagine. Letters and/or an occasional telegram will be the only bridge between their two worlds.

Life resumes its normal pace, Miep once again lives with her parents and every day travels to college in The Hague. Her studies go smoothly and during summer vacation she takes a course with the Wycliffe Bible Translators in Germany. The course is part of her preparations for the future. It will help her when she has to master unknown tribal languages.

Miep follows the reports about Indonesia and the controversies about New Guinea in the newspaper. However she knows that her husband is in God's hand and she is at peace. His calling is with the Papuans.

At the end of the year she receives a request from her husband, "Miep, would it be possible to do your exams earlier than June?" Gerrit is concerned. When the transfer is implemented and New Guinea becomes part of Indonesia, will his wife be allowed to enter the country?

With her brother Kees, Miep goes to Leiden. On a slip of paper she has the address of the Inspector for Home Economics Education. She hopes to find out if it is possible to do her State Examinations earlier than June. Miep has never heard of something like this and is doubtful. "But you never know; yes is always a possibility." Miep rings the door bell and the inspector opens the door. "Come on in," she says. As Miep enters the room she notices the wallpaper has a bamboo motif, potted tropical plants and Oriental paintings on the walls. When Miep explains the reason for her visit, the inspector understands the situation. She, herself had been an Inspector of Education in Indie for many years.

The inspector decides on a plan. She will contact one person from each examination committee and arrange for Miep to take her exams. The only requirement for Miep is to travel to the various cities where the committee is meeting. "Just go home and do not fret. I will arrange everything for you." Miep is relieved and grateful and thanks the Lord Who went before her.

The inspector's plan succeeds: Miep takes the exams and passes with glowing results. After passing the last one, Miep travels to Rotterdam to let Rev. L. Rijksen and. Rev. A. Vergunst know the results and to say farewell, as she was leaving in two days. Congenially, Rev. Vergunst tapped her on the shoulder and said, "Miep, I must be honest. I am really proud of you."

The flights to Biak and New Guinea are full. Missionaries and others who are studying in The Netherlands want to be back in New Guinea before the transfer takes place. The planes in the opposite direction are also full with Dutch dignitaries and business people. Only a few more airplanes will fly to New Guinea and after that it is 'wait and see'.

Mrs. Kuijt emerges from the KLM aircraft in Biak on April 17, 1963. Despite the early hour, the climate envelopes her like a damp woollen blanket. The sun rapidly climbs to its zenith. Palm trees reach dustily upward to the sky. The customs officials can barely manage the bustle at the airport. Patiently the passengers wait in line. When Miep finally passes through customs her husband is there. After fourteen months of being apart they embrace each other. They are together again. 'The Lord has done great things for us, where of we are glad.' Together they travel from Biak to Manokwari where Miep is introduced to several missionaries. From there they travel further to the Wisselmeren (Wissel Lakes) and then to Hollandia.

By this time, nearly all the Dutch have left Hollandia. Rev. Kuijt guides his wife through the dusty tropical city to an office where residence papers must be arranged.

Together at last!

Miep at home in Irian

The couple is allowed to stay in a home belonging to CAMA. This mission organization bought the home from departing Dutchies. The bottom floor is the CAMA office and the upper floor is for the Kuijts. While in Hollandia, Rev. Kuijt continues to look for a suitable mission field.

Pole house in Sentani Lake

In the meantime, Zeth and Adri have left Kosarek; Junus is staying on the coast and the guru has been called back to Hollandia because his wife needs to have an operation. Kuijt asks the delegates to make a decision regarding the future. Rev. Aring suggests three possibilities: He could merge with the ECK and become a pastor of the church; he could look for an affiliation with one of the faith missions; or he could work independently. The relationship between Kuijt and ECK has deteriorated especially with Dr. Vriend from Angguruk. Kuijt has the impression that ECK will not give up Kosarek. In Kuijt's opinion, ECK will not give up any region. Later this proves to be correct.

According to Kuijt, working with the ECK is no longer possible. He also has misgivings about developments in the ECK, including their contacts with the World Organization of Churches and several of their liturgical practises. Kuijt is inclined to establish an independent mission work. He also wants to join The Mission Fellowship (TMF) in which several mission organizations work together.

The delegates do not agree with Gerrit's idea of joining the Fellowship. Is there not a good connection with the ECK? They have the impression that joining the TMF will mean becoming part of "The Faith Missions." It takes a lot of effort for Kuijt to convince the MB otherwise.

TMF will look after all our paper work like work permits, residence papers; purchase food, materials or whatever we are in need of in the interior; manage contacts between the government, receive and send telegrams etc. Because our work will be in the interior, we will not be able to go to the coast regularly.

The Mission Fellowship is not a super-organization in which you lose your identity or independence. It can be compared to the United Nations. Groups and individuals come together for discussion and the greatest opponents meet with each other. Although they are all members, they are still independent and keep their own ideologies.

Membership in the Fellowship must officially be requested by the MB but no request comes from The Netherlands. Therefore, Kuijt is accepted on a personal basis as an observer in the TMF.

Kuijt receives an opportunity from the UFM to look for a field in Oksibil.

View from the air

In the meantime, the MAF takes him on several survey flights. Above the Broekhuyzen-Yalimo area they can see quite a few villages from the air. A quick calculation tells Kuijt that there must be about four thousand people in the area. No other mission organization is working there. To continue on to Nipsan will not be possible at this time. The local people have denied him entrance. Kuijt continues tirelessly and unwaveringly to look for an unclaimed area. Some surveys are made and others are cancelled because of weather conditions. The ECK offers to help Kuijt settle in Lere. He does not accept their proposal. According to him there are too few people and it will never become their own mission field. "Now a National Minister will occupy that place," writes Rev. Locher in his journal. "The ECK is not planning to extend another offer to Kuijt."

The plan is for Kuijt to first start working in the area of Broekhuyzen-Yalimo. A year later a new missionary couple could come and take over the work started by the Kuijts who then could try to go to Nipsan. "I continue to regard Nipsan as a God-given terrain but we must be like Paul and for the time being plan a different course."

Preparations are made to go into the Yalimo Valley. Food and other items are packed and numbered so that drops can be requested by specifying the desired numbers. Kuijt continues to help Miep build up her physical stamina.

Mrs. Kuijt on a trek

> *We may start from a deserted mission post in Wolo. The UFM has worked there already but had to withdraw because of hostile tribes. We cannot start from the Wamena direction because we would have to go through an area that is inhabited by a cannibalistic tribe. The CAMA has already been chased out of this area five times. We do not know what is in store for us.*

Being very cautious, Kuijt adds, "If there are any changes to the plans mentioned, you will hear about it." This last comment makes the MB especially nervous. Plans are constantly changing. To top it all off, there is the issue of affiliation with the TMF. They wonder, "Who is driving the bus?" It seems that all their directions of what they want have not been received. Again time plays a negative role. At the MB meeting on September 27th they have to deal with six letters from Rev. Kuijt and in November an additional four more letters come up for discussion.

At the same time that Rev. Locher's message is discussed at a Board meeting there is also a letter from Kuijt announcing that they are moving via Wolo into the Yalimo region.

> *Should this new undertaking succeed, with the help of the Lord, I have the following to share or rather to propose: Suppose that in six months we have a station in Central Yalimo; could you provide three mission couples? They do not have to be theologians at the state of simplicity in which these people are. They could be evangelists for example. I write this simply because I cannot forget Kosarek/Nipsan. It is my earnest desire to return when the time is right and they are willing to receive us.*

"Why did he not stay in Kosarek in the first place?" The delegates ask themselves. "Why did he not expand the work there?" Okay, for now they will compromise but he must concentrate on settling in Kosarek. The ECK will not hinder him in that and there is no necessity for him to join the Fellowship.

A letter pertaining to this is sent to New Guinea. At the same time, Rev. Kuijt wrote:

> *We are starting to wonder why we have not heard from you. We are still waiting for your official opinion concerning the Fellowship. On Thursday, we are leaving for Wolo. Everything so far has been organized. The plan is to start our*

trek from Wolo to the new field, which will take about two days. The terrain is not as difficult as between Anggeruk, Kosarek, and Nipsan. Miep is also trekking along. We hope to be in Wolo for three weeks to contact the people in the area we have to pass through. They are known to be very hostile to white people and especially to the message of the missionary. How the situation is in the new area is unknown. May the Lord be gracious to us. Two coastal boys will go with us and at Wolo we will be joined by a Dani-boy from Kelila (a UFM mission station). The young man has a unique name, Roti, which means bread. We have come to an agreement with our boys that they will earn 125 guilders per month, of which they will pay us 50 guilders for their food. Roti will earn an axe or a hatchet each month. These salaries are established by the ECK.

Rev. Kuijt in Kosarek/Nipsan

A few days later, the group is flown into Wolo. Rev. Kuijt and the two boys make contact with the Wolo people, who demonstrate that they are willing to receive them.

We were given a hut to sleep in; this saved us the trouble of building a shelter. The homes that were here have all been destroyed or burned by the locals. They salvaged the nails which are very desirable and they knew there were lots of them in these buildings. Every day there is a gathering in the open in which Kuijt brings the Gospel message in Indonesian and Roti translates it into the local language. Kuijt also holds a daily clinic for the people. The most common affliction is yaws, an infectious tropical disease, which is easily remedied with one or two injections. On Saturday, I treated one more patient with these ulcers. His physical appearance was gruesome with sores over his entire body. We gave him an almocilline injection. His mother came back with him after a week. What a difference. Now his ugly sores are mostly gone and he is laughing again. He thanked us by giving us a sweet potato. What a blessing these medicines are.

The MB delegates stress the temporary nature of the work in Wolo and do not want to invest a lot of money there. After all, this station will be abandoned again. They express their concerns in a letter:

We want you to go back to Kosarek. You have become acquainted with the area and you are enthusiastic about the people and the manner in which they received you so you must go back there.

The ECK is not opposed to that as we have heard. Therefore, we will continue to work with the ECK. As far as we are concerned, we have always worked together favourably. We are thankful for their advice, which we always have and still do receive from their experienced mission personnel at Oegstgeest and those who have worked within the framework of the ECK. From the outset, our mutual understanding was to stress the autonomy of our own work and that we would not allow our work to be absorbed into ECK. With full acknowledgement of our situation they have continued to offer a helping hand and, with great patience, they have always sought a solution to our problems. We hope to be able to continue to work together in the future.

Kuijt, you will undoubtedly understand that our patience is running out. In fact, nothing has been accomplished during the time you have been in New Guinea. You have only been wandering from place to place. Every time you try something different. We are set on Kosarek and we are staying in contact with ECK. If this does not work out, it will be the end of our work in New Guinea and the end of your service as a missionary minister for the NRC. We have come to the decision to call you back if you do not show cooperation and bring about a change in the near future.

This letter is signed by all the members of the MB. The sharpness of this letter was undoubtedly influenced by a visit to the board from Rev. Rigters. He informed them that he is disappointed with the behaviour of Rev. Kuijt and that mutual friction has arisen between them. Rev. Rigters fully agrees with the decision to focus on Kosarek and to demand that Kuijt returns immediately.

A disconcerted Mrs. Kuijt stands beside her husband. He has the letter in his hand and reads it again.

Go back to Kosarek; nothing has been accomplished; they have lost their patience; will call him back; dismiss him…

All this, just as they are ready to leave for a new area! Now they have a chance to start their own mission field. Kosarek will never work out. The ECK claims this area and it will be impossible to have an independent mission there. The sharp tone of the letter hurts him deeply. Why is there so much misunderstanding? If only he could sit around the table with the delegates, he could help them to understand that working with the ECK will never give them the opportunity to become an independent NRC mission. Oh, he can understand the problems of the delegates. They are inexperienced and form their opinions from a distance. They have no other sources of information except Oegstgeest. Sometimes it is difficult when the deputies ask you to implement decisions you know they will regret later.

Everything is ready. The MAF plane is waiting on the airstrip. The items that were used in Wolo but cannot be carried on the trek are loaded into the plane. This letter is received just as they are ready to start their trek. "What now, Gerrit? Do we unpack everything again and stay here?"

"No." He folds the letter and puts it into his pocket. "We are going! Later the delegates will certainly understand our decision. Let us hope and pray."

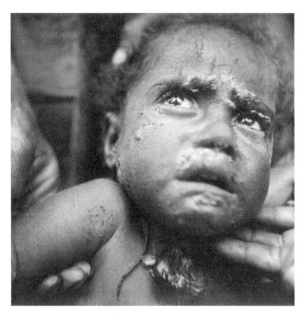

Child with yaws

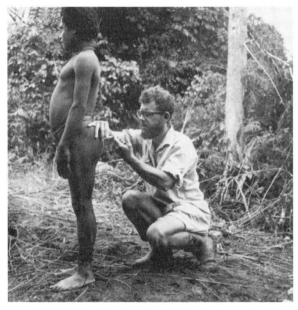

Kuijt does not hesitate for one moment:
his calling is with the Papuans

Miep steps in to play the important role of mediator. First she sends a short "cry of distress" from Wolo. She explains that if they were to go directly to Kosarek as the delegates demand, she would have to remain behind for probably at least a year.

> *The place is unreachable by foot for me. A strip has to be built in Nipsan on very rocky terrain. They have to find workers which are hard to find.*

She and her husband are now at the point of departure to the newly chosen valley and it is too late to make new arrangements. A few weeks later, she writes a long letter to the MB. This letter helps to clear the confusion and misunderstanding among them.

She explains that her husband is eager to return to Kosarek-Nipsan but others, including Rev. Aring, strongly advise against it. This is not the right time. "It is not at all certain that Kosarek can become a mission station from the NRC and that the ECK will not claim it for themselves."

Ultimately it is decided to first start working in West Yalimo and later use this place as a starting point to Nipsan.

Miep writes:

> *Do you understand our request for more workers? Gerrit longs to go back, even now. He is doing everything possible here to get this strip finished so that this place can become our base.*

> *I truly hope that you can form some idea of the situation here. I understand very well how difficult it is to comprehend the situation as I experienced the same while still in Holland. Now I have been confronted with the reality and have a better understanding as I have seen the land and the circumstances confronting us... I think it would be to your and our advantage if one of the delegates (and I think especially of you Rev. Vergunst) could come out here. At least one of you would then have a realistic impression of the situation and would be able to understand how and why we have made our decisions. I know a trip is costly but for you to continue in this way is not good and for us neither, especially when we receive such letters.*

> *I hope you are not offended with me and should you have any questions, please write. If you do not receive a satisfactory reply,*

please ask again. For us everything is so obvious but in respect to you, our explanations may be unclear.

*Village in
the jungle*

*Work on the West
Jalimo strip*

Her letter prompts the MB to send the following telegram:

We are happy with latest correspondence-stop-stay in West Yalimo-stop-Our thoughts are with you-stop-wait for other letters from us-stop-Cordial regards. Vergunst.

Chapter 9

Home!

Twenty people and one pig: it is not a particularly impressive procession! Nonetheless, it is a militia of Christ en route to capture souls for the Great King. Roti and four native UFM evangelists, including Timin and Tapulabuk, accompany the two white people, Rev. and Mrs. Kuijt. At the last moment, UFM also sent along five carriers. The rest of the group comes from Wolo. At the end of the line, the piglet trots along, contently oinking.

> *We have had a great deal of pleasure from that animal. I never knew a pig could be so faithful. She follows us like a dog. Later when the pig reached the age to mate, no partner was to be found for her, with the result that she ended up in the cooking pot.*

Up to the moment of departure, it is uncertain whether Timin can be part of the group. His wives refuse to give him permission to go along. He makes a special trip from Wolo to his home in Kelila to convince them that it is very important for him to go with Tuan Kuijt. Must not the Word also be brought to Yalimo! Timin and his wives! If you were to ask him how many wives he has, he will look at you frankly and say, "One. Before the missionaries came, we did not know the Word of God. Now we know that the Word does not allow us to have more than one wife."

The group is ready to depart without Timin. However, on the day of departure one more MAF plane lands in Wolo, and who steps out? Timin. He has with him a note from missionary Powers which says, "Timin has convinced his wives."

The sun is already at its highest point when the procession is set in motion. Not only men walk along with them, there are also several women and a girl. This is good because it is unbelievable how much women can carry. It is customary that they carry the heavy loads. When they go to the gardens the men carry an axe on their shoulder while the women carry their baby in a net which is hung from their forehead onto their back. And on the walk home they usually carry a few extra nets with sweet potatoes and on top of their head some pieces of fire wood.

Rev. Kuijt leads an open air devotion in Wolo, with the translation done by Roti

When the group has only gone a short distance, a quarrel ensues between a man and a young girl. A number of the men start striking the girl. Kuijt interrupts the disturbance but the men surround him and shout *At maluk!* (She is bad); *An mendè* (She is mine!). Helplessly the girl looks to Rev. Kuijt. He is at a loss how to handle the situation. Is the man her prospective husband? It turns out he is her father who does not agree with the girl accompanying the group. Finally, the Missionary and his wife take the child into their protection. Mrs. Kuijt walks in front of the girl and Rev. Kuijt behind her. The men behind him push forward and try to grab the girl but the Missionary does not give them an inch. Then the men try to negotiate. Roti interprets the demands of the men and responds with Kuijt's reply. The Kuijts have offered to take the girl with them to give her a good upbringing. The father gives in and the argument is settled.

The first part of the trek from Wolo to Ilugwa is over easy terrain, so the going is not difficult. "If you are faced with high mountains right from the start, your courage will rapidly fade. It is remarkable how the Lord in His providence works out all things. He does not test us beyond what we can endure and with the trials He also sends deliverance. I am especially thankful for my wife as this is her first long trek!"

The men become restless; they look around and listen sharply. They are nearing the war zone with the Ilugwa. The accompanying men and women must absolutely return if they do not want to get into trouble with the Ilugwa people. The rest of the party continues.

At about five o'clock we came to the first kampong (village). Some of the elders came to meet us. They signalled that we were to follow them. And what did we see when we came into the compound? The inner courtyard was filled with cooked potatoes and vegetables. Everything was neatly laid out on freshly cut grass. The women who had so loving prepared the food sat nearby. We were both humbled and encouraged by such a welcome. The people of this kampong had heard about our coming and welcomed us in this way. After asking God for His blessing, we began to eat. After trekking through the heat of the day the meal was thoroughly enjoyed.

While we looked around, we noticed several people who had ugly tropical skin ulcer called Yaws and through Roti, we understood that they wanted medicine. It was possible to give some help but the ones with yaws needed injections and had to be disappointed. We explained to them that they should come to Yalimo once we are established there. We thought, 'They will never do that.' But we were pleasantly surprised after we arrived in Yalimo. Scores of people who suffered from the skin ulcers came to us for treatment. We were so thankful to God that we had enough medicine with us to give the needed injections. At one time this was a disease for which little could be done but after the introduction of penicillin these people can be healed. A single injection of two cc is enough to heal them from the foul-festering wounds. Not only did the patients come from Ilugwa, but they also started arriving from Kobokma, which is a good day's trek away. Even as far as from the Archibald Lake, when they heard of our arrival. Information travels fast here!

His hand is infected with yaws. They had no remedy for this disease

During the mealtime the natives try to communicate with the missionary and sometimes even use their hands and feet to get their message across, or they ask Roti to translate for them. Gradually it becomes clear to Kuijt what the commotion is all about. The natives want the missionary couple to stay with them. It is not because of their love for the mission or the Word but purely self-interest. They know that wherever the missionaries settle, an airstrip will be built for the big birds to land. This will bring many benefits: food, tools, building supplies and medical help. No, the missionary couple should not go on but should stay with them. "Here is a good location for a strip and we are willing to assist." Rev. Kuijt must disappoint them. The UFM has claimed this area and plans to start mission work there in the future. Yalimo is their final goal and that is where they intend to go.

That night we slept in a native's hut. It was neatly prepared and they had placed freshly cut grass on the floor. Wearily we fell asleep only to be awakened on and off by unwelcome little critters, and the bitter cold. However, the cold was not the worst; the fleas were something else!

Luckily, Rev. Kuijt had an excellent remedy for fleas—*Flint*, an insect spray given to him by a fellow student Karels.

The morning sun rises early from behind the Yalimo mountains. The sun determines the time of day as well as the plans for the workday. With the rising of the sun, sleeping is over. The group prepares to set out. The natives again offer food; sweet potatoes, the main staple of the interior people.

This time a number of Ilugwa men walk along. The terrain is not too difficult yet, but it is hilly and the ground is covered by hard grasses. But the terrain soon becomes rougher and more mountainous. They struggle through the jungle, sometimes needing to bushwhack their way through. All day the light under the dense canopy of the forest is obscured.

Travel becomes even more difficult as the area becomes more unforgiving. It means climbing around or over rocks and slogging through muddy areas. Suddenly Mrs. Kuijt loses her footing and the carriers scream. She wonders why; she only lost her footing. But when the carriers push some bushes aside she sees a deep ravine at her right side! Now she understands why they screamed. She is a hair's breadth away from death!

Transporting a pig

Every once in a while the pig squeals pitifully. When Kuijt looks back to see what is going on, he sees how two carriers have tied the legs of the animal together and are carrying her upside down with a pole over their shoulders and the pig in the middle!

Miep cannot go as fast as her husband and regularly he and his group disappear out of sight. She asks him to slow down and he does but soon he is off again. Some carriers stay faithfully by her side. At regular intervals the couple must stop and rest. Kuijt and his group wait for her to catch up. At one time he asks, "Can you still manage, Miep?" and she answers, "Sure, Gerrit." What else can she say. There is no other alternative but to carry on!

By late afternoon, she is exhausted but she forces herself to persevere. The thought that "every step I take, I won't have to take again" keeps her going. Finally, they come to a provisional shelter that has been set up by travellers who have passed through earlier. The group is too large for everyone to sleep inside so some stay outside and sleep, dozing around a fire. The Kuijt family and some of the helpers sleep inside. There is not much room in the crowded hut but that does not matter. They can keep each other warm. They immediately fall asleep from fatigue.

It is cold in the morning in the mountains. When Mrs. Kuijt comes out of the hut, Rev. Kuijt is already sitting by the fire and has managed to make some tea. The excess tea is poured into a canteen to be used along the way. The carriers are hoisting up their packs. They will be mainly going downhill today, which may appear to be easier than climbing but going down is gruelling to the leg muscles and the knees—at least if you are a white man. Apparently this does not apply to the natives; they walk over roots and tree trunks as if they are strolling on the boulevard in Katwijk. It is beautiful to see how, burdened with the heavy packs, they move over tree trunks sometimes as high as three and four metres above the ground. They literally spread out their toes and cling to the tree trunks.

The trek progresses slowly but surely. On their own, the Papuans would go much faster. Suddenly Apuk hurls a stone up into a tree and a bird plummets to the earth. It is a beautiful bird with black velvety wings and a gorgeous yellow collar and beak outlined vividly in blue. "Apuk, how can you kill such a beautiful bird?" Apuk answers unperturbed, "I am going to eat it."

At last they reach the top of the mountain and the path starts to descend. They hope to arrive at their destination before too long. Unexpectedly the group comes out of the jungle and is faced by a rapidly flowing river. On the other side, three warriors stand on a rock. They have painted themselves with pig fat and soot and are decorated with feathers in their hair. One has a pig bone running through his nose. Proud and self-assured they stand there.

Mrs. Kuijt watches from the boulder she is resting on. One warrior separates himself from his group and skips adroitly from rock to rock across the river. For a moment, the missionary and the warrior face each other. *"Wah, wah, wah!"* It is a greeting and Kuijt answers: *"Wah, wah, wah!"* The warrior reaches out with his hand to touch Kuijt's throat. He remains motionless. The man has good intentions and tickles his beard. As if it is the most ordinary thing in the world, Kuijt in return does exactly the same thing to the warrior.

The group does not stay but treks on. "This must be the right valley, Miep," says Rev. Kuijt. However, they cannot see much. There is not exactly a forest but boulders and very tall grass obstructs the view. The group passes right by the strip site. Sometime later they come to another village where the men stare at them suspiciously. They have never seen white people. Later on the Kuijts came to know that they were considered to be ghosts. Others thought they were worms that crawl into the ground at night and come up in the morning, which explains why they are so white.

Yet they do offer them a piece of sugar cane, a treat to chew. The group continues their trek and a number of villagers accompany them.

When they arrive at another village, Rev. Kuijt decides to ask for accommodations. They find themselves in a small valley named Kulkulè. This valley contains several villages most of them not larger than five to seven huts. Langobarek, the war chief, gives them permission to stay and even offers them some cooked bananas and his own hut to sleep in. This is unheard of because men live with the men, and women live with the women. Extremely tired, Mrs. Kuijt lays down in the hut and, without looking around, she falls asleep on the floor. She is unaware that she is in the hut of the war chief and that according to the helpers the large number of arrows near her, represents the number of his victims. She is also unaware of the collection of sacred objects treated with the greatest respect by the war chief, Langobarek. In one place there are more than one hundred pig jaws blackened by the smoke of the fire: these are thought to possess magical powers. The ancestors live in the jaws and their spirits deal out both good and evil.

Contacting MAF in Wamena to request assistance

While his wife sleeps, Kuijt stays awake, convinced that they have gone too far. The next day he makes radio contact with MAF and asks if a pilot can come and show him the direction to the strip site. A bonfire will be set to let the pilot know where the group is. Indeed it is clear that the Yalis have guided the group in the wrong direction. They have to retrace their steps. Kuijt finds the strip site. This must be the place. But where are the people? Everything looks deserted and abandoned. The rumours about the coming of the missionary have proceeded. Everyone has fled into the jungle. After some time a few Yalis come towards the couple. After they have investigated the situation, they disappear again.

There is not much time to rest. Immediately Rev. Kuijt starts to inspect the strip site. It will take lots of work. There are trees to be removed; the slope seems to be okay, but the boulders! Some are as large as a house. How is he ever going to remove them? Prayer arises up to God to provide the wisdom necessary to tackle this problem. Is He not the Almighty one? With Him nothing is impossible. No, he will not give up. With full assurance that he has been directed to this place, his helpers and him diligently start to work.

One of the rock formations found on the strip site in Pass Valley

This now proves that pioneer mission work is different from the work carried out by a minister in a congregation. Ah, this is actually no different than Paul on his mission journeys. Just read in the Acts of the Apostles to know what is involved in spreading the Gospel.

In journeying often, in perils of waters, in perils of robbers, in perils of mine own countrymen, in perils by the heathen... In weariness and painfulness... (2 Cor. 11: 26,27).

After that comes the preaching; then the miracles of healing.

The first weeks the Kuijt family lives in a native hut where they have to bend down on entering. Once inside they have to sit or lie down. By the end of six weeks they have built a grass shelter suitable for their height.

It would be nice if you could see how cozy it is. We do not have a table or chairs and we sleep on dried grass on the bark floor. Our windows are openings in the grass wall and the curtains are made of empty rice sacks sewed together. They are closed at night to keep the insects and the cold out. It appears that the roof is not totally waterproof.

Entrance to the grass house and open-air clinic held in the doorway

The Kuijts' first home, made from grass

Work has begun on the strip. Trees are chopped down and smaller rocks are removed. Under the unmoveable boulders, pits are dug and a fire is started under and around the rock. For days on end the fire burns and heats up the rock until the rock splits with a loud bang. Sometimes during the night, Kuijt is awakened by the noise and hopes that some damage has been done to the rock so it can be tackled with pickaxes and sledge hammers the next morning.

In the meantime the natives have returned to their village. Contacts are made and pigs eaten as a sign of friendship. In trade for some shells or an axe, the people help with the building of the strip. The price paid for labour is much too demeaning and it actually bothers Kuijt; one shell for several hours of work! That is nothing! But shells are very valuable in the interior, they are used instead of money and only the rich wear them.

Chief Liok and Kuijt greeting each other

There is also opposition. One day Liok, the chief, comes with some sticks and places them in the ground across the part of the strip that has been finished. "That's long enough for a strip," he says. "Let the big bird come and land now. You absolutely will not get more land. The rest is for our gardens."

For a proper landing strip you must have at least four hundred and fifty metres; they have only finished two hundred! "What now?" asks Miep? "Pray!" answers her husband. The work comes to a halt. They gather together to pray for the Lord to change the Yalis' hearts. The next day no work is done. But at about five o'clock someone walks onto the strip. One by one, Kuijt pulls out the sticks and places them into the ground twenty metres further on. The missionary is being watched from of the forest, and all his actions are being observed. Patiently Kuijt and his helpers wait.

Nothing happens. The following morning the workers start again. Kuijt again moves the sticks. This continues until one day he simply pulls the sticks out and throws them away.

When Liok notices that the white man and his helpers tenaciously continue to work on the strip, he does not interfere but monitors every move. So many questions arise in his thoughts. Is that second white person really a woman as the helpers of the white man claim? He cannot believe it. He knows that the two white people stay together in the same place at night. Liok is used to men and women sleeping separately. What about the long hair he has seen? Only men wear their hair long. When they go to battle or after they have won the fight, they show their hair off by greasing it with pig fat and making tight curls. No, this cannot be a woman. Finally, he asks the white man and the answer is, "Yes, Liok, she really is my wife."

The little pig that had supposedly eaten a snake

"Tuan Kuijt! Here is a little pig for you, kill and eat it; it is yours." The animal struggles but Rev. Kuijt has a tight grip on the rope.

"This is a nice little animal to fatten up." he says. "Then we can eat it together, the workers and the Yalis."

"Oh no, Tuan, you must shoot it and eat it now."

Surprised Kuijt looks at the generous giver and wonders why he is so insistent. A pig is a valuable possession. Rev. Kuijt has made up his mind to fatten it up first before eating it.

No Yalis come to see the group for several weeks. They go around Kuijt's house in a wide berth. Later they understand the reason why this was happening. According to the people, the pig had eaten a snake. If the pig had been killed and eaten right away, the participants would have died.

Metre by metre, they gain ground on the airstrip. At the same time the Gospel is taught.

> *On Saturday evenings we get together for a meal with the boys from Bokondi and Kelila and afterwards I read from the Indonesian Bible and then repeat it again in much simpler Indonesian; Roti translates where necessary. On Sunday, I had a short service in the Indonesian language for the coastal Papuans and Roti, while the boys from Bokondi and Kelila had their own service. Sunday is a real day of rest for all of us as we all work very hard during the week. There are even a few people from the area who come to listen.*

The service had already started and Mukani, a village Chief, walks in. He has a commanding presence which is due to his status. He sits down and quietly listens. Usually he is the one who talks and others listen. Kuijt has a weak spot for Mukani. He and his helpers temporarily moved into his abandoned village after their arrival. The chief took this in stride and was thankful for the axe he received as a token of gratitude.

> *He is a good-natured man who has several wives and owns a few pigs. He has already earned another axe for the work he has done. This brings him even more respect among his people. Mukani is a man who biblically speaking does not forget to offer lodging to strangers. Of course, he does not know that there is such a verse in the Bible but still, this is what he practices. Something like what Paul says: "People who do not have the law are a law unto themselves." Mukani is always prepared to receive strangers who come from neighbouring tribes. While working we noticed that he is the one who moves the heaviest loads and helps the others where ever possible.*

> *Is it in the way of God's providence that He brought us to this man's compound? 'Holy in Thy habitation is Thy way, Lord of creation. There's no God, O God like Thee...' In*

retrospect, you see these things. Often I notice how the Lord also leads these people by His providence while they know nothing about Him. Indeed if the Lord sees and hears the sparrows, pigeons and swallows, then He also hears these people. The Lord knows when they are hungry or when they are grieving. He hears their crying and lamenting, although they do not know it themselves.

What a privilege to tell them about this God, Who brought the world into being and Who afterwards did not cast off the world and leave them to fend for themselves, but to tell them about the living God, Who sees their sorrow and troubles, so that they may give themselves into His hand.

Mukani and his little son

Friendship is established with some Yalis

The first months consist of working on the strip, winning the confidence of the people and providing medical care. The Gospel is being told in simple terms by Rev. Kuijt and his helpers. Patients with yaws come from the surrounding valleys to the missionary for help.

> *It may sound strange, but we can smell where the people come from. Kobokma people have a peculiar unpleasant odour for us as they rub their skin with the sap made from bark of a certain tree. The people from Ilugwa have a different smell again.*

It takes time before the people from Abenero come. The breakthrough comes when Engenma, a village elder, brings one of his wives who has a serious case of yaws. She is the first woman from Abenaho to receive an injection. The problem is that Kuijt will have to touch her when he gives the injection and that is not permitted in their culture. No man may touch a woman in public. He tries to explain the procedure. Imagine if Engenma does not understand what needs be done. The result could be disastrous for the newcomers. Engenma with his wife enter Kuijt's home. She trembles with fear and to encourage her, her husband holds her head against his chest and wraps his arm around her and tells Kuijt to go ahead as he trusts him.

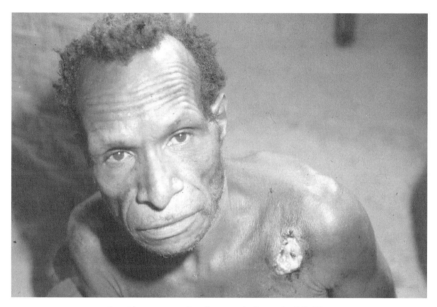

Another example of yaws, infested with flies

Just this past Saturday we had five more patients from the Ilugwa with yaws. There were some children as well who did not make a peep when the thick needle went into their body. We have to use thick needles because the almocilline is oil based and consequently is thicker than penicillin.

Once again, Kuijt and his Dani helpers are on their own. No Yali is too been seen. Suddenly a large group of Yali warriors run up to the strip but not to work. Oh No! They are dressed up and painted and they carry either a spear or bows and arrows in their hands. They run up and down the strip. It is a threatening sight. Kuijt and his helpers have no weapons and are defenceless. What now? The missionary asks his wife to get his film camera and calmly he takes some pictures. When Liok comes up to them, the missionary says to Roti, "Tell him that if he wants to kill us, he can go ahead. He can kill our body but he cannot kill our soul. Our souls will go to heaven where Jesus is." The young man relays the message. Liok who had come up to the group looked at him and threw his bow and arrows on the ground. No, he does not want to kill them. "But they must leave." Kuijt answers, "We came with a message and we have not been able to explain this message to you clearly enough yet. We have not had sufficient time to explain everything to you. So we must stay and we cannot go away."

Kuijt and one of the helpers working on the strip;
the Yalis do not want to work any more

Not long after this incident, another attempt is made to drive the missionary away. A large group of Yalis surrounds the house. They are sitting on the path to the house, on rocks around the house, in the field and on the section of the strip that is ready. The message is clear, "We want you to leave!" The missionary and his wife realize clearly that they are treading on terrain that is under Satan's power. The people, but even more specifically the evil powers, feel threatened and Satan will do all that is in his power to stay in control.

The Yalis think the strip is long enough. No more ground will be given, no more trees may be cut and the Yalis will not work anymore.

"You tell us about Jesus. Well, we do not want Him here."

The Yalis do not threaten violence; all they want is for the white man to leave them. Liok speaks adamantly to Rev. Kuijt. The Yalis are prepared to escort them to the Baliem Valley. At the same time the war Chief Langobarek stands at the "window opening" of the home. Miep is inside and the chief tries to persuade her to leave Abenaho. "I cannot do that," she answers, "My feet are very sore." "No problem," says Langobarek, "we will carry you." "No, Lango, we are going to stay!"

Kuijt radios MAF and asks if they can do something. Promptly, Don Beiter flies out and does a few dives over the people. The Yalis' attitude suddenly changed, some fled and about fifteen men immediately started working on the strip.

The Yali people are forbidden to have contact with the missionary couple. But in the evening when it is dark, some regularly come to visit and secretly disappear into the night again. The chiefs argue, disagree and point an accusing finger at one another about who is willing and who not to provide more land. After a great deal of negotiation and many questions, the owner of land near the top of the strip offers to sell another hundred metres of land for the price of an axe. The payment does not have to be made until later because the owner is afraid of the anger of the tribe against him. At the other end of the strip another sixty metres of ground is also sold but that owner is not as easily frightened and immediately accepts an axe. The chief, who has been the greatest opponent, sells the missionary thirteen large trees, which are needed to keep the fires going around the rock formations on the strip. Work can now continue.

A number of boulders are literally impossible to burn away. If they remain as they are, they will obstruct every aircraft that attempts to land. Everything has been tried: burning, chopping, rolling—nothing works. It is enough to make one lose hope. To add to the rock challenges, the radio breaks down. "Well, Miep," says her husband, "we are going to Wamena. We will take the radio along and see if we can bring back some dynamite. That is what the Dutch have used to make roads and I think I know where to find it. If I can get permission from the authorities, the work can be done with explosives."

But Miep does not feel up to the trek. Climbing up and down those mountains is too gruelling for her so she decides to stay behind. The agreement is that if she needs help, she will spread a white sheet on the completed part of the strip. "Fasten it down with stones; then the MAF pilots can see that you need help."

Working on the strip, fires heating the rock, and a MAF drop

Daily, Mrs. Kuijt visits the work site on the strip and works alongside the natives. When there is a tropical rainstorm she lets the men seek shelter inside her grass hut. She sits on the grass bed while some forty-five Yali men sit with her in the small room. They begin to sing, first softly and gradually the tempo is faster and the singing becomes louder. The floor vibrates from the noise. Constantly Miep hears her name repeated in the song. She starts to feel uncomfortable. "Gerrit is on his way to Wamena, and I am here all alone and without a radio. How irresponsible," she realizes "but I cannot change it now." Calmly, she waits for whatever will transpire.

Suddenly the singing stops. One of the workers looks outside. It is no longer raining. He signals to the others and they all run outside and start to work again. The Lord watches and gives peace. All those who trust in Him, will not be put to shame. She is certain of that. Rev. Kuijt writes:

> *You should have heard and seen the Yalis and the Danis scream and dance with the first explosions. Of course, we clearly explained to the people what was about to happen and the dangers. That is why we started with a few test explosions. The older ones were frightened and pulled up their noses in a sign of disapproval. But the youth had it figured out. "Tuan, Tuan, bum phano!" (Sir, boom, good).*

Mukani began to address me as Anombeije (our father). Maybe he was thinking of the heavy loads of wood he has been carrying. However, we were all thankful for the dynamite and its results. It definitely made a deep impression with Ngalabuk. After the first real explosion, he stormed down the hill and stood where he had seen a giant boulder totally shattered. The Yalis and Danis stood at a respectful distance from the area where the explosion was to take place. The vicinity was declared a danger zone. Dynamite used for peaceful mission work! What a blessing.

Mother and daughter

But when Rev. Kuijt is ready to begin the Sunday service on the air strip, no one shows up. The place is too dangerous in the eyes of the Yalis. Where are all the evil spirits that used to live in those rocks? Are they angry, are they dangerous, will they come for revenge? Spirits do not like to be mocked, especially when you blow their dwellings to pieces.

Father Kuijt in Katwijk presents a special request to the MB. Kuijt senior has already sent thirty-five red handkerchiefs to his son. Now he has been asked for another one hundred. This is a bit much for Father Kuijt so he makes a request to the MB. His request is not in vain and the handkerchiefs are shipped and Kuijt is thankful for them.

> *The Ilugwa always supplies us with carriers. Red handkerchiefs are in great demand with these people. They will walk two days to get one.*

That is quite pricey considering they will also walk two days for two shells or about six cents. The delegates have no idea why these handkerchiefs are so popular with the Ilugwas but they make fashionable decorations for their dancing feasts.

In the distance behind the mountains, a faint "zoom" can be heard and slowly it becomes louder. Some Yalis stare in the sky and discover the small dot. Rapidly they get out of the way. It is that time again. The big bird from the white man is coming. You have to keep your distance. The bird comes right towards you and opens its belly. If you are in the way, you can be pelted by a large burlap bag stuffed with grass and goods that are dropped from the plane.

Fear of the airplane soon disappears and the Yalis become accustomed to the danger. When the Cessna from MAF has finished its drop on July 25, 1964, it does not immediately return to its base. The pilot flies over the strip several times, lengthwise and across. Then the missionary hears from the radio: "It looks very good. Mike Papa Foxtrot. It looks very good." A warm feeling fills Kuijt and he can't say more than, "Thank you very much." Then chief pilot Hank Worthington, an old hand in the mission world, flies away. But Kuijt knows enough. This is very encouraging. The last work must be completed and then the area will be accessible. Ten months have gone by while they have lived here in total isolation. Of course there are always people around them. They have their own place in our hearts and lives. But contact with other whites has been solely via radio and the supply of goods and food is only by means of air drops. Only once did they travel to Wamena together when Kuijt needed to have his medical check-up for his lungs and Miep had a severe toothache.

The help given by the Yalis varies greatly throughout this time. Some days they are working with full force and on other days they all stay away. Mrs. Kuijt explains:

> *We did not know the reason for this behaviour until this evening. All around us murders are taking place. A man who came here this afternoon said that more than ten people have been killed in our area. We do not know if this total is accurate, but that killing is going on is for sure. It is terrible how*

brutally these tribes can treat each other. The area we are in as well as the Ilugwa area where we trekked through on the way here is known for its hostility. We found out that the people who are killed are also eaten. People who die a natural death are burned. The Chiefs are chosen by being the ones who killed the most of their enemies. You would not believe how sweetly they can sit beside you!

The last loads are always the heaviest. Of course, the use of dynamite helps to save time. The last seventy-five metres of the strip can be cleared in four weeks. Otherwise this might take at least five months. But Rev. Kuijt is at the end of his strength; he hardly eats anything anymore and is intensely tired. He has lost quite a few kilograms and does not look good. His wife is anxious.

I try to keep Gerrit away from the work but he cannot leave it alone. He has to set an example. If Gerrit looks like he wants to sit down the others are already sitting. You cannot blame them as it is very hard work!

Jozua Rumabar, a coastal Papua has decided that he will go on a vacation for no less than four weeks. Actually we cannot blame him. It is hard work and he is also exhausted. He says he will return but you never know. They are so easily influenced. If he does not come back, it will be extra hard for Gerrit. Thankfully we have the Bokondini and Kelila helpers who faithfully keep going. They also have days now when their energy is low. These helpers have more experience in building a strip; they are Christians and can read and write. They have a very positive influence on the locals, also in spreading the Gospel.

Gratitude wells up in Kuijt's heart; first of all to the Lord. The undertaking has had trials and tribulations, but neither the devil nor people could hinder the fact that a firm footing has been set in Abenaho. *Soli Deo Gloria.* Alone he would never have succeeded.

The MAF has been of indispensable service. The pilots were always ready to help out. Also invaluable was the helpfulness of the UFM, especially the mission posts of Bokondini and Kelila. From those bases new workers were made available time and time again.

If that had not been the case, the work of the strip would still have stretched endlessly before us because the people in the valley have not always been there for us.

The Kuijts on a little trip.
Note Mrs. Kuijt's hat and walking stick in the left foreground.

Across the width of the strip stand seven Papuan boys, each holding a stick in their hand. A cross bar is fastened to each stick, and the boys jump on that to see how fast and how deep the stick penetrates the hard ground. In this way they test the hardness of the strip. When they are done the sticks are put away. Also, the smoothness of the surface needs to be checked. The slope is about ten percent, which is acceptable. The MAF has done its required tests from the air. Now MAF pilot Clell Rogers will make the trek through the jungle to do one more final inspection on the ground. Clell even takes his wife with him. On the last portion of the harsh trek his wife has to be carried on an improvised stretcher. When darkness falls and the MAF couple still have not arrived, some Yalis ask the missionary for flash lights and small kerosene lights and go out to meet them. Thankfully Clell and his wife arrive safe and sound. "Once and never again," is their comment about the trek through the jungle.

Thankfully we could offer our first white guests a warm room in our grass hut (our one and only room) and the difficult trek was soon forgotten. I must admit that we did keep our guests up rather late that night. But you must understand, after such a long period of isolation...

Lunch is being served—no chairs and table available yet

On Monday, August 31, 1964, it is busy near the strip. Kuijt walks around nervously. All of us know that this is a historic occasion. There are no guarantees that the first landing will be successful. The Cessna Mike Papa Alpha appears over the mountain ridge and circles above the landing strip. The Yalis huddle together at a distance; nervously they peer at the sky. The *urulu* is coming, the bird is landing. Several times the pilot skims low over the strip. Then he decides to proceed with the landing and the wheels touch the ground. The aircraft bobbles and bounces but comes to a stop after a hundred & fifty metres. The little door opens and a laughing Hank Worthington pokes his head outside. He gives a thumb up! It is a success! Abenaho, known as Pass Valley in the aviation world, has been opened. Filled with thankfulness, Kuijt shakes Hank's hand.

In the meantime the Yalis come near the plane. Carefully one of them sticks out his hand and feels the skin of the plane. Others follow his example and the entire plane is touched. Janbenago asks, "Tuan, where is his heart?" The pilot kindly shows the heart of the bird, the engine. Several Yalis start to dance. A milestone has been reached in the mission work.

An example of a landing strip
high up in the mountains cut out in the jungle

Hank walks with the missionary and others the complete length of the strip. Within the hour he is ready to take off again. There are two extra people onboard: Rogers and his wife. The plane wobbles as it gains momentum and speeds down the strip. With plenty of room to spare, the Cessna rises and the plane disappears over the valley in the direction of Naltja.

Next week we hope to have a plane come in five times. The first will bring a Government Representative of Aviation who will inspect the strip. If it is approved, planes can deliver whatever we need. My wife and I are looking forward to finally have a table and two folding chairs. Until now we have been sitting on the floor or lying on the bed to do our writing. For some of you it will be a relief when I can type my letters again... Do not forget the mattresses. All of which, will come in as soon as possible.

Finishing touches have to be made to the strip. Along the sides, ditches are dug to carry away the rain water. After that the strip will require regular maintenance.

Just think of the grass that grows. Someone told me that about six goats can keep the strip clean. So we will try to get some.

Chapter 10

Cast Your Bread upon the Waters

The morning devotions and the weekly services attract only a few Yalis besides the Dani evangelists and helpers from Bokondini, and Jozua the coastal Papua. The Yalis do not show up except for a few children and sometimes Mukani.

Mukani is wounded from an altercation with Uluayè about a tree. They fought each other with burning pieces of wood. As usual, others get involved and the fighting leads to shooting with bows and arrows. As a result Kèra and Olat are also wounded.

Kokpan, a friend of Kèra, informs Rev. Kuijt what happened and both wounded men are asked to come and see him. Kèra comes but Olat does not show up. By radio Kuijt contacts the mission doctor in Pit River and he agrees to take Kèra and do the necessary surgery. A plane is arranged and the doctor successfully removes a six centimetre arrowhead from his back.

Several weeks later Olat shows up and Kuijt again makes the necessary arrangements to have him flown to Pit River. The operation is successful but unfortunately he died the following day. Olat had told his people he had swallowed a spirit and this must enviably be the cause of his death. See there it happened again! Olat is dead!

After I passed on the news of Olat's death to Kèra and Kokpan, they were visibly shaken and Kokpan trembled so badly that he could barely swallow. You wonder what will be the consequences for us in our work. Let us be silent. God has spoken.

It is Easter Sunday; Kokpan attends the service and drinks in the words like water. The sermon is about Christ's suffering, His death to pay for our sins and the resurrection for our salvation. Gradually the tribal

134

people lose their fear for the white intruders. At first the women would flee whenever they saw a white person; now they come to the door to sell sweet potatoes.

Kokpan, who was the first believer

It is not possible at this time to start primary schooling yet, but medical care is now accepted on a limited scale. The local people are afraid of the medicine. Kuijt builds a small clinic which includes a storage shed.

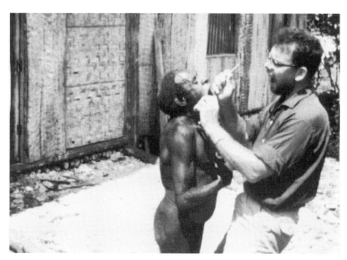

Rev. Kuijt working as a dentist:
he is just as involved with the procedure as the patient

Now that the airplanes can land it is possible to bring in sheets of corrugated aluminum, a material unknown to the Yalis. It is still too premature to build a church. It is not a problem to hold open-air services on the strip.

*An undernourished child, who is unsure
whether to take the medicine offered by Miep*

Jozua, the evangelist who has been here since the beginning, just returned from a holiday to the coast and agrees to stay at least another year in Abenaho. Kuijt thinks this is an excellent opportunity to continue further into the valley and to leave Jozua to oversee the work here. The MB is pleased with Kuijt's endeavor but would like him to permanently settle in Abenaho and dedicate himself to evangelism and teaching. Rev. Rijksen writes:

> *Honestly, Gerrit, I do not want to be harsh but in all love I must remind you that your mandate is not to claim more areas for the NRC but to be a Missionary. Your mission is not to raise the Banner of the NRC but the Banner of the Cross and to be the means in God's hands to bring the Light to those who live in darkness. We strongly advise you to leave other places out of the picture for the time being. I know that when you see the heathens*

killing one another your heart must be burning with compassion to preach the Gospel, to tell them of the love of Christ and to let them know the word of God and His grace so that people will forsake their practices and embrace the Gospel of Christ.

The MB understands how hard it is to bring the Gospel in Abenaho; it is like plowing on a field of rocks.

But Gerrit, you know that not only the people who eagerly accept the Gospel, but especially the enemies of God must be reconciled with Him.

Kuijt assures them that he will certainly not venture out on his own. Deep down in my heart I hope there will come a time when you and I can say "Amen" together for the opening of Nipsan. We will cast ourselves on the Lord and watch for His Godly deeds.

Again Kuijt seizes this opportunity to request more mission workers so that more effort can be put toward this goal.

I am convinced that if we truly want more workers to come here, they will be admitted. Don't we believe in the power of an Almighty God with whom all things are possible?

There is a tremendous amount of work waiting to be done.

I hope you do not assume we are sitting here doing nothing. We are doing everything in our power to reach our ultimate goal. But never compare our work with yours. Your task is to prepare your sermons as well as your congregational duties (although I know that can be varied and very time encompassing). Here we are jack of all trades, guiding and working along with the locals on the airstrip, attending to gardening, building projects, doing linguistic work, etc. In addition there is a great deal of correspondence which is a requirement of all missionaries. During the year that we have been here, we have not had time to read one book. I believe it is your responsibility to inform the church goers of this reality.

Mrs. Kuijt tires easily and has problems walking. The doctor on the coast diagnoses that her Achilles tendons are too short and so she walks only on the front of her foot instead of using her whole foot. It is necessary for her to undergo surgery in Port Moresby, Australian New Guinea.

A cordial letter is received from Rev. Vergunst passing on warmest wishes on behalf of the MB: "We wish you well, Miep. The Lord is with you. You are a brave woman Miep; we would like to express our deepest respect for you and your work." However, the operation does not take place as Mrs. Kuijt is pregnant and that explains her tiredness. The surgery is postponed until their furlough.

Another agricultural project ; long poles for the climbing green beans

One of the many projects

The MB urges Rev. Kuijt,

We want you to live in a decent home. We don't want you to spend the rest of your life in a grass hut, especially now with a baby on the way.

However, the Kuijt family is content with their house.

All I can say is that we are comfortably situated. We just had visitors and the lady complimented on how cozy our home is despite the fact that, besides the windows and roof, the house is made from tree bark.

Rev. Kuijt with his two-way radio and world receiver on top. The necessary current is provided by a car battery

The missionary is more concerned that the locals still do not want to listen to the Gospel than about the size of his house. Chief Liok has forbidden the children to attend school. Kuijt decides to start first with the chiefs but after a few days they have had enough and tell the missionary it is easier for children to learn all those letters and numbers. This opens the way to begin teaching the children.

In the meantime, Rev. Kuijt continues his linguistic work. He writes to the MB.

Although these people are viewed as Stone Age people by our standards, their language is as complex as Latin,

They are astonished and respond,

>   *This definitely indicates a higher level of development than was initially assumed.*

When Rev. Kuijt is on the coast he purchases goats, chickens and ducks. The goats will be used to keep the strip clean and the chickens will be kept for their eggs. The Yalis are more interested in the chicken feathers that enhance their appearance during their dances than the eggs.

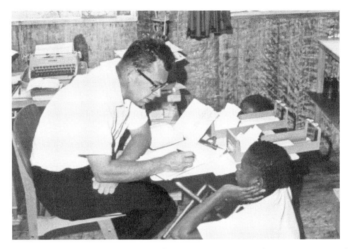

Rev. Kuijt with two language informants. To the right is Sabonwarek

Rev. Kuijt visiting a village. Note the many grass huts

Much less innocent are the axes and parangs (bush knives) which Kuijt has paid to the Yalis in exchange for their work done on the strip. While he is away, an old village feud breaks out near Abenoho. Now the weapons are not bows and arrows but parangs and axes. When the wounded come to Kuijt for medical care he refuses to help them because he had warned them over and over again to stop fighting. They purposely engaged in this fight. "We have noticed that while we are here they go to war with neighboring tribes; while we are gone the fights are more local."

Rev. Kuijt spends a month in Jakarta together with approximately one hundred missionaries from Irian. The Indonesian Government invites them to take some courses. President Sukarno himself, meets with the missionaries. When Kuijt returns from Jakarta to Irian he immediately travels on to Karubaga where there is a small RBMU hospital. The Scottish missionary doctor greets him and tells him he has arrived just in time "as it looks like your baby will be born today." Their first child, Klazina Geritha, is born on June 22, 1965. Via the radio, Kuijt immediately informs Jozua in Abenaho but in his excitement he forgets to tell him it is a girl.

Klazina, comes home - the first white child ever seen by the local people

After several days the couple returns to Abenaho with their new daughter. Both Yali men and women are waiting for them on the strip.

141

They are curious and want to see the baby. With utter amazement they put their hand to their mouth and call out, "At *kuluon werek* —She is white! She is white!"

Proud Father with his Daughter, Klazina

The Yalis consider the baby part of their tribe; therefore they want to give the baby a Yali name, *"Phiphikè"* or woman of the Phiphi, a high mountain between Ilugwa and Abenaho. Chief Liok sends Rev Kuijt out of the house and remains behind with mother and baby. He then moves his arms and hands above the baby and mumbles something, but Miep does not know what he says. He ends his ceremony by blowing on the baby. Mother Kuijt is very thankful that he does not attempt to touch the baby.

Rev. Kuijt's livestock includes a white boar. It is his intention to breed this pig with the local Yali black pigs in order to get a better breed. Unfortunately, they will not allow their pigs to be bred by a white pig from the *other* world so the missionary decides to purchase the local black pigs, breed them and hand them out to the Yalis.

Goats and pigs husbandry; cross-bred black mother pig with white piglets

The goats supply the milk which little Klazina needs to supplement her feedings. The women are allowed to watch Klazina being bottle fed in the hopes they will become interested in raising goats.

No money in the world will entice them to drink one drop of goat's milk now but we will wait and see.

Later on several motherless babies are kept alive by feeding them goat's milk.

When Mrs. Kuijt needs to go to the coast because of a terrible toothache, she asks her husband if there is anything she can do for him while there. "Yes, come back with a goat," was his answer. "No way!" she replies. But while at the coast she cannot forget his request and when she returns, low and behold after the plane comes to a stop, out comes not only Miep, but also a goat!

Raising livestock, gardening and offering medical care are all part of pioneering mission work. Rev. Kuijt tries to teach the people how to grow European products but an Irish potato or a plate of brown beans are foreign to them and they are not ready to eat them. This also applies to the medical work. Many have benefited from the treatments they received from the Kuijts but the work is still in its infancy. At first they were scared of the injections but after seeing the results from penicillin shots for yaws they do not fear an injection any longer. The time comes when they ask for an injection instead of explaining what their problem is.

However, there is no place for the Word of God yet. There are only Kokpan, Kèra with the scar on his back, Dakma and some others who attend the church services. "In the beginning God created the Heavens and the Earth. And God spoke: Let there be light." "Oh," says Kokpan, "Then our forefathers have been wrong." Kuijt asks him what they thought about this. Then Kokpan tells the story. "Before you came here we believed that the origin of day and night was caused by a rat called Namok. He hunts at night and with his long tongue (because he has no legs) he crawls up to the tops of the trees and lets the night come. When he goes back down the tree with his long tongue he then lets the day begin."

Mrs. Kuijt feeding an undernourished motherless baby

Open-air service on the strip. Coastal helper Jozua and Miep are sitting on the left side. Other helpers and one Yali are seated. Standing is Roti, bringing The Word.

144

The Gospel causes havoc with the heathen spirits and idol worship. It is difficult to comprehend if you are a Yali; their tales have been passed on through oral tradition from one generation to the next. It is no wonder that opposition against the Gospel increases. Last week nine children attended school now none. There are no children to be seen in the neighborhood. Ndomeli, our house help from Bokondini, pensively tells Rev. Kuijt about rumors that are going around. The natives in the valley are busy collecting all the axes, bush knives, knives and mirrors that the missionary gave them over the past few months. They are planning to return them all.

Now I must say it is not a good sign if they want to return everything you gave them. It is their way of telling you loud and clear that you are not welcome and that it would be better to leave right away.

Ndomeli also tells him that the people are saying that since the missionary's arrival the sweet potatoes are not as big as they used to be. Kuijt is concerned. Did not Liok recently walk around the house making gestures with his hands, then sat on his haunches as he hit the ground? Apparently, in doing so, he put a spell on everything that belongs to the Kuijt family.

Liok knows very well that this would not scare us but it will have great significance to the locals.

So this week the airplane arrived as scheduled and we expected them to come. But no one showed up. While sharing this information with the pilot, we saw groups of men hiding in different places at the beginning, along the side and at the bottom of the strip. If they wish to harm us they could end our lives in an instant. We are totally at their mercy. Although I have a very old rifle, I have no ammunition. But as a missionary to now start shooting these people.... We can truly say we were spared again. Our time is in God's hands.

Furlough is fast approaching. The MB urges Kuijt to make the necessary arrangements with the government for his return. After repeated discussions whether to join the TMF or not, the MB makes the decision to ask for membership with the TMF.

Ndomeli is reluctant to go home; he looks at the photographs on the wall and finally picks up his sweet potatoes and vegetables and goes into the dark night. The Kuijts and Kokpan are seated at the table. Suddenly there is a blood-curdling scream. Everyone freezes. The screaming continues. The door is thrown open and the curtain pushed aside. In stumbles Ndomeli. His *baju* (shirt) is soaked with blood and his eyes are bulging out of his head. Stuttering and stammering he tries to tell them what happened. While walking to his hut about thirty metres away he is brutally attacked by three men, one in front and two from behind. He does not have a chance to protect himself as he is thrown on the ground and hit repeatedly with an axe by one of them. Blood is streaming from four deep gashes in his back.

Arèn, a Yali boy who was near Ndomeli's hut heard the attackers talking and recognized the Ilugwa language. "Is he dead?" They ask each other and then run away. Thankfully Ndomeli is not dead but ends up with several nasty wounds. Kuijt cleans the wounds and tries to stop the bleeding. After consulting with the doctor at Karubaga the next day, it is decided that Kuijt must stitch the wounds himself as there is no MAF plane available. If complications arise, Ndomeli can still be flown to Karubaga.

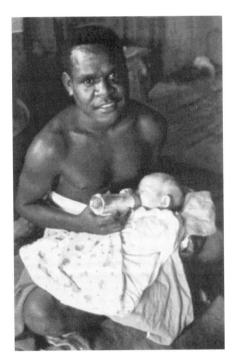

Ndomeli, who is bandaged up because of four wicked gashes on his back from the attack. Mrs. Kuijt gives him baby Klazina in the hope that it will take his mind off the pain.

The operation is successful and Ndomeli recovers. But is it safe to keep the young man? Kuijt reluctantly decides to send him back to his home in Wolo. The Kuijts have become very close to the young man who is about eighteen. Ndomeli has always been a hard worker. He not only helped around the house but assisted Rev Kuijt in translating, his behavior shows he is a Christian.

We can truly say that he puts his life in the Lord's service by coming here. The scars that he carries on his back are the scars he bears for Christ's sake.

Wolo and Ilugwa are at war; it is a running battle between the two tribes. Each death must be avenged regardless of who is the victim. The Wolo tribe has murdered more people from the Ilugwa; therefore ambushing Ndomeli, who originates from Wolo, became an easy target to even the score.

On Sundays Kokpan always repeats the words spoken by Rev. Kuijt to the hearers. For instance the story of Zacchaeus: "A very rich man lived in a certain place." The missionary shows paper money and explains what you can do with it. The man's name was Zacchaeus. As he had a great deal of money he also had many pigs, steel axes, knives, mirrors and beads. One day he was caught stealing. He ran away and climbs into a tree to hide but he could not hide from God. The Lord Jesus who knows everything also knew that Zacchaeus had stolen. When Jesus came close to the tree where Zacchaeus was hiding, Jesus told him to come down out of the tree immediately as Jesus wanted to go with him to his house and sleep there, as night was coming. Zacchaeus was terribly afraid but when he told Jesus that for each pig he had stolen he would give back four pigs in return, Jesus said to him that he was a good man. Jesus had given Zacchaeus a new heart and instead of going into the place where he would be eaten by the fire he would be with Jesus in a place called heaven. If we are like Zacchaeus and receive a new heart we will love Jesus and not steal and lie anymore.

The story of Zacchaeus hits home. One day Miep sees a young boy, Nacharalma, taking a cooked sweet potato. The boy hurriedly tries to eat the potato but no matter how he tries to cover it up, there is no denying what Miep has seen. Nacharalma is reprimanded. To Mieps amazement, the boy returns a few days later with four sweet potatoes! She felt very small.

Slowly there is change among the people and their wariness begins to diminish. More people attend the services held in Kuijt's house. Deep thankfulness fills Rev. Kuijt as he counts forty men and boys; even Liok who is totally chained to his heathen worship is there. Yes, he still practices all kinds of incantations but God can still convert such a person. Would it not be wonderful if this happened before Liok dies? From a human point of view, the missionary has arrived in time to bring the Gospel to this old man. Kuijt realizes that these people are in the power of Satan himself and demons, the evil spirits of the air which instigate resistance to the work of the missionaries. What else can you expect? The darkness cannot have fellowship with the Light. In this invisible world a battle rages between life and death.

The first classes take place in the Kuijts' kitchen.
The young man with the hat is Kokpan.

There sits Liok with his head bowed. Does the story of Noah make an impression on him? Because of sin all mankind drowned as they did not listen to warnings of the Lord God spoken through Noah. Rev. Kuijt addresses the little children but also Liok. "Liok, don't you want to listen to the voice of God? Are you going to condone plundering and killing by your warriors? Wouldn't you rather turn to God and be saved?"

The following Sunday there are sixty-five attendees and, for the first time, twelve women and children. On the third Sunday the service has to be held on the airstrip as two hundred Yalis have gathered to hear Kuijt's message. Is it the Spirit of God at work? A prayer arises in the heart of the missionary, "Please bless the labours in this vineyard. Oh Lord, it is our time to go on furlough to the Netherlands, but you do not need me. Please bless the preaching of Jozua who will continue here, that it may keep growing."

Mission day while on furlough in Holland

Once again the loud drone of the ship's horn is heard. The ocean going cargo/passenger vessel Karimun is ready to depart with Rev. Kuijt, Miep, and baby Klazina. Filled with awe the missionary looks back.

Almost four years ago he arrived in Hollandia. He experienced prosperity but also adversity. He fought with the three-headed opponent the devil, sin and, not in the least, his own human nature. So far the Lord has made all things well. "Holy in Thy habitation are Thy ways, Lord of creation. There is no God, Oh God, like Thee, clothed with strength and majesty."

His kingdom will expand also in Irian. No one can stop this. Living in the tropics takes its toll; both Kuijt and his wife experience this. The Indonesian Government has provided them with re-entry permits valid for up to one year.

It is a few months later that they set foot on Dutch soil; Kuijt knows they will stay at his parents' place. Katwijk-home, Abenego-home? He sighs, Irian has become his homeland and the Papua's have his heart. Rev. Kuijt carries deep in his heart the many souls who have not heard the word of God. If the Lord wills it, they will return to Irian.

Chapter 11

Turned Away from the Idols

The police officer looks directly into Rev. Kuijt's eyes. "We are not certain but, if the rumours are true, your going to Abenaho can be quite dangerous. A hostile chief from the Baliem Valley and his warriors are supposed to be on their way towards the mission post and their intentions do not seem peaceful. Their main targets are the two coastal Papuans, Jozua Rumabar and Melki, who are both working there." The officer sends two policemen along with Kuijt to investigate the situation.

They are flown into Pass Valley, the name given to Abenaho long before the missionary came there. Mrs. Kuijt and baby Phiphikè will come later. The village chiefs led by Liok, are waiting by the strip to welcome the Tuan. At first glance, the situation seems peaceful. Liok speaks first, "War! Naturally our tribe is very upset. The neighbouring Kapiè tribe has killed and eaten one of our men. Retaliation is required." Langobarek, the war chief nods in agreement. It is necessary to seek revenge for the death of Kweakma. The score must be evened. The police officers absolutely forbid them to carry out their plans. The agitated tribal chiefs try to negotiate with the police officers to change their minds. The missionary proposes compensation from the Kapiè tribe rather than revenge. The Papuans raise their voices in protest but the officers remain adamant. There will be no revenge!

The Sunday worship is poorly attended. Liok has become a faithful attendee, at least when he has no other plans. It seems he has some understanding of the spoken word but he also wants to benefit in a material way. "If you do not give me an empty burlap rice bag I will not attend church this Sunday." The missionary refuses because he does not want to have "empty bag" Christians. "I am certain you do not experience this situation in Holland," the missionary wrote to the MB.

Service in the Kuijt's home where the walls were made of grass

Their reply was: "It is clear that you have never been a minister in Holland. You think we do not meet "empty rice bag Christians"—well there are lots of them. There are people who wish to benefit from the church—not in the spiritual sense but only in a materialistic way. We all struggle with the empty-rice-bag syndrome and must constantly fight against becoming stingy and greedy."

Kuijt realizes that the Papuans are the same as Leidenaars and Katwijkers (and the same as you and I).

By God's grace once in a while we realize and detest the materialism that cleaves in our hearts. I would almost say that I have met this Liok somewhere before.

Jozua has renovated the house. The grass section of the house was torn down and replaced with tree bark and an aluminium roof. Both coastal Papuan's have worked extremely hard but there is little left of the livestock. The goats died, the number of chickens declined; even the white boar did not survive. They buried the pig but after a few days the people regretted their decision so they dug it up and ate it. Only the piglets are still alive and seem to be thriving. The school is also not a success yet; the number of pupils remain the same.

Rev. Kuijt listening attentively to the locals.
Note in the background the bark wall of the house (no more grass!).

Jozua does his best, and soon the children can count to one hundred and recite the ABC's. When Rev. Kuijt returns from furlough, the children, with glowing faces, sing Psalm 81 in the Indonesian language, which Jozua has also taught them.

Kuijt concentrates on the work in Abenaho but he has not forgotten Nipsan. When he hears that the UFM wants to work in Nipsan, he is disappointed. He still holds in his heart the hope that in one way or another he will be able to work there and reach the people with the Gospel. Now it seems that this will not be realized. He does not dare hope that the Nipsan Valley can be considered a mission field for the NRC. It is with profound anguish that he lets go of Nipsan. UFM is prepared to work only in Nipsan and for the time being to leave Kosarek alone. Rev. Kuijt commits this into the hand of the Lord. However, at UFM's annual meeting, a proposal to start work in Nipsan is rejected.

Once again Rev. Kuijt sends an urgent appeal to the Mission Board for more workers.

We are desperate for helpers. Is there no one in our churches
who is qualified to come over and help? Do the other Reformed
Churches have people who are willing to come? Our church is

officially registered with the Government and people from other denominations could, via our mission, come to Indonesia and retain their independence. Thankfully here we do not distinguish between churches as you do in the Netherlands. More people will also help to alleviate our loneliness; we seldom receive white visitors. When they do come, rest assured that they will receive a warm and generous hospitality at the Kuijt residence. At Christmas we received a visit from two German missionary nurses from the Baliem Valley. It seemed as if we were on holidays as well.

Another time Rev. Kuijt writes,

With Miep, the baby and me, everything is fine. However it is lonely, which takes its toll…

One evening Rev. Kuijt and his wife hear voices speaking Dutch outside their home. Who in the world can that be? After opening the door they face two Catholic priests who are making a trip to search for herbs to be used as medicine. An enjoyable evening ensues; they are interested in how the work is going. It was a pleasant break for Rev. and Mrs. Kuijt to have company and being able to talk with Dutch people and they invite them to spend the night. Later on the MB heard about this and were concerned. They wonder if the looking for herbs was the real reason for visiting Abenaho or if they are trying to extend their territory. Kuijt does not share their concern but can understand them.

I have sent one of the priests a book called, "Rome in the Light of God's Word" by Rev. Zijderveld. We are on friendly terms and hope this will remain (which it did). While here they promised me some rabbits which we can pick up on our next visit to Wamena.

In 1964 Rev. Kuijt writes;

Hostility seems to be the order of the day. During the past weekend, we have experienced a lot of turmoil. On Saturday we heard rumours that there had been fighting again and thirteen men had died. The war chief supposedly also was slain. That night I was unexpectedly called out of bed to find a lot of people up and about at that late hour. They asked me for matches to light torches and a flashlight battery which I gave to them. We knew that warriors were wounded. It is a tradition in this area to sacrifice a pig in order to restore the health of the wounded warriors. The next morning we received a leg of pork as a thank you for our help. We then heard that Langobarek was seriously wounded by an axe.

Early morning devotion. In the background is the Kuijt's grass house

In church that day we told the people how God has no desire to take Langobarek's life but that he was spared so he could change his way of life. We pointed out that pitching battles is from the evil one. "Yes," added Kokpan, "and does going to war give you potatoes to eat? It is much better to work than to fight."

After the service we told the people to get Langobarek. His injures were even worse than those of Ndomeli's and he was in a great deal of pain.

One of the wounds was so deep and gaping that I was reluctant to stitch the wound shut. But it was better not to let him wait another twelve hours in order to see a doctor. It was already 24 hours or more since he was wounded. Thus without anaesthetic, I proceeded to stitch him up; thankfully we were able to pull the tissue together. Now we have to wait and see whether he will heal.

Kuijt asked the local people to pray for Langobarek because,

If he heals, it could be the spiritual turning point in the valley.

Several months later Rev. Kuijt writes,

Langobarek has completely recovered. On Sunday he attended the church service and I was asked to cut his hair as he declared he wanted to follow the Lord Jesus. However, a few days ago I noticed he was treating himself freely to some salt. He said he was not feeling well and eating salt would help him get better.

Langobarek healed from his axe wounds

Gradually Sunday worship services become an important part in the lives of the Pass Valley people. Approximately seventy men including a large group of women gather for the outdoors services. This gives reason to rejoice. With the help of Kokpan, Rev. Kuijt preaches in the Abenaho language. When necessary, Kokpan clarifies Rev. Kuijt's message, because the language has so many conjugations.

More and more, whenever I give Kokpan the opportunity to provide clarification, he tells me that the people fully understand what I have said; that he does not need to add anything.

Our students have learned to sing Psalms 81, 100, 116, and 134; of course everything is still informal and it happens every so often that we sing the songs over and over again as the women enjoy listening to them. When Jozua returns we will have to add a part of the service in the Indonesian language again.

It seems especially on Sunday that our open-air services are interrupted with a downpour so we are thinking about building a little church. This building will have a dual purpose—to be used for church services and as a school. A sawmill donated by people in the U.S.A. has arrived and cutting boards for building projects proves to be a success.

Rev. Kuijt , a man of many talents, cutting down a tree for the sawmill

In our public worship services we have another "praying man." His name is Milibaga. He starts the service with singing and then Kokpan prays while I stand in the middle with my "elders" on each side.

On Sunday we spoke again about the conversion of Paul. He hated the Christians at first. We tried to explain in simple terms what Saul was like in his former life and asked Kokpan's father if he wanted to be a Christian. His answer was: "Anindi" which means, "I want to". Later on, in another service when we spoke about the importance of attending Sunday worship services, he was no longer sure he wanted to become a Christian, as he likes to skip services once in a while.

Mrs. Kuijt is expecting their second child. When the time comes to deliver the baby, she, her husband, and Klazina are flown to Angguruk.

While waiting for the baby's arrival, Kuijt and Dr. Vriend discuss all kind of subjects including medical information that will help Kuijt treat patients once back in Abenaho. Kuijt discovers that there are quite a few similarities between the language of Angguruk and that of Pass Valley. Kuijt knows that the MB is trying to find an agriculturist. His response is:

He has to be prepared to do all kinds of work. But at least please send a person who has received a call from the Lord to come here. Then everything will work out.

When the question is raised whether or not to start an agriculture school in Abenaho, Kuijt's answer is,

No, right now there is no need for such a school, maybe in fifty years. Let us be spared from becoming a social organization but keep the proclamation of the Gospel the main reason for us being here.

There is great joy when the baby is born—their first son. Mother Kuijt proudly holds baby Willem Johannes in her arms. He was born March 22, 1967, delivered by Dr. Vriend in Angguruk.. Phiphikè has a little brother and Rev. Kuijt has a son. The MB gives permission to baptize the child in Abenaho even though it is not an established church. A large group of Yalis attend the church service.

Above all I believe that our child is also part of the people of this valley.

In Angguruk the local people call the baby "Yalinap" which means "Yali-man". The people of Abenaho are ecstatic with the birth of the baby boy! This means that their Bapa (father) will have a successor. What is even more delightful is that the parents have given the baby the name "Wim" (abbreviation for Willem). The Yalis pronounce it as "Wiem" which in their language means: "War". This proves that the little boy really belongs to them.

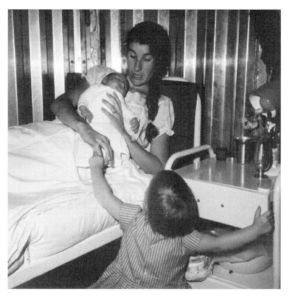

Mother with baby Willem and daughter Klazina

Rev. Kuijt has personally given a donation to the Pentecostal Assemblies and that is his own business. However, the idea of having a picture and a testimonial appear in the Pentecostal periodical, *World Prayer Front* is too much for the MB. They comment:

> *We hope you were able to stop the publication of this article. Not only do you bring yourself and the entire mission but also the NRC into upheaval and God's Name is blasphemed. You must realize that these actions bring discord.*

It appears that a certain Van Dijk who was originally a member of the NRC and now belongs to the Pentecostal Assembly informs the MB of Kuijt's sympathy towards the Pentecostal movement. Another time he writes about Kuijt's leaning toward the Pentecostals and that the missionary believes he must be baptized by the Holy Ghost and that he must speak in tongues in order that he may heal the sick in the name of Jesus and so that he may bind and command the forces of hell to leave his mission field.

Rev. Kuijt does not blink an eye at the allegations. For a while he had received the magazine *Power from on High* but that had stopped because the postal cost was too high. He did sent a donation with the explicit instructions to use the money to distribute bibles behind the Iron Curtain.

But having written a testimony for the magazine? This is totally unknown to him.

> *This probably relates to a leaflet from Tante Joan. She is involved with World Prayer Front. I do not share their views but I do admire their activities. Tante Joan asked whether she was allowed to share something out of our newsletter and a family picture. Why not? Now and then there are articles and pictures of us in other newspapers as well.*
>
> *I do not subscribe to the beliefs of the Pentecostals that the doctrine of election is a false doctrine. Consequently this is where we differ; concerning conversion, rebirth, etc. But God forbid that you and I deny the work of God's graces should it be present in an individual's life. Then we are in error.*
>
> *It would go against my conscience if I were to condemn people because of their different church backgrounds. The Lord may save us from judging people. There is One Who judges!*
>
> *As far as Van Dijk is concerned, I imagine that he and his fellow believers pray for us that we would be delivered from the errors of the NRC. I think that the wish has become the fruit of the thought. As he wrote himself, it would create quite a sensation.*

However, Kuijt would not be Kuijt if he did not add that a photo of Rev. Huisman had appeared in the magazine, *Power from on High*, on April 7, 1967.

The number of people attending Sunday worship services increases to about one hundred. Some of them complain that they have to walk too far to pray—this is how they describe the church services. It is no different than in The Netherlands. For one person it is too warm, for another it is too cold; for one the service starts too late, and again for another it is too early. Rev. Kuijt requests that four Dani Evangelist families from the Baliem Valley come to live among the Pass Valley natives. It is his hope that they will be an example by their lifestyle and testimony. He places the families in outlying villages which causes some villagers joy and with those who still reject the Gospel it causes unrest. "Are these people coming to eat our sweet potatoes? Isn't it enough that we have Tuan Kuijt, Jozua and Kokpan who already bring us The Word?"

The steaming cooking pits

When rumours are heard that the Baliem Christians are threatened, the police steps in. An entire evening is spent in Kuijt's home deliberating with the locals as to how this situation can be resolved. Analek and his men are responsible for the threats. So should they take them prisoners or burn down their village, or is it enough to kill some pigs? The following day action is taken; pigs are killed and Analek and his men are forced to participate in negotiations which results in peace. And also, between the men of Kapié and Abenaho peace is restored. The gathering is closed with prayer, and singing Psalm 81.

Njanji bangsaKu
Dan bersukatjita
Bagi Tuhanmu!
Ialah kekal
Allah Israil,
Kekuatan kita.

("Unto God, our King, Joy and strength of Israel, Lofty anthems sing; Glorious are His ways, To His Name give praise...")

The war chiefs from Kapiè and Abenaho solemnly shake each other's hand and promise in the presence of many witnesses and before the all-seeing eye of God that they will no longer fight with each other. Of course Langobarek is also present. The people of Kapiè are astonished to see that he is alive as they had celebrated his supposed death by dancing and feasting.

Women dancing

Once more, pigs are butchered and eaten. This time they are feasting to celebrate the peace and to forget the past. Christianity expands through the Pass Valley like yeast—it gradually grows. Their change of heart is expressed not only by words but especially by their deeds.

One example is Ngaialima, a man who had to be flown to Angguruk for medical help. Before he left, he publicly led us in prayer for the first time. This was the same man who used to go around with a black greased face and a long spear in his hand ready to start a war dance. But if these

162

men would have to appear before the MB, they would say, *"an nakel"* which means: "I am scared". They would be lost for words.

Another example of change is when, on behalf of the people, Kokpan asks Rev. Kuijt what the Good Book says about the proper time to kill the pigs. In their culture killing pigs was often related to satisfying the evil spirits. "So what must we do now?"

> *One evening we could hear singing nearby. We listened attentively and realized we were not hearing the old heathen songs but a Psalter. Open saith the Lord, wide thy mouth believing....These natives were singing the familiar Psalm 81 and when they finished they began to sing Psalm 116, I love the Lord...*

Would it be possible for Jozua to take responsibility for the mission post of Abenaho so that Kuijt and his wife could go to Kosarek-Nipsan? Kuijt cannot forget his first love; he is convinced they are waiting for him there. But the time is not right because in Abenaho there is still a great deal of work to be done. Many times he has pleaded with the MB but also at the Throne of Grace to send more evangelist workers from The Netherlands. In The Netherlands all efforts to recruit mission workers seem to be futile.

How must we proceed from here? Kuijt sends Jozua to the coast to find Christian evangelists who are willing to come and help with spreading the Gospel. On Sunday, services are held in four different places to hundreds of listeners. They have also started a post and a strip in Landikma, a six-hour walk for the people from Abenaho, where there seems to be great interest for the preaching and every service is attended by about five hundred people. At three sites they are busy building churches and the Gospel message seems to be spreading. The missionary pastor yearns to see spiritual fruits. Since there has been peace among the tribes, there is more trade taking place which proves to be a blessing, as now approximately two thousand people are reached by the Gospel.

Little Wim is still not baptized. Rev. Kuijt would like to first teach the people the meaning of the Holy Baptism so that they will understand what is happening.

> *I started teaching about baptism without first informing Kokpan. If ever I have seen a man look stunned, it was Kokpan;*

the necessity of baptism was incomprehensible to him. I intended to explain this while performing a wedding ceremony that all children born from this union should be baptised. However, this was very difficult for them to comprehend. Still, I thought that they should know something about the baptism ceremony..

"Miep, will you please come here," Kuijt calls as he holds a letter in his hand. She comes over to see what is going on. He informs her that, "the Lord has heard our prayers. A new mission couple has been accepted and their name is Fahner, They are newlywed and his wife is a teacher."

*The Fahners are an answer
to prayer*

Rev. Kuijt immediately advises the MB about his plans to build a house for the new couple. Oh and by the way this issue about my slides! He understands that in The Netherlands his slide presentations are not always well received because they show "naked" people.

Well, look you must understand that I cannot dress these people first just to take some pictures. It is normal for these people to walk around naked, as it is the norm for us to wear clothing.

Kokpan is getting married! What news! He was unable to find a girl to marry him as he lives and associates with white people. This is viewed by the Yalis as playing with fire. The people were indifferent to him and no one wanted to give their daughter to him in marriage. Later he was offered a seven-year-old girl but Kuijt advises him not to accept the offer. Kokpan obeys. Lo and behold, Abalokè suddenly wishes to marry him! Rev. Kuijt immediately starts to teach Kokpan about a biblical marriage. He tries to convey what marriage means and that a marriage must be consecrated before God. Kokpan does not comprehend everything and assumes that he and Abalokè must pray together and then they are married. So that's what they did in their hut. The idea of getting married in the church scares him but he agrees, the marriage takes place the following Sunday. Kokpan promises not to live together with his fiancé before the wedding ceremony.

A large number of the congregation, at least two hundred people wait on the air strip. But Abalokè is not there. The shy girl stayed at home with her mother and did not dare to come. Kuijt thought he had prepared everything, the marriage service and an appropriate prayer. And now the bride does not show up. He is really perturbed and he shows it by walking to his house. The people sit and wait. "Now he is going to talk on the radio," one of them says. In other words, he is going to tell the radio that everything went wrong! Here again is an example of how they think. Radio, police and religion are all one to these people.

The missionary just sat down on his chair when Liok, the chief comes in. "Tuan, come with us and we try to do better next time."

The following week Abalokè is present. She receives a new name, Sarah. The reason for this change is that she wants to break with the past and start a new future with Kokpan. The bride and bridegroom come to their wedding dressed in their usual attire; Kokpan already wears clothes and Sarah comes in the customary grass skirt.

Kokpan and Sarah stand in front of the congregation. The missionary places his hands on their heads as he says a short but powerful prayer asking for God's blessing on the young couple. He also asks that if they receive children, the Lord will bless them in His mercy.

A week after the wedding Sarah's father suddenly passed away. Kuijt is very upset.

What now! One week ago Sarah was married and now as

punishment her father suddenly dies. The people will not be able to understand this; pagan culture and the new religion are still easily mixed together.

Kokpan getting married

Sarah is very sad. According to custom, she ties a string tightly around a finger so that later it can be cut off at the middle knuckle. It took some explaining from Rev. Kuijt to convince her that Christianity does not condone this custom. She finally decides not to continue this practice.

I sometimes wonder how long it took our forefathers to overcome their traditions before they reached the stage at which the NRC is now. That cannot be a question of years, but generations.

166

*After the loss of a loved one, part of a finger is removed
as a sign of mourning — Abalokè must have lost many loved ones.*

The education program is expanding, We now have two classes with fifty students and, along with Jozua, Herman Imbab also teaches. Mrs. Kuijt has a class of fifteen girls. The work is blessed, but Satan does not sit still. At a mission post close by, Rev. Bentz and his helpers are savagely attacked. Four of the helpers are killed and eaten. Bentz is wounded with three arrows in his body and needs to be taken to a hospital.

In the Baliem Valley there are influences from other churches. Rev Kuijt warns the people that they should only pray directly to God.

Every two weeks they try to have a MAF airplane come into Pass Valley. The aircraft bounces up and down on the strip before it glides to a stop. Every time a plane lands a prayer rises in Kuijt's heart asking the Lord to spare the pilot and the plane. On October 19, 1967, things go wrong. Pieces of the wreck are scattered in the middle of the strip. The plane flipped over and the pilot is hanging upside down in the aircraft. Before Kuijt can run down the hill he has already crawled out and was checking the damaged plane. When asked if he is okay, Jerry Reed replies, "That's the second one within a year." He has been in an accident on the strip in Karubaga that destroyed a plane borrowed from the Australian MAF. Kuijt's reaction is, "Did I give him the proper wind and weather information? Did he misjudge the condition of the strip?" But Jerry assures him that it had nothing to do with any of those issues. He is unfamiliar with this air strip and, afraid to run out of landing room; he breaked too hard, which caused the propeller to hit the ground and the plane to go head over heels. For some of the hostile natives this again is more proof for their superstition. Did they not spread blood on the strip as a curse? And there you go, now this accident happens.

Pilot Jerry Reed checking the damage to his plane

Yesterday the plane made a stop in Apalapsili, where Bentz works. The guru there confided that the people had killed a child of one of their enemies and that they were going to eat it on the strip after we left. I was filled with disgust and did not know what to say! I asked the guru, "Do you allow this? If I was here, I would be adamant that this practice be stopped!" The guru also confided to me that six hundred people are attending church, and yet he allows this poor child to be eaten on the air strip. When I left, I emphasized my disgust by saying, "Enjoy your meal," and then I blew my nose as a sign of great disgust.

In our area I have no tolerance for this type of human degradation; in the Name of Christ I abhor this. I have to agree with Brakel, "You must thoroughly shake them up spiritually, verbally and physically, so to speak." Everyone will be reprimanded, including myself.

Meanwhile another dance is going on in Angguruk. A woman is riddled with arrows but miraculously she is still alive. Yet nothing is done for the poor woman. I can only describe it with one word: Ugh! This is not true mission work.

The reference of Kuijt to Brakel's remark does not go unnoticed by Rev. Vergunst. "We found the reference to this expression quite remarkable, but seeing that we do not have a concordance of Brakel's writings, we could not ascertain whether it has been taken out of its context. Please let me know where you have found this, because I would like to refer to it in my sermons too. But of course I first have to know where it is written." However Kuijt cannot help him there; he can only recollect that he heard Professor Wisse use the expression about fifteen years before, even naming the book, chapter and paragraph where it was found but he cannot remember this. The physical part I added myself in my mind.

The success that Rev. Kuijt has with his animals varies. The goats are thriving, but the pigs do not have enough to eat, and most of the ducks are dead. The remaining animals have been carried to Landikma where the altitude is about four thousand feet lower with a more moderate climate. Ducks are hard to keep alive, unless you give them a lot of attention and medicine. Of the forty rabbits that they started with, only three have survived and one of them is a male with three legs.

While the Kuijt family is on furlough, seven goats died or have been killed and eaten and two geese have suspiciously also disappeared. But giving up is not in Kuijt's vocabulary. He is concerned about the health of the people, he wants to bring more variety into their diet and raise the protein level, which is too low especially in the women and children.

He would really like to have a few cows, sheep and geese to add to his flock, as these animals will eat the grass. He distributes fifteen young pigs among the people, and then he starts to build stalls for cows. A piece of grass is surrounded by an electric fence.

The electric fence installation is a great success. A Yali accidently touched the wire and got quite a shock.

Mrs. Kuijt is again expecting. This time the pregnancy has some complications. She needs to go to Angguruk with her husband and children to await the baby's arrival. Dr. Vriend delivers Gerrit Paulus on May 25, 1968. Phiphikè already realizes that she has a new brother, but little Wim is too busy with other things. The Yali people are very proud that their third baby is another boy! His name sounds a lot like Bapa Kuijt's name, his parents shortened his name to "Gert". The Yalis cannot make the G sound, so they call him "Hert".

Baby Gert

Gert does not receive the typical addition of a Yali name, like his older sister and brother did. The Yalis are worried because Bapa Kuijt is talking of leaving them to go to Nipsan after the arrival of the Fahners. The Yalis are not at all happy about this. What is this anyway? The Bapa and his family belong to them! The Kuijt children are their children too! No, for the time being they will wait and see what the Bapa will do and the baby can always get a Yali name later.

Several days after the birth of baby Gert, there is a severe earthquake on the island. Everyone is afraid; Kokpan is convinced that the hour of Christ's return has come. The next day he leads a worship service in Angguruk where fifteen hundred people listen attentively to what the Word of God teaches about the final day of days.

Fifteen students are now enrolled in the Bible school that Kuijt has started; they are being used to spread the Gospel into the distant villages.

When I listen to how the Yalis pass on the message they are taught during the week, I am amazed at how these young men, who came from a stone-age culture, bring the Word. I also instruct the students to ask questions from the listeners while they speak. This past Sunday, Lannilekma made good use of this advice. I am noticing that these people really have incredible memories. Winnimukè ("angry woman") especially knows a lot. It is an advantage for them to hear the message being delivered in their own language by their fellow tribesmen.

It is also a joy to us that these fifteen students and their wives have set up their homes near us. This way they are always close. Kokpan built his house similar to ours, including a bathroom.

In Landikma, things are going well. Jozua hopes to have three hundred metres of air strip completed by the end of the month. There is a good turnout at their services.

*All-purpose house in Landikma - note the size of the stones,
which were removed from the strip site*

On December 13, 1968, chief pilot, Hank Worthington, one of the most experienced MAF pilots, circles in the air above Landikma. The previous week the first landing was postponed because the strip still appeared to be too rough. For several days Kuijt and his helpers work hard to smooth out the surface of the strip and this time they are ready.

We were expecting the arrival of the plane at nine o'clock. Fifteen minutes before that, we stopped all work to pray with all those who were present. The anxiety rose as the minutes slipped by. We had set up the radio outside to see every manoeuvre. The people were instructed to sit at the upper end above the strip. Simson would direct the plane while I would man the radio. A large pile of wet grass was burning so that the pilot could see by the smoke exactly which direction and how strong the wind was blowing. Wooden blocks were ready to put in front of the wheels after the plane came to a stop. Suddenly the call was heard: "At waga!", "he is coming!" First came a test run. The plane circled around and approached the strip from the top, touching the wheels on the strip, rolling down to the bottom where it took off again. It turned around and came back, lower and lower, until the wheels touched the ground again now at the very bottom of the strip and taxied to the top where the plane came to a stop. The engine was turned off and the blocks were placed in front of the wheels. The pilot stepped out of the plane amidst joyful greetings from the Yalis and with a heartfelt handshake from me. Now Landikma was officially opened. Great was our joy, as we walked down the strip. We told Hank Worthington that we had promised the people to pray with them when he had safely landed on the strip. "Of course," Hank replied.

Three of us in turn led in prayer, Kokpan was after me and then Mepdanbuk, an elderly Christian from Landikma. Then we sang Psalm 116, "I love the Lord, the Fount of Life and Grace, He heard my cry...." The Lord has made all things well.

There are now nine churches in which six Dani Evangelists can be found, all originating from Pyramid in the Baliem Valley. A Bible School has been established with about seventy students who are also involved in bringing God's Word. Four gurus are working in various areas, the first Bible selections have been translated by Fahner into the Yali language and a number of Bible school students are beginning to read. God's work continues.

Chris Fahner concentrating on translating the Bible into Yali

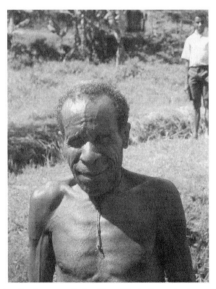

Mepdanbuk, one of the first Christians in Landikma

Baby Gert suffers from an odd rash on his skin. While the Kuijt family is on a two-day visit with the Bentz family in Apalapsili, the rash worsens rapidly, soon covering his entire body. They ask Dr. Vriend for advice via the radio and he tells them they must come immediately to the clinic in

173

Angguruk. The doctor wants to see what this rash looks like, especially because there appears to be no explanation behind the symptoms. Mrs. Kuijt is flown to Angguruk with the other children and Gert is examined. Ointment is made by Dr. Vriend and is used on a trial bases as the source of the rash is still unknown. It eventually cleared up.

The trip to Angguruk offers Miep a break from her many obligations on the station. Another benefit to being in Angguruk is that she can talk with other women.

With the arrival of the Fahners it helps to alleviate the loneliness. They arrive in June 1969, but a few months later, on the advice of Dr. Vriend, they need to travel to Medang to await the birth of their first child.

The second period of service has almost come to an end and a furlough of six months awaits the Kuijts. A much needed break is in order.

When Rev. Kuijt asks permission to travel via the U.S.A., the delegates reply curtly:

> *We have no objection to that. Gerrit, it is up to you if you would rather travel on a yacht or a row boat, whether you want to sail around the Cape of Good Hope or whatever other country, but you must realize it will make the travel time longer and period of rest shorter.*

Kuijt does not mind as they got a good rest on the boat!

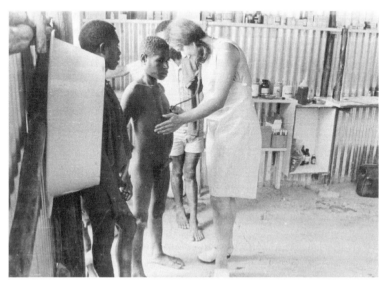

Nurse Marry van Moolenbroek takes over the medical duties

Kuijt finds that they have the worst furlough rules of all missions. There are grumblings about money; "they can tell beautiful stories at Mission Days and in the *Paulus* magazine about all the money that is rolling in, but in the meantime we are in financial poverty." However, Kuijt is very happy to hear that in The Netherlands they are collecting funds to cover the cost of the MAF airplane that was wrecked in the crash. He also rejoices when he hears that two nurses have been accepted: Janny Hofland and Marry van Moolenbroek.

> Even more encouraging is the invitation he has received to come to Ulfugufug, where the peope have a desire to burn their fetishes. Ulfugufug was the last stronghold of the power of Satan in the Valley but now God's Word has become so powerful among the people that they want to get rid of the old ways.

According to evangelist Simson, the village is only about a half-hour walk, but it takes Kuijt two and a half hours. Little Wim also goes along although it doesn't take long before he has to be carried.

> When we entered the village, tears sprang into my eyes. The people had butchered four big pigs and placed them as an invitation at the entrance to the village. This was the sign that they were really serious about what they are planning to do.

To a large gathering the missionary preached very fittingly about Acts 19 which tells of Demetrius the silversmith.

> I was sympathetic to the old people who were sitting there. All their life they have put their trust in pig's tails, pig's teeth, certain stones and you name it. Now these items will be burned. I asked them if they could part with them. Full of joy they declared that they will only trust in Jesus and beside Him they will serve no other.

A little later, with the flames ablaze, the people threw in their fetishes. They returned to their cooking pits filled with joy and together they eat the meal of sweet potatoes and pork.

Concerning the topic of baptism, Kuijt remains somewhat reluctant. According to Kuijt, baptism in Irian is believed to be reaching a plateau, as a final step for spiritual life.

> You must agree that I should not baptize people here just to please churches in the Netherlands, Canada, and the U.S.A.

Burning of fetishes

Preparing sak, a fruit found in Landikma
and an excellent source of vitamin B

I am unwilling to "make" Christians by baptism. As we can see it at this point, baptised Christians would have an elevated position above the others, giving the impression they are better. I am emphasizing that they must lose all their self-righteousness and try to impress on them that because of Adam, they are not one bit better than the rest of their fellow villagers who have pig's teeth in their huts.

Of course, Rev. Kuijt looks forward to the time when the first Christians will be baptized.

How precious is the sacrament of baptism, when we may in truth be buried with Christ and also be raised up again in newness of life. It will be a glorious day when these Yalis may be added to the Lord's Church, and may receive the sign and token on the basis of their conversion and the indwelling of the Holy Spirit.

We are working on a mission field and are speaking to adults, yet it is remarkable that it is usually the younger ones who are open to the eternal word of God. The older ones are too ingrained in their unbelief and superstition.

Ah yes, we have Kokpan, who could have been baptized long ago. But we had to be cautious, because Kokpan would have been singled out. Besides, I believe that Kokpan in his un-baptized state has won more souls for Christ than he would have, humanly speaking, if he was baptized as the only one.

Rev. Kuijt hopes that the instruction at the Bible School will be an incentive to have a desire to be "buried with Christ" by baptism. It is a step that is not to be taken lightly.

We feel a change coming among the students; they realize that baptism is serious. This became clear when we had to remove a student from the school who was found to be living common-law with his girlfriend. We then prayed with the young couple in the church, who realized the seriousness of the situation. The couple were invited to give their confession of guilt in public. The unanimous decision is clear: they will not be allowed to return to the Bible School. A precedent must be set. Otherwise, after any disciplinary action they will think, "Oh well, next year I will go back again."

Rev. Kuijt also has inner conflict regarding infant baptism. The ECK has given the missionaries in Yalimo the liberty to decide for themselves whether or not to baptize infants. The MB points to the Reformed Confession, in which infant baptism received a prominent place.

In this regard, the uniqueness of our mission must be in the forefront.

On Sunday, December 28, 1969, the Yalis from all the surrounding villages come to Abenaho. Climbing up and down the steep trails, they gather at the airstrip. Beside the strip a deep pit has been dug and filled with water for a baptismal font. The church service takes several hours this day, for ninety-six adults receive the seal of baptism by submersion. They are baptized in the Name of the Father and the Son and of the Holy Ghost. The first to enter the water are Kokpan and his wife and, as a sign of the washing away of sins, each disappears completely under water for a moment. The Bible school students with their wives follow and finally other new Christians are baptized. The foundation of their belief in baptism is to be found in 1 Thessalonians 1:9 ...".and how ye turned to God from idols to serve the living and true God."

Baptism in Langda with Rev. Kuijt and Missionary Louwerse

The children are baptized in the church building by receiving the token of baptism by water on their foreheads.

I have personally interviewed each candidate to question them on their reason for desiring baptism. The main reason given was that before we came they had no knowledge of the way of salvation but, by the instruction they received, they have been convinced of the truth of God's Word. They have turned away from their idols and burned their fetishes and now wish to place their trust in the Lord. They themselves attribute this change to the work of the Holy Spirit, Who dwells within them. There is a clear knowledge and understanding of our deep fall in Adam, of salvation through Jesus Christ, and the application of the Holy Spirit. They also believe in the second coming of Christ on the clouds, when He will judge the righteous whom He has given a new heart, and the wicked who have remained disobedient.

I truly believe that some have received a new heart by the operation of the Holy Spirit. They are so attentive when I speak from God's Word that they seem to devour every word.

Before we started the baptism ceremony, many publicly confessed their sins, some with tears streaming down their faces. Many have made the firm commitment to follow the doctrine that has been taught them.

In February, baptism is done again and another hundred and fifteen adults and forty-four children are baptized. Afterwards the Lord's Supper is celebrated. The Word goes forth and it will never return void.

Chapter 12

Faith can never expect too much

Nipsan. It has never been far from Rev Kuijt's thoughts. Now that UFM is willing to return this territory to the mission of the NRC, it is gladly accepted back. Although the tribal people are not known to be a peace-loving people, Kuijt has never lost his love for them and for this area. Fierce people living in complete paganism in stone-age darkness are found in the Nipsan valleys.

Fahner cannot see himself opening up this territory. He wishes to concentrate on Bible translation. Both nurses will continue their medical work in Landikma. Mr. Louwerse and Looijen, who recently have been accepted in the Netherlands must first prepare themselves for mission work and then spend time acclimatizing. However, both men have been accepted to do practical work, one as an agriculturist and the other as technologist.

The pioneer spirit of Kuijt is revived in all its intensity. The people of Abenaho and Landikma can be saved under the Lord's blessing while they are hearing the message of the Gospel daily. God's spirit will continue to work in those for whom the Scriptures say, "and as many as were ordained to eternal life, believed." (Acts 13:48)

But in Nipsan the Name of Christ has never been proclaimed. It is a territory that must be brought under the influence of the Word of God. Rev. Kuijt makes the decision to go himself with the approval of the MB.

Kennecott, a mining company, sometimes makes use of mission strips. The company is willing to return the favour and promises to fly the missionary and his party to Nipsan in their helicopter. The cost for these flights is quite high. When Kuijt learns that the people in Middelburg in The Netherlands are raising funds to pay for these endeavours by collecting recyclable paper, he exclaims: "Bravo, Middelburg!"

Kuijt is reminded of the farewell service in Rotterdam when Rev.

Vergunst requested the congregation to sing: "Forever trusting in the Lord, take heed to do His will; and shalt thou dwell within the land, And He thy needs shall fill."

In whom else can he place his trust other than in the Lord, especially when opening a new mission field? How will the Nipsan people respond? The first time Kuijt entered Nipsan (after walking through the jungle from Kosarek) the heavily armed warriors had formed a human wall in front of him and held him at bay so he could not verify where to locate the possibility for a strip. To persist would have meant certain death because the Nipsan warriors made their intentions abundantly clear. But deep down inside, he could never forget them. He firmly believes that he once will work among the Nipsan people. Their welfare is a burden on his heart.

The food staples are packed in gunny sacks, tools are bundled together; axes and bush knives are taken along as payment for work. Remaining space in the large sacks is stuffed with grass to prevent breakage and the bags are sewn closed to prevent damage upon hitting the ground

· *The greatest importance is whether we are inwardly prepared by the applying work of the Holy Spirit. We pray that His commandment may be brought to practise.*

Kuijt has selected his helpers who will assist him; primarily Bible school students from Abenaho and Landikma, among which are Sabonwarek, Milibaga, Bola, Jomare, and others. They have all been baptized. They are "the best", and they are well aware of the reason why they are going—to bring the Gospel. They also realize the potential dangers and that they might not be warmly welcomed. Wherever the Word comes, enmity is encountered. Herman Imbab (a coastal Papuan) and little Wim are also coming along, and Mrs. Kuijt and the other two children will follow a few days later. She knows that her life and the lives of her children are in God's hand. Should the Lord wish to end her life he does not need a Nipsan arrow. She has no desire to stay behind in Abenaho but prefers to be at her husband's side in "the battle" rather than hearing at a distance about tensions, dangers, and problems. She knows that the family will be required to live in tents. The children are unaware that they also are used in the service of the Lord. Their presence can have a positive influence. It shows that the missionary does not come with evil, but rather with friendly intentions.

With full confidence, the pioneer missionary entrusts the work he has begun to Fahner and his wife. She demonstrates that she is an excellent teacher. Many students can read and write and those who have this ability are sharing their knowledge with others. The nurses, Van Moolenbroek and Hofland, are doing a first-class job in providing medical help. New workers will arrive in the future. Rev. Kuijt gladly leaves the further development and intensification of the mission work to all of them. He believes his task is to bring the Gospel to those who have never been reached before and to bring them the only Name given under Heaven unto salvation.

Mrs. Fahner teaching her students

There are indications that the local people will again try to resist the establishment of a mission post, therefore, Kuijt requests a few policemen to accompany him. The chief officer in Wamena agrees. Even the Bupati, the resident Government Representative, concurs.

Naltja, a UFM mission station will be the base. The resident missionary, Rev. Cutting wants to go along on the first helicopter flight to Nipsan and return on the second. He wants to find out whether the language in Nipsan is similar to the one in Naltja. Perhaps he can help to make the first contact. Now everyone waits for the flight to Nipsan. How will it turn out? They will be going to people who are not waiting for them rather the opposite. Conversely there is an irresistible urge to face the unknown by faith to which William Carey said: "Expect great things from God, undertake great things for God." Faith can never expect too much.

The helicopter is ready. It is clear that the pilot has no patience or time to spare. The outfit is thrown into the helicopter but the pilot limits the amount. Then the pilot refuses to take little Wim along. He is adamant. His "no" is final and so father Kuijt brings his deeply disappointed son back to the edge of the strip. Mrs. Kuijt is standing there, carrying Gert while also holding Klazina's hand. Mrs. Cutting takes pity on the little fellow and takes him in her arms. Pandemonium immediately erupts. Wim is not so easily left behind. He hollers, "Pappááá, don't leave me! Why are you leaving me?" His child's cry cuts the missionary to his heart but perhaps it is for the best that Wimmie stays behind. They do not know how they will be welcomed by the Nipsanners. They may be met with a volley of arrows which happened to Rev. Zöllner and Rev. Roth. But Wim does not give up, he tries to pull himself loose from Mrs. Cutting and cries out in Dutch, "Let me go or I will bite you!" But Mrs. Cutting who understood no Dutch just smiles sympathetically at him. She is therefore totally unprepared when the boy proceeds to do as he said.

"Oh Lord, please help to change the heart of the pilot," Kuijt prays. He does not know how to resolve this situation. Unexpectedly the pilot says, "Okay, bring him along but keep him on your lap." The missionary could have cried for joy and proceeds to call. "Wimmie, come. You may come along." Wim cannot believe it. So Papa Kuijt runs to his son scoops him up and together they climb into the helicopter. Herman Imbab refuses to get into the helicopter and mumbles something about his backpack and stays behind. Later he has to trek for three days through the jungle with the other helpers to reach their destination.

The helicopter rises into the air causing a cloud of dust on the ground. After flying for approximately fifteen minutes, they see their destination. The helicopter descends rapidly and the pilot looks for a suitable spot to land. While the men are full of apprehension, little Wim talks non-stop, asking all sort of questions. When the heli lands, the doors open and the passengers and baggage quickly off-loaded. The heli takes off immediately for the second load of additional baggage and other helpers.

A long-awaited desire has become a reality. Pioneer Kuijt has placed his feet on the ground of a new, unreached territory.

As the missionary takes his first look around he sees a small hut that seems to be occupied. As he walks toward the garden hut there is a man crouching in front of it. He looks like a skeleton; thin as a rail and shaking like a leaf. With deathly fear he looks at the white people. This man appears to be an outcast living alone away from his people.

Nipsanners, one of them with sweet potato vines
which are planted for the new crop

Then missionaries Kuijt and Cutting, together with Milibaga, kneel down thanking God for bringing them here and ask for protection and blessing. In the meantime Wim is out exploring his new surroundings.

No matter how many times Rev. Cutting tries to call with hands around his mouth to amplify the sound, there is no response. Again and again he calls out but to no avail. He wants to let the people know they have come with good intentions, but all is silent.

Again the heli departs from Naltja now with two police men and the radio on board. Within ten minutes they are back. Cumulus clouds have formed and the heli cannot get over the mountains. Because of this the first group will have to spend the night without a tent, radio, or food. Later in the afternoon a MAF plane flies over low enough to confirm that the men and the child are okay. The group waves to the pilot and the pilot reports the good news back to his base.

Once again the missionary walks to the hut still occupied by the shivering man. The man cowered against the wall. Kuijt tries to calm the man's fears and asks with gestures if they can join him in the garden hut. Even though space is limited everyone finds a place. He holds Wim close and everyone makes room for Milibaga and Cutting. As a result they are like 'birds crouched on a perch,' but at least they are relatively dry under the leaking roof and have some protection. Mrs. Kuijt spends a restless night; she tosses and turns and asks the Lord to protect them.

The following day several more flights take place and Rev. Cutting returns to Naltja. The policemen, one helper and the radio are flown in.

By Sunday, Mrs. Kuijt is informed via the radio by Bentz that her husband is experiencing some difficulties, not because of the Nipsan people or because of a sudden illness. It is the police who have problems dealing with the isolation as well as being surrounded by savage murderers. They ask for the heli to come and pick them up. They also complain that there is not enough food and the accommodation is lacking and so on and so on. However, Kuijt cannot request a helicopter to come as the frequencies vary from his radio. In addition, the weather is not favourable for flying. Via his radio, Rev. Kuijt speaks with the Chief of Police who talks to his men and succeeds in calming them down. Dr. Vriend advises to give one of them some calming medication. After a week the helicopter suddenly shows up in Naltja. Now Miep and the two children, Klazina and Gert are flown in and the police are flown out.

Again a new period of isolation begins. They are together with the helpers from Abenaho and the coastal Papua, Herman Imbab but the radio is the only form of contact with the outside world.

> *Yet our hearts rejoice in God. He knows about us and whatever He does with us is good. We are in His hands. I am amazed that our children are doing so well and the God of Daniel is still alive, Who helps us to thrive on water, so to speak. (Dan.1:12) The little ones are healthy and Miep and I are doing well. It is a miracle that we have not been greeted by a volley of arrows. It was a blessing to have Wim with me at the beginning. He played near me without being aware that we may have been in danger of death. Soon the people were calling him, Wimmie and bringing him cucumbers and sweet potatoes. We firmly believe that God was with us. No, you will not hear any complaints from us but we may truly say: "I rejoice in God and praise His infallible Word."*

Progress is being made on the strip site. Contacts with the local people are limited because of their hostile attitude. Kuijt gives strict orders to more than forty Yali helpers not to leave the camp, although there is some trade with the locals who offer to sell sweet potatoes in exchange for some contact articles.

Klazina, Wim and Gert with their Tante Marry

Klazina, Wim and Gert

Against the missionary's instructions and without his knowledge there are a few boys who regularly go to the village of Nipsan to buy sweet potatoes. One day three boys reported sheepishly to Kuijt that they went to

Nipsan and were shot at. Jesaja was hit by an arrow. The wound did not appear to be too serious and they put him in their hut. But his condition deteriorated rapidly so now they have come to tell the story. When Kuijt sees the boy the situation is already hopeless. Apparently there is internal bleeding and a short time later the boy dies. "To keep the enemies from rejoicing, we burned his body in the early morning," writes Rev. Kuijt.

The people in the immediate area deny that they are responsible for the killing but blame it on a Nipsanner who lives in a nearby village. They also warn that the enemy will be back to 'finish them all off' the following day. A helicopter comes to take Mrs. Kuijt and the children to safety in Landikma and several police officers are flown in.

It seems that Rev Kuijt's camp is situated on the border of a war zone. The people on the one side are friendly while on the other side they are hostile.

> *But I fear that by bringing the Gospel to the "friendly" side, their friendship might also soon change to antagonism. We have not entered any of the villages yet and I do not give permission to do so in the near future. We find ourselves in the front line of the battle. Abenago and Landikma are heaven compared to this area.*

When the police pay a visit to the village of Nipsan they are welcomed and given sweet potatoes. But this does not mean there is peace. Yesterday, a heli was attacked by arrows. The MAF advises Rev. Kuijt to obtain a gun to protect himself and his family. The police bring a message to the Nipsanners; the Landikma people do not demand payment for their fellow tribesman, Jesaja, who was killed. When the Gospel changes hearts, the desire for retaliation falls away.

In the meantime the building of the airstrip progresses and on August 8th, 1971 the first landing takes place. Klazina needs to leave for Sentani located on the coast to attend the Sentani International School run by missionaries; it is now possible for her to come home twice a year. A strip is not only convenient but also essential.

A MAF plane makes an unscheduled landing. Everyone is surprised and goes to the strip. They were not notified via the radio. When the plane comes to a halt, the pilot Bob Donalds, climbs out. He has been to Naltja and is on his way to Sentani but decides to make a detour to try out the strip in Nipsan. He had not yet landed there and did not know the terrain. In retrospect this impulse is later seen as being guided by the Lord.

Looijen and the Yalis from Abenaho and Landikma,
along with some locals working on the strip in Nipsan

Klazina's seventh birthday celebration with her brothers, Wim and Gert, and Mom.
Note: the outside walls of the kitchen are not grass!

Sabonwarek and Rev. Kuijt welcome the pilot heartily and walk to the kitchen to have a cup of coffee. Kuijt mentions that lately it has, thankfully, been quiet. The murder of Jesaja has made a deep impression and creates unrest among the workers. Besides this, nothing special has happened. However, yesterday four axes and a bush knife were stolen. The helpers cannot accept this action so they take three pigs from the "friendly" neighbours as collateral. They trust that this would encourage the thieves to return the axes and the bush knife. But this action is not well received by the neighbours, who start waving their bows and arrows and hollering excitedly that they are not the thieves. After a couple of hours, the missionary tells the boys to return the pigs. Lo and behold, three axes are soon returned but not the fourth axe nor the bush knife.

Nipsanners dancing

After a visit of about an hour, the pilot, Herman Imbab and the Kuijt family walk back to the airplane. When they are still thirty meters away from the aircraft, they hear a hoarse cry, "Tuan, watch out, we are being attacked!"

At the top of the strip a large group of warriors appears and within seconds arrows are coming towards them. It is a horrendous sight; black war vests made from rotan sharply contrasting against the green grass. Slowly the warriors approach. Bob runs to the plane and calls Mrs. Kuijt and the children and hurries them into the plane. Herman runs to the house to grab Kuijt's buck-shot rifle. Kuijt refuses to board the plane and remains with his men. However, the engine does not start, and arrows pierce the walls of the plane.

When an arrow strikes the ground between Kuijt's legs, he grabs the gun from Herman's hands and opens fire in an attempt to scare the attackers away. This does not help and the attack intensifies forcing the missionary and his helpers to back away. In the meantime Bob finally succeeds in getting the engine started and a few moments later the airplane lifts off. By radio, Bob calls for police assistance from Wamena and then he starts his own air offensive. He skims low over the warriors who drop to the ground or run into the forest for safety. But some keep shooting at the aircraft. For nearly an hour he continued to dive into the people, barely missing the ground with the wheels. In the meantime a second airplane arrives with Jerry as pilot and Bob turns his plane into the direction of Naltja.

Pilot Jerry has not landed on the Nipsan strip before nor has he performed any drops. A landing with four police officers on board without checking out the strip first is a risky undertaking. Kuijt prays for the safety of the airplane and its occupants. Thankfully they land safely. When the warriors see the police coming out of the plane they disappear into the hills and remain out of sight. Peace is rapidly restored.

A warrior

In the meantime, Bob and his distraught passengers land in Naltja. There were no passenger seats in the plane as the Naltja flight was only hauling cargo. Miep and the children were thrown back and forth as the pilot made his dips and turns. They desperately clung to each other with each dive. It did not take very long before the first one started to throw up and the others soon followed suit.

In Naltja, the Maynard family welcomes Miep and her children warmly. They are given the luxury of a fresh bath and clean clothes. Via the radio they hear that the situation in Nipsan has calmed down.

Kuijt questions himself, "Is it wise to continue here? Is it not wiser to vacate this post where the animosity is so prevalent? Personally we have experienced so much here already. We wonder what will be next."

The camp is now surrounded with a barbed wire fence and the attackers are not seen any more. The friendly neighbours come to express their concern immediately after the attack but then they also disappear. He wonders whether the people will ever be receptive to the Gospel. The Nipsan people view the missionaries as being responsible for failed crops and sicknesses. Neither the white people nor their helpers have been invited to participate in eating a pig or a meal together. Still he does not believe that he should return to Abenaho or to Landikma.

Miep writes a letter to the MB in which she defends what has taken place. She understands the questions about whether the theft of a few axes and the knife has to be settled in such a harsh manner. Of course, she writes, we listen to the advice of people with experience. Cutting has stated that the natives are known for their thievery. When they steal something, immediately take some pigs from them and the goods will be returned. Do not accept the theft!

> *In areas like this the missionary sometimes has to act as both a government official and as the police. This is not always easy. In this particular situation, something had to be done.*

Shortly after, Rev. Kuijt enters a period of uncertainty A violent lightning bolt strikes which not only causes havoc in the camp, but also strikes Kuijt, himself. "Up to now the hand of humans was against us; is now the hand of the Lord against us as well?"

> *If I could only believe that it was Satan! He is the prince of the power of the air (Ephesians 2:2) who does his utmost to break down our work. This is one of his last bulwarks and he has very little time left. If I can believe this, then I can take courage to carry on. But if it is the Lord, I will pack my suitcases today and leave.*

> *When I see the tent I am reminded of that night when I was*

awakened by my frightened helpers to prepare for an enemy attack. Looking at our kitchen I am reminded of that terrible event on Sunday when lightning struck at least twenty times. Several pieces of equipment were blown to pieces and we no longer had any contact with outside world; we could not transmit nor receive. Poles were splintered, and the electrical current ran all along the beam above my head; even the chair I was sitting on is damaged.

When I was struck by lightning, I thought my leg had been severed from my body because I had no feeling in it. There was no time to think, however, as a fire had started in our grass kitchen. Crawling over the ground I tried to put it out. Our bathroom, which is also made from local material, was on fire but the boys managed to put it out. The tent where we slept looked like a bomb had exploded in it... I could see that the lightning had travelled straight down the pole in the middle of the tent. One of the storage tents was hit in three places.

The two-way radio transmitter-receiver in the tent, later hit by lightning

Thankfully Miep and the children were not here: they were taken from Naltja to the coast after the attack. But Kuijt does not have the liberty to leave Nipsan. His work is here, this terrain is where he is called to labor.

The work on the strip continues as it now only has the minimum requirements. Even the soldiers, who were flown in, work on the strip to lengthen and widen it. Again dynamite is used to blow the large boulders to pieces. Gardens are also planted to grow sweet potatoes. Henk Looijen has started to build a house for the Kuijt family.

*The settlement. The big tent is used as sleeping quarters for the Kuijt family.
The two smaller ones are for storage. Behind the tents is a bathroom
(the nicest one in the valley) The kitchen is in the front.*

*In front of the kitchen. All the workers with their wives
and children, with Miep, Marry and Klazina*

Kuijt persuades some of the people from neighbouring villages to come to the station. His intention is to offer one representative from each village an axe. Though many came, there is no one from Tapla, the people who committed the theft. Also, no one came from the Nipsan village either. They are the people who have murdered Jesaja. To those who did come, Kuijt indicates that he does not want to take revenge. About a week later the people from Tapla show up to make peace. They bring meat and they receive several axes. But the Nipsanners stay away. Are they afraid of retribution? There is very little interest in hearing the Gospel although there is one couple, Sarabang and her husband Imag, who listen and ask questions. Very slowly the Word makes an impression on the people.

> *It was overwhelming to behold, that the ones who attacked us are now the first to build a "little church", made from local materials. Despite their poverty, they slaughtered two pigs for the occasion.*

> *Last night a delivery took place in our kitchen; the birth of a son to the wife of one of our helpers. With approval from both parents, the child has been named Arie, after the secretary of the MB.*

History has never recorded whether Rev. Vergunst was pleased with this honour!

Sabonwarek faithfully works in the village of Nipsan. Using local materials, a primitive gathering hall is constructed where he teaches approximately sixty-five young people. In the village of Tapla, a school is built where Obed works and teaches a group of young people. Herman Imbab teaches students in a little school near the strip. In several villages, the people come to hear the Word of God. Altogether about three hundred people are attending the services, while about one hundred and fifty children are taught in the schools. Rev. Kuijt has again given the wise instruction to the teachers not to start with the children right away as this could offend the leaders and elders of the villages. Extend an invitation to the adults first. After trying out the school, they will say, "Let the children go to school. It is easier for them to learn." This approach works here just like it did in Abenaho.

Sabonwarek teaching students

Once again an MAF airplane has an accident although it is not on one of our strips this time. The pilot is miraculously spared. Rev. Kuijt remarked:

> *As far as I am concerned, they can keep the flying! Thankfully there are still people who are willing to serve and be available for the exceptional work of the MAF.*

Jan and Janny Louwerse opened up Langda
and accomplished a great deal in their first year

On June 12, 1973, Rev. Kuijt and Jan Louwerse, who has married nurse Janny Hofland, open a mission post at Langda. By heli, forty people are flown in and are welcomed by the locals. A token of their friendship is shown by handing over freshly picked green tobacco and lit homemade cigarettes which were then shared. This does not agree with Kuijt. He reacts with a bad coughing spell but he does not give up as friendship sometimes requires sacrifice.

Once again one of Kuijt's helpers is attacked now by one of the inhabitants of the Iliktom village. Immediately the other helpers pursue the attackers. They think that their mate is killed and, in turn, they intend to kill a member of Iliktom village. The law of the jungle again takes over: an eye for an eye and a tooth for a tooth. But peace is restored with the people of Iliktom and together they eat a pig, which has been cooked in a pit.

Again it is time to go on furlough and Rev. Kuijt decides to spend this furlough in North America. There he plans to take flying lessons and at the same time serve the North American congregations.

The post will be under the leadership of Herman Imbab; a number of Bible school students will keep bringing the Word in the surrounding villages. Although there is not a great deal of interest, the presence of the mission is accepted. Nipsan is a delicate little plant. Hopefully it has the strength to mature.

Chapter 13

The Gospel Saturated in Blood . . .

Stealthily, a Nipsan warrior creeps towards the generator shed. He knows the door is always unlocked and he enters unhindered. Within minutes he emerges carrying the radio transmitter, dragging the cord and the microphone over the ground. He shoves the radio in a hollow under a large rock nearby. The tall elephant grass covers any view of it; without a sound the warrior disappears into the night.

Vegetation, including some elephant grass

Being unsuspecting of anything, Herman Imbab leaves his house with the intention to walks toward the cow shed. Some of the workers are in the neighbouring villages. One is invited for a pig feast and the others went to evangelize. Tuan Kuijt is in North America and Herman is taking care of the day-to-day running of the settlement, so the Tuan will be pleased upon his return. Herman has already worked with Rev. Kuijt in other places and there is a strong bond between Herman and the Kuijt family. Herman is like an uncle to their children. The Gospel has changed his heart and he now has no other desire but to follow Christ. With dedication he performs his tasks.

As Herman walks around the corner of his house he suddenly sees a bush knife coming towards him. But it is too late to react. The force of the attack drops him to the ground. More warriors brutally assault him and soon the ground is red with blood. Within seconds he is dead. The warriors angrily yell, "Away with those strangers who cause nothing but disaster! Away with their God. Away with the message they bring!"

Herman Imbab

Stefanus, another helper, approaches the camp unaware of the danger and is also attacked and brutally murdered. The hut in which the evangelists' children live is set on fire. Little Mina, the daughter of Obed and Debora, and the adopted daughter of Orpa and Abraham are killed.

On the site of the murders, a feast is prepared. The warriors perform their rituals and butcher the body of Herman. His head is carelessly kicked to the side and his scrotum nailed to a pole. The body of Stefanus is cut into pieces. When the bodies of the helpers of Rev. Kuijt and the servants of the Lord have been eaten, the cow shed is emptied and the butchering party continues. Animals are slaughtered, cooked and eaten.

Finally, the warriors vent their hatred by burning the buildings. Everything is destroyed; nothing of the settlement may remain. The God of the white people must never be mentioned here again! The spirits will only be satisfied when their work of destruction is completed.

For several days, there has been no radio contact with Nipsan. At the other stations everyone is becoming increasingly concerned and wonder what the matter is. Is their battery dead? Is the radio broken? The MAF is requested to fly over Nipsan and take a look. When pilot Pablo Pontier flies over Nipsan, he sees immediately that something is very wrong; he tilts his plane to have a better look.

To his shock he sees no people about; all the buildings have been burnt to the ground. He circles his plane a few more times and cannot believe his eyes; the entire settlement is completely destroyed. He cannot land because of obstacles thrown on the strip. By radio he reports his findings.

Pilot Pablo Pontier views the massive destruction from the air.
Part of the cowshed still stands

Via Kosarek, reports of the attack come in. The drama unfolds as the extent of the tragedy becomes known. The eleventh of May, 1974 will be recorded as a black day for the work of the NRC in Irian Jaya.

Rev. Vergunst rips open a telegram from Jayapura. The sender is Hans; a name which means nothing to him. But the content of the message does. "Nipsan station destroyed—all killed by population." Rev. Vergunst is shocked. Nipsan destroyed? The last reports were so positive; in the different villages approximately seven hundred people came to hear the Word. Immediately he calls the President of the MB Rev. H. Rijksen. A short time later the two pastors meet with the secretary, Mr. Schouwstra, in the consistory at Gouda. Although they do not have any other information than what the telegram states, they decide to inform the parents of the missionaries.

Rev. Kuijt and Miep are currently in Choteau, Montana where their daughter Wilhelmina Maria is born on April 30, 1974.

Halfway around the world, physically far removed from the tragedy, our fourth child, a beautiful baby girl, Wilhelmina, is born on April 30th, 1974.

Kuijt had accepted an offer from his friend Henry Bouma to come to Choteau, Montana during his furlough in 1974. The Boumas are prepared to pay the cost of the lessons for the single engine flight training. It was only eighteen months ago that he had written to Rev. Huisman, that he was quite content to leave the flying to the MAF. But since then he has realized how valuable it would be for him to be able to pilot a small plane if or when needed.

However, when he shared his plans with the MB, the brothers had serious reservations. A flying minister!! Inconceivable!!!! Does Kuijt have any idea of the dangers of flying? They make it very clear that they consider this flying business to be Kuijt's personal responsibility. Kuijt accepts this.

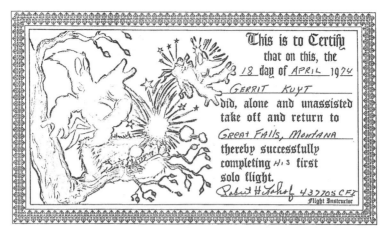

On April 18, 1974, Rev. Kuijt does his first solo flight

Eleven days after the birth of Wilhelmina, the MB decides to inform Kuijt that they want to send him back to New Guinea immediately. Rev. Vreugdenhil, the new missionary, who is studying the Yali language, shall also depart as soon as possible for Irian Jaya. Rev. Vergunst will prepare an article for the *Reformatorisch Dagblad*, a daily Dutch Christian newspaper, to inform its readers of the situation.

They reach Rev. Kuijt by telephone. On this particular day he is actually in Corsica, Montana, far from Choteau where he and his family are staying while he pursues his flight training. To get the necessary flying hours for his pilot's license, he and Harold Bouma fly Harold's Cessna on Saturdays to various congregations where he will preach on the Sunday and then fly back.

"What! Nipsan!*"* Kuijt is in shock, "Nipsan destroyed? How can that be? Everything was going so well. What happened? Herman and the boys would do everything to prevent this from happening. Was it not God's work? Where are all the evangelists? No one knows?" He promises to try to get more information and, if necessary, to go back as quickly as possible.

Rev. W.C. Lamain is also shaken by the tragedy that occurred on the Nipsan station and the setback that his Brother in the ministry and the mission of the NRC has to experience. He immediately telephones Rev. Kuijt to express his sympathy on behalf of the American NRC and sent a letter to the MB. He brings the needs to God in prayer in his congregation and has them sing Hymn 265: 'Jehovah reigns in majesty; let all the nations quake.' He writes:

> *If the Lord truly lived in the souls of these workers, their souls*
> *will live forever. The devil has only a short time left, but the gates*
> *of hell shall never prevail over God's church.*

Missionary Looijen

After the first rumours of the murders, missionary Looijen flies to Nipsan with the MAF. As the plane circles over the station the pilot and Looijen try to get a better understanding of the ramifications of the destruction. The strip is still obstructed so they cannot land. Then three soldiers start out from Kosarek and they arrive in Nipsan after a three-day trek. After they have cleared the rubble off the strip, an airplane can land again. It is Rev. Benz from Apalapsili, who is the first to visit the demolished settlement. Via the radio he reports that he has found one survivor; Orpa the wife of Abraham who hid herself for a full week in the jungle. With the arrival of the soldiers she dares to come out of hiding. She was wounded by six arrows in her legs and head and left for dead. Now her greatest sorrow is the death of her little adopted daughter and the uncertainty about her husband. If he is still alive, he definitely would have returned by now. Rev. Bentz takes Orpa with him to Apalapsili and informs her that her husband Abraham unfortunately was killed and eaten in the Hablo village on Saturday, May 11, 1974. Orpa is transported to Angguruk for treatment of the arrow wounds.

On May 17, Looijen is flown into Nipsan. After examining the area, he sits discouraged on some charred boards from the cow shed. He will stay in Nipsan with ten police men. Using his knee as a table, he writes down his impressions.

> *The airstrip is still completely intact, but nothing remains of the buildings. The only place that provides any shelter is the cow shed. The three walls of the shed are destroyed so the building is a write-off.*
>
> *After walking around, we found Herman's head which is severely disfigured. From one of the surviving boys who managed to escape we learned that Herman was the first one to be murdered. Near his totally destroyed house, we found the place where he was butchered; his intestines and body parts were still there. Herman did not have a chance to reach the radio; it would have been useless anyway as the radio had been stolen. I noticed the microphone and, as it is connected by a cord to the radio, I found the radio as well. The radio had been cleverly detached from the battery and the antenna; it no longer worked. We sent it to Sentani for repairs.*

There is another survivor, Matthias. When it became dark, he managed to flee to Kosarek and there he told the horrific story of the massacre. He tried desperately to protect his wife Dogwareke and their son Marcus with his bow and arrows. When they were killed, he fled into the forest. Looijen found only the skull of Marcus and a body part believed to be from Dogwareke. Asaf also hid behind Matthias, defending himself with stones. Asaf's wife Endahambik and his little daughter were both killed. Near the strip, Looijen found the little girl's body filled with arrows, her skull severed in half and the grass skirt of her mother beside her.

Asaf arrived in Kosarek on Saturday. He could not continue any further as his feet were raw. A Chief from the Nipsan village protected Philippus who was also able to flee to Kosarek. He hid in the water behind a waterfall near a hanging bridge. For two days he managed to cling to a rock with his head barely above the water. He had received an arrow in his calf. Somehow he managed to limp to Angguruk.

Pilot Pablo brings Looijen and soldiers to Nipsan

The place where the bodies of some workers were cooked and eaten

When Looijen returns to Pass Valley, he gives a grim report. The reality hits like a bomb. The people scream and wail in anguish. Why did the missionary not tell them sooner? These were children from Pass Valley who have been butchered and there needs to be revenge! Looijen must ask for planes so they can fly to Nipsan and can see to it that blood will flow. An eye for an eye; the people demand retaliation.

With great difficulty, Looijen finally succeeds in calming the people down.

"I explained to them that it would be impossible to find one pilot who would fly them to Nipsan for that purpose and the police for sure would not condone their reprisal. These arguments finally stop them from carrying out their demands." Many relatives of the murdered individuals live in Ilugwa and Waktangu. Most of these relatives are still opposed to the Gospel message and now they have proof that the Gospel is dangerous. "See what happens when you start to obey the Bible?" The families threaten to kill Looijen, the chief Kahelima, and Kokpan in retaliation for the murders of the people in Nipsan. Indeed, on Monday about seventy or eighty warriors from Ilugwa arrive in Pass Valley smeared with clay as a symbol of grief. It is only because of the two police officers that they restrain themelves. How did this happen just as the work was beginning to take hold in the Nipsan area? It is a question they ask in Irian as well as overseas.

Can it be the generation gap where the older ones feel threatened by the young people who are receiving education? Did it have something to do with the attitude of the Bible School students? Or did it have something to do with dominant behaviour toward the Nipsanners? Orders were expected to be followed up without any question; apparently sometimes these were accompanied by threats and physical punishment. Not long ago a little boy was taken to the hospital in Angguruk with a broken arm. Looijen had forbidden the use of corporal punishment. But the helpers only adhered to this rule as long as Looijen was at the station.

Could it be that the Nipsan people were upset about the gardens? The helpers had planted their gardens but they were destroyed by heavy rain. So new gardens were planted to supply the necessary food but this time they used land which had not been purchased by the mission.

There could be other reasons why this tragedy took place. Did it have to do with the death of the man that Amos killed? For this incident ample payment has already been given though the Government still wants Amos to appear before a judge in Wamena. Another possibility is the flu epidemic that "spread as a wild fire" through the interior of Irian Jaya. This took a heavy toll everywhere especially on the children and elderly. Church attendance and cooperation by the people declined.

Pass Valley man smeared with clay as a sign of mourning

Not everyone in Nipsan knew of the plans for the massacre. Several chiefs, who likely would have disagreed with the attack, were kept in the dark. This was evident when two chiefs from the Nipsan village tried to protect the boys.

How it happened is evident; why it happened is still uncertain. The NRC Mission of Irian Jaya must draw up the balance sheet. The list consists of: Herman killed beside his house; Abram in Hablo; Bola in Silekaihek; Mandi in Walmag; Stefanus in Nipsan; Obed in Tapla; Dogwareke in Walmak with her son Marcus; Deborah in Tapla; Mina, daughter of Obed and Debora, together with the adopted daughter of Orpa in the hut in which they were burned. Twelve cows, thirteen pigs, three cats and a dog, all killed and eaten.

The Nipsan area is closed down. Without special permission from the Bupati, none can enter the area. The strip is again barricaded and when a plane flies low over the area it is welcomed by a volley of arrows. It is impossible to return to Nipsan now. In October, the Bupati wants to visit Pass Valley to further investigate the matter and speak with the survivors. Besides not being allowed to return to Nipsan, Kuijt is emotionally unable to return. For the time being, he will be a substitute for the Louwerses in Langda and later for the Looijens in Pass Valley when the missionaries are on furlough.

Arrival of Bupati in Pass Valley

Children are playing near the airstrip. A little boy practises archery with his bow and arrow and a young girl is sitting in the grass with her baby brother on her lap. Other children chase each other. Suddenly they all stop as the soft rumble of a distant airplane gradually becomes louder. Quickly they run to the shed where the airplane is supposed to come to a halt. From the other direction, Kuijt and Vreugdenhil approach, followed by Mrs. Kuijt. Everyone is curious and comes to the strip. When the Cessna comes to a stop, the little door opens and out steps the Bupati. He is dressed in Western clothing. More people descend from the plane. Introductions are made and handshakes are given. Busily talking, the group approaches the school.

Psalm 116 is sung; even the Bupati joins in. A Bible School student says a short prayer then the Bupati begins to speak.

The Bupati is an important man. He is not only the Chief of Police in his district but he is also the Justice of the Peace. The Bupati introduces his other guests: his commander in chief, a lawyer, and the Bupati's secretary.

The Bupati tells the people that outside the Pass Valley area there are people living even farther away than a Yali can go. You must not view these people as enemies; just like you in Pass Valley, they are Indonesian citizens. This means that you all have to abide by the Indonesian laws and therefore, you all have the right to be protected by the Indonesian government.

Then the lawyer addresses the group. He says no one may act as a judge. Everyone must leave justice in the hands of qualified authorities who represent the Indonesian government, where you can also bring your grievance. The lawyer hopes that they will all abide by the law so no punishment is needed in Pass Valley. The Bupati adds, "We must chase the devil out of our hearts and be watchful that there is no food for him in our soul."

Then he comes to the point of his visit. He hopes that the questions he is going to ask will be answered honestly and openly. Timidly, Kepala Kahelima is the first to step forward. He asks the Bupati if he has discovered the reason for the destruction of Nipsan. The secretary dutifully writes down this question. When Bupati in turn asks if Kahelima has any more questions on his heart, he responds by asking when the guilty ones will be sentenced and when the police will go to Nipsan.

The Bupati has anticipated this question and he has already consulted with the missionaries as to when they anticipated returning to Nipsan. At the moment no pilot can land there. They contemplate possibilities that are mentioned. Finally the decision is made to postpone the reopening of Nipsan until the spring of 1975. By then the new MAF helicopter will have arrived in Sentani.

As for sentencing the accused; first they have to take a few Nipsanners into custody and question them to determine their motives. Other discussions follow. If the Ilugwa tribe threatens them, can they defend themselves when in danger? Can those who fled to Yiwika be brought back under police protection?

When all questions have been answered, Rev. Kuijt takes the floor and directs their attention to Sabonwarek who wants to say something. Sabonwarek has spent several weeks in Langda after he has been threatened in Pass Valley. Now he has returned from Langda with Rev. Kuijt. Sabonwarek and Teofilus are accused in Pass Valley as being the instigators for the tragedy in Nipsan. Sabonwarek uses this opportunity to challenge his accusers. Let them speak up and inform the Bupati of their accusations. They are all witnesses to what happened and they know Sabonwarek is innocent. All remain silent. Finally Kahelima forces Asaf to tell the story. He recounts the situation in Nipsan from the moment that Rev. Kuijt left on furlough. The church attendance dwindled rapidly and then the Bible School students burned several huts and took pigs from the people in the village and ate them. They thought this would compel the people to come back to church. This method is often used by the police but of course the police only do this when the individuals take on a threatening attitude. The helpers wanted Tuan Kuijt to find the church full of people when he came back so he would be very pleased with his boys.

Six witnesses tell their stories; Orpa also talks about her escape. At the end, many garden huts were destroyed or burned and at least twenty pigs were stolen and eaten. "This was the straw that broke the camel's back." The Nipsan people had had enough. Away with those boys and away with the Gospel! Truly, this is a black page in mission history.

Many years later, after Rev. Kuijt receives his emeritus status and is doing volunteer work in Bali, he reads a fax from his wife, in which she mentions an article in the latest *National Geographic* about Irian Jaya and the annihilation of the mission at Nipsan. The article states that missionary Kuijt and his assistant Herman Imbab supposedly had extramarital relationships with the women of the local population. This enraged the men of Nipsan and a massacre ensued. Oh, this story was not altogether new. Robert Mitton included it in his book, *The Lost World of Irian Jaya*. The *Periplus Travel Guide* mindlessly repeated the fabrication, and now the *National Geographic* is carrying it. Rev. Kuijt knows where this story originates from. Pilot Pablo, the first to land on the Nipsan strip after the massacre, discovered Herman Imbab's scrotum nailed to a post. Dr. Vriend subsequently drew the conclusion that adultery must have been a factor. Looijen sternly questioned the survivors on this score. Nothing ever pointed in this direction. But, meanwhile, the rumour has taken on a life of its own and Rev. Kuijt is also implicated. Will there never be an end to all this slander? Not only the mission representatives in the Netherlands wonder whether something ought to be done but also Wim feels that the limit has been reached. "If Dad does nothing about it, then I will start a lawsuit."

Kuijt takes time to consider his actions. Would he prefer to suffer damage to his reputation or go to court to defend his reputation? But does the issue not go beyond the honour and good name of Gerrit Kuijt? Is it not ultimately the Name of the Lord that is slandered? Gerrit decides to initiate a court action. He first traveled to Irian Jaya, collected his faithful helper Sabonwarek and went to Nipsan. There he asked frankly and directly whether there is any truth to the accusation of adultery. The tribal chiefs and not only those who have become Christians, but others as well deny it vehemently.

Next the missionary travels with Sabonwarek to Singapore. He would have preferred to bring the chiefs along as well, but this is not necessary. When the lawyer in Singapore asks Rev. Kuijt how many children he has, he replies, "Five." "No," says Sabonwarek. "Six! I am his sixth child!"

The outcome is that the *National Geographic* has to put the record straight and *Periplus* must publish a new edition which excludes the accusations. The revised edition has indeed been published.

Chapter 14

Seeking New Directions . . .

Missionary Kuijt sits somberly in front of the mission home of the Langda post. The attack on the station in Nipsan deeply affects him; the loss of his faithful workers and families grieves him profoundly. Not long ago, Mandi, their trusted and faithful house helper, while on a brief furlough in Pass Valley, said that he believed Nipsan to be the place where God wants him to be. "If I am to be killed, I will go to my Heavenly Father," he said to his friends when they warned him of the dangers of working among the Nipsanners. This comforts the missionary, yet questions remain.

Rev. Kuijt was convinced he was to bring God's Word to the Nipsan people. Now the path seems to be blocked by the hellish attacks of Satan. Would God's promises ever fail? Has he deceived himself?

He is also bothered by the differences of opinions with the MB. The members think the massacre in Nipsan could have been prevented if Kuijt had been there. Missionaries of other organizations in Irian thanked the Lord that the Kuijt family was absent at the time for they certainly would have been killed too. Over the past few months some harsh words have been exchanged between the MB and Kuijt.

For a while it appears as though Kuijt will be dismissed permanently. Thankfully this did not materialize. At the end of August he receives a letter from Rev. Vergunst informing him that the MB is pleased to continue working with Kuijt and to disregard the past and move forward.

However, the differences in opinion are still there. This pains Kuijt, especially since he feels such a bond with his brothers in the ministry. Kuijt knows that he is not always right. The whole situation really bothers him but ultimately there is nothing left to do besides praying and asking the Lord to open possibilities where there now seem to be none.

*During their stay in Langda, Rev. Kuijt continually thinks about
what took place in Nipsan. Here he is with Wilhelmina
on his way to check on the work being done to extend the strip*

Barefooted Gert crossing a vine bridge

The missionary can understand why these differences of opinion can arise so easily. MB members must direct the affairs of the mission work but they are far removed from the field. He is convinced that they make their decisions with heart-felt love. The cause of the King is also very important to them but they often lack the necessary insight because they do not have to deal with the everyday challenges of working on the field. This came to light when MB representatives Rijksen and Vergunst visited the mission field the previous year. They both gained a better insight into the situation and activities in Irian Jaya.

Klazina, Wim and Gert home on vacation

Wim and Gert with the Langda people

The Kuijt family has lived in Langda since the middle of August, 1974. Due to the destruction of Nipsan they do not have their own mission station; at the moment they are filling in for the Louwerse family who are on furlough in the Netherlands. Rev. Kuijt writes to the MB in his first letter after arriving in Langda:

> *What Jan and Janny have built up here in a little over a year is amazing. An airstrip has been built and a storage barn erected with extra space for medical work. There is also a small, single-walled wooden house. Janny Louwerse has made it cozy and there is room for the three Kuijt children, who will be coming home for the Christmas vacation. Even a crib has been made for baby Wilhelmina.*

Mrs. Kuijt is thankful for her new quarters. After living in so many different shelters; this is a good home.

The Langda station has been open for a year. Rev. Kuijt remembers clearly how he, Louwerse, and forty Yali helpers from Pass Valley went to Langda. The first encounter with the local population was friendly. The people had put their weapons on the ground. It was unfortunate that this friendliness reflected a sense of duty rather than a sense of acceptance.

Kuijt and his wife are warned by the helpers from Pass Valley to be on their guard; there are regular massacres in the area. Shortly before the Kuijt family arrived in Langda, twenty-three people had been murdered. Rev. Kuijt writes, "The inhabitants here prefer human flesh to pork. Our boys advised me to wear long pants to try to curb their appetite for cannibalism. We observed their habit of gauging the size of our arms and legs in Nipsan but we treated it as some sort of a joke. We now have different thoughts. We are being measured to be eaten. They also admire long hair; Miep is advised to keep her hair up."

But he does not notice much of an appetite for the Word of God here. Church attendance in Langda is meager. "This past Sunday morning there were thirty-two people in church; in the afternoon only eighteen. A possible cause can be that the Langda people have so much other work to do on Sunday." A few months after the arrival of the Kuijt family they request that the morning service be held at 6:00 am so that they can go to their gardens afterwards.

You may think, "Is this work necessary on Sunday?" But we have to realize that a change must come from one's inner spiritual condition. If this does not exist, we can do much damage by insisting on the change. In the afternoon service Kuijt pretends to be oblivious to what is going on around him. The service is seen as an opportunity for companionship and relaxation. It is a time to braid bracelets, which occupies many of the listeners. Others sit comfortably with a home-grown cigarette between their lips and listen. No opportunity is lost to interrupt him. But the missionary accepts this as a positive sign. "It is proof that they are listening and thinking."

Following the sermon they are told to pass on the message that they have just heard. "But Tuan Kuijt," they complain, "Do you realize how difficult this is?" Bent over, as though they have a bow and arrow ready to shoot, the men encircle the missionary. "If we go to the other villages and tell them stories from the Bible, we will get shot with a full blast of their arrows."

A Langda girl with traditional nose decoration

A beautiful head-dress

I want to look like Tuan

This initiates a lengthy discussion about the "dangerous" commission. Rev. Kuijt does not excuse them from their mission although he advises them to stay well out of the archers' range.

Church attendance increases and in March 1975, Kuijt writes that in the morning one hundred and twenty people attend the service but in the afternoon the church is pretty near empty. Then the missionary goes out to the Langda people. In the open air he conducts a meeting which despite cold or rain, is attended by about fifty people.

When the Louwerse family returns from their furlough, the Kuijt family moves back to Pass Valley. Here, they will take over from the Looijen family while they are on furlough.

While in Pass Valley the Kuijt family lives in the comfortable home of the Looijens, which is especially enjoyed when the children are home for their summer vacation. Klazina is home before the boys. An unknown illness with symptoms of low fever and extreme tiredness goes around among the students. These children are sent home earlier.

There is much work to be done in Pass Valley. Every morning Rev. Kuijt teaches at the Bible School where he instructs the young men who will later on go out and sow the seeds of the Word. During the afternoon there are other tasks to be done, and people come to ask Kuijt for his advice and acquaintances come to visit.

Langobarek the warlord also visits. There is a special bond between him and Kuijt but it grieves the missionary that not much has come from Lango's promise to become a Christian. Langobarek has a request. He needs an axe. Could the Bapa give him one? Tomorrow he must go to war and this time axes will be the weapons.

Kuijt tries to persuade him. "Instead of making war, it is better to come to church. Please come, Lango!" In the end Langobarek shakes his head sadly, turns around and walks away. Kuijt turns to his wife with tears in his eyes. "Miep," he says, "Did I do the right thing?" His wife is silent; she does not know either. The next day the sad news comes to them, "Lango has been killed in action!"

Time rushes by; the furlough period for the Looijens is already over. The Kuijt's moved back into their former home made of bark. But having two missionary couples at one station goes against Kuijt's principles. There are still unreached tribes. Rev. Kuijt prays for the Lord to open new doors. In their hearts the missionary and his wife hope for a new opportunity to return to Nipsan. They cannot believe that the work there will be lost forever but they also know that they must wait for God's time.

On December 3rd, 1975, another beautiful baby girl, Cornelia Debora, is born in Angguruk, delivered by Dr. Gert Scheepstra. The whole family is ecstatic. Baby Cornelia is named 'Oeni' by Wilhelmina, who is holding her.

1976: the Kuijt family
L/R Gert, Wim, Mrs. Kuijt, with baby Oeni, Wilhelmina (in front), Rev. Kuijt, Klazina

First they will go to Bomela where Rev. Kuijt acquires a new work terrain. Louwerse has made a few orientation trips from Langda to the Sayn Valley which includes the village of Bomela. Here people also still live in accordance to the practice of their ancient culture: an eye for an eye, a tooth for a tooth. The local justice system is clear and methodical; there is only one form of punishment. Not only murder and manslaughter but also adultery is cause for the death penalty and insults are cause for revenge. Regularly there are wars among the various villages. Every death must be avenged. The endless cycle of revenge holds the valley residents in a stranglehold. Even if it sometimes takes a year before retaliation occurs—usually unexpectedly— it definitely will take place.

After these initial scouting trips by Louwerse, the decision is made that Bomela will become the fifth NRC mission station in Irian Jaya. Once again, here is an area where Christ's name has not been heard and where the work has to be started from the bottom up in extremely primitive circumstances. Who is more qualified to carry this out than Kuijt? The missionary agrees to go. All the team members are prepared to lend a helping hand to start this new station. Louwerse ensures that a piece of land is leveled for the building of a simple dwelling. In addition he also organizes a shipment of building materials to be flown in with the new helicopter that was purchased by the MAF.

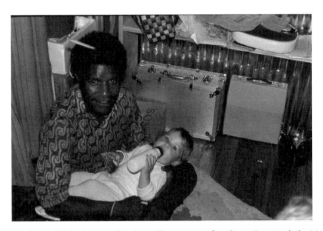

Endog, a very faithful helper, gifted in all areas, is feeding Oeni while Mrs. Kuijt is attending a meeting with the Bomela people

Looijen and Rev Vreugdenhil are willing to frame the new house. After a two-day trek on the mountain trails, they arrive at Bomela accompanied by a group of helpers from Langda. They are given a friendly welcome although the missionaries are uncertain why the locals are constantly pinching them in their calves and buttocks. Is this their manner of greeting or is this an omen? The Chief of Bomela reiterates a number of times how happy they are to see them but the construction team has an uneasy feeling.

A few days later they realize this feeling was not unfounded. On Sunday morning Rev. Vreugdenhil conducts a meditation in the open air for which various valley residents show interest. Following the gathering, the population of Bomela withdraws to their huts to prepare food. Suddenly the missionaries hear a terrifying scream. Then it became quiet. Vreugdenhil, Looijen, and their helpers watch as the body of a woman is thrown out of a hut.

After two-and-a-half weeks of work, three rooms of the home for the Kuijt family are ready. Vreugdenhil and Looijen depart and the Kuijt's settle in Bomela. For the fourth time in New Guinea, they are at a place where the natives live in a pagan manner.

Everyone works hard to get a strip in Bomela

As at the other posts, Kuijt immediately starts with the construction of an airstrip. The ground in Bomela is swampy. The biggest concern therefore is how to remove enough boggy soil until there is a solid base on which an airplane can land. The locals show little ambition to help. However, he receives a great deal of support from the Landikma people who came along to help. Thanks to their efforts, the strip is ready after eight-and-a-half months. Bob Breuker makes the first landing on May 3, 1977.

This albino lives in Bomela. The cap was given to him by Rev. Kuijt to protect his head from the sun

Contact with the local population develops positively from the very beginning. One week after he started in Bomela, Kuijt writes that the people are very friendly. One reason is that the big Chief of Bomela, Yuan, offers his collaboration and friendship right from the first encounter. He encourages his people to bring food for the missionary family and ensures that their belongings are watched overnight. He even urges his fellow villagers to attend the Sunday meetings. This is encouraging.

However, Kuijt soon concludes that the people of Bomela are more interested in material gain than in spiritual food. They show little interest in the devotions which he conducts every morning except for the time when an MAF helicopter lands during the open-air assembly. Within seconds a number of valley residents come to see if they can get some of the rice that is being delivered. "They suddenly are prepared to feign interest. Quietly they listen to the meditation and the prayer." After six months Kuijt writes in his report: "Putting it succinctly, we can state that the spiritual situation in Bomela is altogether sad. The best way to describe it is: dead in sins and trespasses. There is no hint of spiritual hunger. On the contrary, they are resentful of the piercing Gospel. They are indeed crazy about goods. For the only comfort of which the Heidelberg Catechism speaks, is no place whatsoever."

For Kuijt and his helpers it is especially disappointing that this definitely must also be said of chief Yuan. At the least provocation he uses deadly force. Kuijt writes in one of his letters.

> *His dog had a small wound on its nose. He immediately suspected Ayam (meaning: chicken) and Obeyakib (nicknamed Obed) as the guilty ones. Ayam, who is blind in one eye, narrowly escaped the four arrows shot at him. Obed was less fortunate. The first arrow Yuan aimed at him hit him in the leg. Tingto, the most prominent of Yuan's four wives, decided to get involved, but she paid a bitter price for doing so. Yuan angrily bit a piece of flesh out of her cheek and her arm! As my wife dressed Tingto's wounds, Tingto said, "Yuan has the devil in his heart."*

*Chief Yuan promised to look after Mrs. Kuijt and the children,
Wilhelmina and Oeni when Rev. Kuijt was not at home
and that is exactly what he does*

Despite their initial reluctance, a change is eventually apparent in the way the people of Bomela listen to the Gospel. In the spring of 1977, Rev. Kuijt writes that about fifty people come together for the morning worship. It might have to do with the absence of Yuan. He is gone on a trip to Langda for some time. It is noteworthy that it is the young people who especially show an interest in the services. "They seem to be interested in listening to something that is new."

About one year later Kuijt reports that things are going well in Bomela. There have been some Sundays that there are more than one hundred people at the services and even Yuan now comes regularly to listen to the missionary. Yet he remains an unpredictable factor: when the slightest thing perturbs him, he prevents the people in his tribe from going to worship.

Wim with Oeni

Yuan's sister is baby-sitting Oeni

When the Kuijt family again goes on furlough in the summer of 1977, there are many reasons for giving thanks. Kuijt writes to his mission friends:

> *When we came back to Irian Jaya three years before, we were discouraged. So many of our faithful workers and evangelists were killed and all avenues seemed to be blocked. But the Lord gave a new mission field in a way that we could not see at that time. Bomela has been introduced to the Gospel and the Lord will lead us further.*

The furlough starts with a visit to New Zealand. At the request of the Board for Overseas Churches, Rev. Kuijt serves the church at Carterton which he has instituted a year earlier. He preaches and serves the sacraments for three Sundays; this time the mission couple wanted to visit each family. The whole family spent this time in New Zealand together with nurse Marry van Moolenbroek. In one of the services Rev. and Mrs. Kuijt's youngest daughter, Cornelia Debora, (Oeni) is baptized.

Then the family travels via the Netherlands to the U.S.A. The MB and their relatives would have liked them to stay in Holland but Kuijt wants to spend most of their furlough in the United States. The children are accustomed to the American school system and English is their first language. When they are on their first furlough, Mrs. de Bruijn, a former teacher from Grand Rapids, came to Holland to tutor the children and during their second furlough the children went to the International School in The Hague. This was very expensive, but necessary for the children to be able to continue their education. Thankfully, the MB decided to help subsidize some of the cost.

Besides, Kuijt does not have time to spend in the Netherlands. His desire is to become competent in flying a helicopter. Rev. Kuijt has already calculated that there are exactly enough days in his schedule to earn the required flight certificate and to fly the necessary hours. No, it is not an ambition to earn the certificate. He writes to the MB in May, 1977:

> *That would stink like pride. I only want to know how to fly a helicopter to reach lost souls and if I have to, I will pull them out of the trees to lead them to Jesus.*

With the help of his friend, Bouma, he has been registered at the flight school in Fort Worth, Texas but ended up taking his training in Metford, Oregon.

The Bouma family belongs to a conservative Baptist church. They make every effort to help Kuijt to become a good pilot. They are even prepared to make a helicopter available for him. This is not a small proposition. The MB of the NRC churches of America and Canada are also prepared to help cover the costs, if necessary. The purchase of a helicopter would be a burden on the mission budget in the Netherlands.

Enthusiastically Kuijt communicates this offer to the MB. To his surprise there is no encouraging reaction from them. Yes, it is a splendid offer that the NRC and personal friends in America are making but what about maintenance costs! And, who will do the maintenance? No, the delegates prefer to keep using the MAF airplanes. As generous as the offer may be, they will not accept it. Kuijt cannot come to terms with this decision. While he does not want to act contrary to the MB, he believes opportunities to bring the Word may be lost if the offer of a helicopter is not accepted.

Five to ten minutes by MAF heli instead of trekking for eight hours or more

Again the delegates remind him that taking flight lessons is his personal business and they will not take any responsibility in the matter. They do not see it as realistic for a missionary to fly his own helicopter. Kuijt accepts this but does not let it alter his plans. Shortly before he leaves on furlough he writes to the MB,

This is a matter of faith and my desire is to trust the Lord in a

childlike manner, believing that also in this endeavor all things are possible. This is not an impulsive desire that sprang up overnight; for three years it has been a deep longing in my heart. There are villages in our area that we cannot reach. I cannot believe that on my next term I will stay at one mission station in a sparsely populated area. I earnestly long for what the Lord will do for me during my furlough. We will rejoice in the Lord and He will give us the desires of our heart. Oh what joy this brings to my soul! Faith can move mountains; would a helicopter be too much to ask of the Lord? Oh my Father is so rich, and He is so able to provide! It is all about His honour and the extension of His chosen people.

However, he has trouble understanding why the MB is so adamantly opposed to his proposal to purchase a helicopter? A helicopter has great advantages over a plane. A helicopter would allow him to easily visit villages and valleys in the area. Up till now every new station requires months of work to construct an airstrip for a small airplane to land. You do not need this for a heli. A level piece of ground or a dry river bed is all that is needed. Just as his fellow ministers in the Netherlands have a car parked in their garage, he would like to have access to a helicopter. Then he could visit and evangelize whenever and wherever necessary. Where now he must trek for a day or more to visit a neighbouring valley or a distant village, it would take only five or ten minutes with a helicopter. To Kuijt it is clear that the purchase of a helicopter will give a tremendous boost to the spreading of the Gospel. The need to reach the people who live in remote places is, as always, his main focus.

He informs the MB in the Netherlands that they do not have to worry about a working relationship with MAF. He has spoken with Dennis Stuessi of MAF who expressed some concerns but is very agreeable. They decide that if Kuijt receives a helicopter, he will have to take care of the import charges but MAF is willing to take over the maintenance. Together Kuijt and Stuessi placed this desire in prayer before the Lord. A mutual agreement is expressed; if the Lord in His grace gives $100,000 (U.S.) the helicopter will be a Hiller. If He gives $200,000, it will be a Hughes. But if the Lord does not give anything, it is also good and nothing will be lost. However one thing is clear: Kuijt will not ask for money, not from the Netherlands, nor from the NRC in North America or anywhere else. If the money comes in, it will be a gift from God. "In the Lord we dare to trust."

Even if there is a difference of opinion between the MB and Kuijt, he holds no grudge. He dislikes conflicts and he knows how easily they can arise especially in mission work and "that they rapidly can grow from a snowball into a snowman."

In his heart he is convinced that he is doing the right thing. The delegates of the Oversea Churches and the MB in the U.S.A. do not allow Rev. Kuijt to preach in the NRC churches and this deeply pains him. But he sees no other option than to complete his flight training. Two months before their departure Rev. Kuijt suddenly is allowed to preach again.

When the Kuijt family returns to Irian Jaya at the beginning of 1978, the missionary has the desired certificate in his pocket. Now all he needs is a helicopter! The Bouma family has already offered to provide one and even the MB is slowly changing their mind. In May, Rev. P. Honkoop and A. Vergunst visit the mission field in Irian Jaya.

While they are on this trip both ministers realize what a great advantage it would be to have a helicopter available for mission work. When Professor Moens plans a visit several months later, Rev. Vergunst writes a letter with a personal message:

> *Gerrit, I recommend that you make sure that the Professor sees the same need for a helicopter that we saw when we were there.*

It is near the end of that year that approval is given and the MB proceeds with the purchase of its own helicopter. An American pilot, Mike Meeuwse is accepted by the MB and MAF to fly the machine, but Kuijt is thankful that the MB agrees that a helicopter is of vast importance to the mission work.

Whatever will become of the Nipsan people? While Rev. Kuijt is busy establishing the station in Bomela, this does not mean he has forgotten them. He is sure that these pagan people one day also will embrace the Word of God. All nations, tongues and people, including the Nipsan people, will acknowledge the Lord is God. Each day he includes them in his prayers. Kuijt's desire is that he may witness the conversion of the Nipsan people. But he is not certain that he will see this being fulfilled.

Though they murdered his faithful helpers, he is filled with compassion for them. Since the bloody massacre two years ago, there has been no contact with Nipsan. From all sides they realize that a time of "cooling off" is necessary. When the message comes that there is a famine in the Nipsan area, MAF is prepared to make several drops with sweet potatoes. How they reacted to these gifts remains a mystery. Via the ECK mission stations in Kosarek and Angguruk, conflicting rumors are heard. Some say the Nipsan people refused the food and after chopping everything into pieces, they left it on the strip; others report that they ate the food. But one thing is obvious; the Nipsan people are fiercely opposed to the return of the mission.

The first MAF helicopter, a Hiller

In spite of this, the missionary continues to try and make contact. Kuijt goes along on several flights over the area to assess the situation and to drop gifts of parangs, bush knifes and axes as tokens of peace. The Nipsan people are amazed to receive valuable gifts when they anticipate revenge. To the delight of everyone on board they can see from the air that the Nipsan people accept these gifts.

In May 1977, via helicopter Kuijt makes a short visit to the Nipsan area. The Bupati, head of the district, gives permission on the condition that two MAF helicopters fly in together. One helicopter must try to put Kuijt on the ground and the second one has to circle around should assistance be necessary. The helicopter hovers above a level piece of ground at Kirikyak. The pilot waits for a few minutes to see if the people of Kirikyak appear but nobody shows. Then he puts his heli down. The people of this village have never been antagonistic. That is why Kuijt has chosen this village as the place to start renewing contact with the Nipsan people. He steps out of the heli followed immediately by Sabonwarek. Many emotions fill Sabonwarek's heart as he remembers how he was one of the first to work among these people. Most of his friends and fellow evangelists are no longer alive. By God's providence, he was not in Nipsan when the massacre took place. Now he is back with the people who also wanted to murder him. A prayer rises within his heart: "Lord, they did not know what they were doing. But they are also people with a soul. Wilt Thou forgive them and show them saving grace? Turn them from their old ways and let them turn to Thee."

Rev. Kuijt with Wilhelmina on his lap in the Hughes heli

Pilot Len Van Wingerden and a passenger in his heli

In the distance they spot a few people at work. The people look in the direction of the helicopter but hesitate to come closer. "I am Sabonwarek," the evangelist calls to them. "Bannesum, the Beard, is here too. Do not be afraid; we will not hurt you. Just come!" Finally the people clamber up the hill and a friendly encounter ensues. Rev. Kuijt stresses that he wants to forget the past and start anew. The villagers indicate that they too would like that.

Renewed contact with the people in the Nipsan area

In a letter to the MB Kuijt writes,

> *All of us are very happy that contact is re-established. I know that many of you have been faithfully praying for a door to Nipsan to re-open. I personally do not believe that Nipsan is a lost cause. If contact with other villages matches the experience in Kirikyak, the work in Nipsan can be resumed in the foreseeable future. We must be careful not to make any rash moves. Caution remains advisable. May the Lord go before us with the light of His salvation.*

No rash steps are taken. In 1978 MAF and Kuijt makes several additional reconnaissance flights and lands in a few places to speak with the local people. In the fall the team and the MB consider the time has come to re-open Nipsan. In the Netherlands the MB requests all the churches of the NRC to remember this event in their prayers.

The return to Nipsan must proceed in two stages. First a prefabricated shed will be flown in by heli from Kosarek. Once it has been put in place, Kuijt and his helpers will restore the strip so that airplanes can land again.

In Kosarek seventeen people are prepared to help carry out the operation with Rev. Kuijt and another ten people will come from Pyramid.

Everyone agrees that it is best not to bring along helpers from Pass Valley. The people there still feel the pain of losing their loved ones who were murdered four years ago. Therefore, the people of Pass Valley have little desire to go along. Sabonwarek is the only exception. He will accompany Kuijt. Before he leaves Landikma, where he attends Bible School, he visits his family in Pass Valley to say goodbye (just in case he does not return from this expedition).

On Monday November 27, 1978, Kuijt flies from Bomela to Kosarek. His wife remains behind with the younger children. She will be in charge of the mission station at Bomela until a replacement takes over. It would not be fair to abandon these people. Besides, the children will come home for Christmas and in Nipsan there is no place to house them. Subsequently Marry van Moolenbroek, who was supervising the daily operation of the station for many years in Landikma, will now move to Bomela.

Nurse Marry

The weather conditions in Kosarek on the first day only allow one flight. Everyone agrees that Sabonwarek and three other men from Kosarek will be the first to go. They plan to go to the village of Tapla which is on friendly terms with Kosarek and hope to spend the night there.

The reception in Tapla went very well and the chief invites the four men to his hut. When Sabonwarek asks straight out whether they will accept the Gospel now, the chief answers, "We will talk about that another time." But as a sign of friendship, he offers Sabonwarek a potato. The evangelist talks with the village elders until the late hours of the night. It is clear after the discussions with the chiefs that Tapla wants peace.

New village for the workers and evangelists

The next morning the heli comes back to Tapla to pick up Sabonwarek and the men. In Kosarek, Kuijt waits anxiously. Will his faithful friend and the three men from Kosarek still be alive? A feeling of sheer joy and gratitude overwhelms him when the pilot calls over the radio, "Everything is okay. Sabonwarek and the Kosarek boys are boarding and I will fly them to Walmak, a one-hour trek from the Tapla village to the location of the strip." Kuijt thanks the Lord for His protection. He would gladly have been on that first flight but the various loads for the heli must be planned in a precise and responsible manner. That day, six flights are made to Walmak, the place where the original strip is located. Some building materials and other supplies are flown in. The following night Sabonwarek and his helpers sleep in Walmak. In the morning the pilot again reports that everything is okay. On the third day, Kuijt can finally be taken from Kosarek to Nipsan.

The population definitely does not appear to be hostile. Kuijt gives two pigs, also on behalf of the Kosarek people, to indicate that his intentions are peaceful. Four axes are given to each village that has sent representatives. Kuijt makes an agreement that the past is behind them and that together they will make a fresh start. "We do not look back but ahead;" Kuijt says. He and his helpers keep themselves strictly to this agreement to not make them *malu* (embarrassed).

With the assistance of his helpers and the local population, it takes over a week before the strip is ready again for landing. The shed is erected within a few days and the tents are folded up.

Killing a pig

The first Sunday following the return of Rev. Kuijt to Nipsan there appears to be some interest in hearing the Gospel. Quite a number of people gather for the open-air service. The second Sunday attendance is much larger. Initially Kuijt and his people are delighted about this. The situation changes after the conclusion of the service. It turns out that the good attendance is because the population wants to attach some clear conditions to the return of the mission workers.

The Nipsan people demand that they be allowed to continue having their pagan pig festivals and dances with the Kosarek people. This is an obvious attack on the preaching of Kuijt who continually warns them against their pagan lifestyle. The ECK who conducts mission work in Kosarek has a different opinion on this. This is all the more the case since the Kosarek people have given the Nipsan people false information. They have told them that the food and gifts that were dropped from time to time were financed and arranged by them. As a result the Nipsan people feel that their villages should actually be looked after by the Kosarek mission.

The Nipsanners are recognized by their many Rotan rings

The people also request that the rattan hoops which are worn around their hips be left uncut. Kuijt knows very well that these ornaments are a part of their pagan initiation rites. Yet, considering the fragile situation, he does not want to refuse this request. "After all, we are doing pioneer work and enter their territory without them inviting us first. The Lord has not commanded us to cut through rattan hoops, but to proclaim the Gospel. Once the Gospel penetrates the hearts, the rings will automatically come off."

The next demand is that the Nipsanners will no longer be forced to drink pig's blood. This appears to be a rumor. Kuijt is unaware of this behavior, therefore can grant this request without any reservation.

A more difficult point to accept is when he is told that the young people will not be allowed to serve as language helpers and not allowed to attend school.

The fact is that the children who went to school were persuaded by the "new knowledge" and started to warn their parents more and more that they must put away their pagan traditions. The Nipsan people do not want this to happen again. They also demand that the family ties which exist with the Kosarek people not be severed. Finally a group of chiefs wants to visit other mission stations as well as the coast to see if it is possible to live a normal life as a Christian. Kuijt promises to organize such a trip.

Sabonwarek is especially upset about the behavior of the Kosarek people. Did they not tell the people that the ECK in Kosarek had paid for everything that Rev. Kuijt's group had supplied? Sabonwarek is distraught about these lies. At the same time he gets the impression that the work in Nipsan will be carried on by Kosarek. Because of all this he wants to give up and go back to Pass Valley. There is no need for him here.

Kuijt is able to turn the negative atmosphere around. He makes it absolutely clear that, even though ECK did help with the work, all the assignments and materials for Nipsan were ordered, organized and paid for by the NRC. He also tells the Kosarek helpers that they better pick up the pace of their work as he is irritated by their lack of ambition.

As a result of this conversation, the Kosarek helpers announce that they are leaving. Rev. Kuijt sends them off with a "thank you very much for your help" and with their leaving the atmosphere improves. Not only Sabonwarek, but also the Nipsan people are visibly relieved.

Bannesum wali (The beard is good) Kuijt is obviously surprised when a villager says this to him on Sunday, December 17th. So this man considers him to be good! Rev. Kuijt does not dwell on it but is pleased with this man's comment. Following the tense situation of a week earlier, this is encouraging, as it indicates that the people do not harbor hatred towards him and approve of his presence in Nipsan.

> *Those first few weeks there is not much interest in hearing the gospel. The congregation varies between twenty and thirty, and a significant number of them are the helpers.*

> *The Nipsan people maintain a wait-and-see attitude. It seems as though their main interest is in material gain. It strikes me that these people are so materialistic. Communists would accept that I wear my own clothes, but Nipsanners would like nothing better than to see me wearing a gourd so they can wear my clothes. The same holds true with respect to food. They would let us go hungry while they stuff their bellies with our rice. The above examples indicate the extent to which the 'cargo cult' has taken hold of*

these people. They covet goods and more goods. It will be a lengthy process to convince these people that prosperity comes through hard work. They want to get everything without doing anything for it.

Every so often the Nipsanners, who are helping with the repair of the air strip and the building of the house, complain that they receive too little food. But Kuijt knows how to handle this. He presents them with the simple facts and usually the Nipsanners cannot think of a good response so they return to work. They must admit that the missionary makes sure that they get enough to eat.

About one month after the reopening of the station, the strip is totally cleaned up, the shed is completed but only the shell of the house for the Kuijt family is ready. Mrs. Kuijt now moves with the youngest two children from Bomela to Nipsan and they make a temporary home in the shed. The three older children are in boarding school on the coast. Kuijt writes to Rev. Vergunst:

We are thankful to be together again. It is as if we are newly married.

Kuijt wants to demonstrate that as a Christian you can still live a normal life. In the spring of 1979, he makes good on this promise. He would have liked to take the Nipsanners to Pass Valley but they are not welcome there. It is indeed possible that the people there might not be able to control their feelings of revenge if the Nipsanners visited them. It is for this reason that Rev. Kuijt decides to take the first group of five chiefs to Sentani and Jayapura. They fly to the coast in a small MAF airplane. Kuijt acts as their travel guide and in the coastal region as their chauffeur. The Nipsanners cannot believe their eyes: brick houses and so many of them so close together! The road from Sentani to Jayapura is a winding road which causes them to get queasy. Every so often they must stop at the side of the road.

The first stop is at a Chinese business and the owner takes them to a restaurant. This group draws attention from other diners, not only to see how these men enjoy the food, but to see how they eat every morsel, literally to the last chicken bone. "If anything spilled on the floor, it was immediately picked up and devoured. It is a shame to waste food." Once the missionary feels the warrior chief poke his arm with his fork. The man invites Kuijt to have another piece of chicken. However, Kuijt has enough with one portion. The Nipsanners have no problem devouring three portions.

After returning to Nipsan, the chiefs are dazed and speechless as a result of what they have been exposed too. The waiting villagers are disappointed as they are curious and have been waiting for the big stories. When the stories are finally told, it is obvious how impressed the men are by what they have seen. The Nipsan people learn from their leaders that they must work particularly hard to build villages and lay out gardens. "Living like Christians is not taking a step backward, but forward" Kuijt hears one chief say. The missionary agrees with this statement as long as the chief means the same thing as Kuijt hopes he means.

The excursion was not without its challenges. Since malaria is common on the coast, all chiefs received malaria profilax. Apparently one of the chiefs was careless in taking the medicine and he got malaria. The missionary is dismayed. If the chief dies, it will be seen as his fault. He has the chief brought to the station, where he installs him in a hut and supervises his medicine intake. Thankfully the chief fully recovers and, partly through this intervention, a cordial relationship develops.

Rev. Kuijt holding a well-attended worship service

The number of church attendees rises to about sixty. There is also a change of view with respect to the school. Kuijt again suggests the possibility of educating the elders who are considered to have more wisdom, not the youth. Following some hesitation, the men take him up on this offer. However, after a few days they abandon their studies. What the missionary is trying to teach them is "of no interest to them." So Kuijt accomplishes exactly what he set out to do—teach the youth.

The class starts out with two students who have taken on the names of Paul and Peter. Soon the number of students doubles and within a year there are already twenty boys enrolled. Kuijt and Sabonwarek teach the classes. It is initially done by oral instruction only because none of the students can read or write. Every week the boys get to hear several Bible stories. They pass these stories on in their villages. Every time Kuijt hears one of the students tell a Bible story he is amazed at how precisely they can repeat it. These people have an amazing memory.

The missionary is also surprised with the intensity of the students' concentration during their lessons. Whenever they become sleepy during the Bible lesson, they take a pluck of grass and dip it in water to wipe the sleepiness from their eyes. Later he discovered that they have a more rigorous method to stay awake. When sleep threatens to overwhelm them, the boys pull out their own eyelashes to stay awake.

Aside from the support of the Bible School students, Kuijt seeks to acquire more evangelists from other mission societies. The need is great! There even appears to be a sort of rivalry among the various villages of the Nipsan region to be the first to receive an evangelist. On June 10, 1980, Kuijt reports that thirteen evangelists have commenced work in Nipsan villages.

In spite of the need for more evangelists in the area of Nipsan, Rev. Kuijt still longs to reach out to the more remote villages. In March of 1979 he had scouted the Bo-Valley to the south east of Nipsan from the air. UFM wants to start in this area as well. Thankfully this problem can be solved. Kuijt had already been in this area during their first stay in Nipsan and had built a small shelter there. Three months later Kuijt records that four evangelists are sent to the Bo-Valley.

Two months later Kuijt arranges a flight by heli over the region north of Nipsan. Later on a discussion ensues with the ECK and UFM missions to establish borders. This does not mean that the area has been opened or a mission station has been established. Kuijt, Sabonwarek and a Selekahek man step out of the helicopter near a village. The heli leaves again to pick up the second group of men and materials so that they can start to build a helicopter pad.

Rev. Kuijt and his helpers looks around. Nearby is a hut. Kuijt peeks inside and sees the face of a terrified woman holding her child. Farther away they spot a few men watching them curiously.

> *It took a considerable time before we were approached by anybody. This was not a good sign. Suddenly Sabonwarek called, "Pendeta, look out! They want war!" And there they came, a row of warriors leaning forward with their bows and arrows ready to attack. What went through my mind in those short moments cannot be expressed. I truly thought eternity was upon me. I had not choice but to make withdrawing motions. No advice can prepare you for such a situation and supernatural wisdom is necessary to handle these critical moments.*
>
> *In the meantime more warriors joined the band. Thank God the Selekahek man had volunteered to come with us. All he could do was scream at the warriors to stop them from attacking. I also heard Sabonwarek yell: "Chang, Chang, Chang" which means: "not allowed." I repeated his cries and it seemed that each time we said the words, the arrows and bows went down a little more. We had no more room left to back away and if the Lord did not do a miracle, we would not survive.*
>
> *But at the last moment deliverance came. An old man approached us with some bananas in his hand. He placed them on the ground where the helicopter had dug up some roots while landing. He hollered to the warriors and then the bows and arrows were immediately put down. What a relief!*

Kuijt advises the heli pilot, which was to deliver the second group of men and materials, to turn around and go back immediately. In a short time it returns again at top speed. Kuijt is convinced that the aviation talents of the helicopter pilot have made a lasting impression on the natives. Quickly Kuijt and the two men step into the heli after promising to drop off some axes as a gift. This is done later on that day. But when they watch from the air, they notice that the natives do not go and pick the axes up. They decide to make another landing and personally hand over other axes. They are barely landed, when an old man walks toward them. Kuijt presents him with an axe.

Later they learn that the tribe is defiant and unwilling to allow the white people in because of an earlier occurrence in Nipsan where strangers had come and taken their pigs. Gradually a feeling of trust develops and Nipsan-north also becomes a field where the seed may be sown.

Christmas Day, 1979. Rev. Kuijt stands in the pulpit of the newly constructed church in Nipsan. The building is filled, and around the outside there are more listeners squatting against the walls. Approximately one thousand people have come together from far and wide to hear the Christmas message this day. The missionary's mind flashes back to one year earlier, when there was no interest in listening to the Word.

The newly constructed Church

Memories lead his thoughts even further back to the destruction of the station and the death of Herman Imbab and the evangelists.

He would have gladly named this new church in memory of Herman Imbab but the MB rejects that suggestion because it reflects the idea of honoring man. Rev. Kuijt agrees but he sincerely hopes the Nipsan people will always remember this martyr.

At the beginning of his time in New Guinea, he did not have any reason to hope for this because there was no indication of remorse with the locals. Thankfully that has also changed over the past year although a sincere turning to Christianity is still far from reality. The locals still use every possible opportunity to have a good time with their dances as the missionary notices when he returns from a visit to Langda only a few days before. These are authentic pagan festive dances. Even one of the Bible school students participated in the dance.

This is what compels Rev. Kuijt to lead this flock on and with enthusiasm and love he proclaims the Christmas message. The Nipsan people will know that a Light has shone in the midst of darkness.

Chapter 15

Phasing out...

"God, our heavenly Father, Who has called you to His holy ministry, enlighten you by His Holy Spirit, strengthen you by His hand, and so govern you in your ministry that you may decently and fruitfully walk therein, to the glory of His Name and the spreading of the kingdom of His Son Jesus Christ. Amen."

The hands of Rev. Kuijt rest on the heads of the two men, Yen Kombo and Thomas Wandik, who are kneeling before him at the front of the big church in Pass Valley. It is January 27, 1982, and Yen and Thomas are being ordained as 'gembalas' or shepherds of the Gospel in Pass Valley.

Rev. Kuijt blessing the two new gembalas, Yen and Thomas

In a few weeks it will be twenty years since Missionary Kuijt was sent out to New Guinea by the church of Rotterdam. Pass Valley was then still unaware of his coming and living in their animism (spirit world). Oh sure, Rev. Kuijt remembers particular instances of animosity and resistance by the Yalis. But when he looks back, he is filled with gratitude and marvels at the loving care of his heavenly Father who has once again confirmed that pagans also will acknowledge His salvation. What a blessing that here, in Pass Valley, a church was permitted to emerge over time so that now the white missionaries can take a step back.

It takes some doing before Yen and Thomas can be ordained to the office of pastor. The first step on the road to independence was taken by the GJPI churches in Irian on December 1978, when consistories were installed in seven congregations. The elders, who took a four-year Bible School program taught by Rev. Vreugdenhil, are now in charge of overseeing the churches. Although the missionaries must provide the new consistories with the necessary guidance—even conducting an orderly consistory meeting is already a challenge—a great deal of work is being taken out of their hands.

But almost immediately the national church wants office bearers to have the authority to administer sacraments. Just as every young person desires to stand on their own two feet without rejecting their parents, so there is a longing for independence in this young church as well.

Through contacts with the Indonesian government it became apparent that they would also like to have their own people assume responsibility for the indigenous churches.

It is impossible for Kuijt and Vreugdenhil to carry out the church sacraments, baptisms and the Lord's Supper at least four times per year at all the different church locations. "Something has to be done."

The office bearers who have been ordained as elders or deacons faithfully carry out the work associated with their offices. There are also those who can provide leadership to the consistories. But to ordain them as pastors is quite a step. Given that most of them are already about thirty years old, which is considered middle age in Irian Jaya, the lack of education of these men is an important consideration. Most "middle-aged" men wouldn't pursue a university education to become a pastor, as is required in the other Protestant churches in Indonesia.

Students following a four-year Bible School program.
In the back is Rev. Vreugdenhil

From the students who complete their four-year study program with Rev. Vreugdenhil in 1978, a small group is selected to continue their theological training at the intermediate level. These are men who not only have the mental capability to follow this program but who have also demonstrated their faithfulness and love for the Lord.

For three years Vreugdenhil instructs them in the knowledge and interpretation of the Old and New Testaments as well as the Reformed doctrine, church policy, and church history.

Kuijt definitely finds it important that the students be taught to interpret the Scriptures. "Personally I would love to see them grounded in the Word of God," he writes to the MB at the start of 1980. Time and time again he must conclude that office bearers and students have only limited knowledge of the Bible. He has questions about instructing them on the basis of the Dutch confession statements. Does it make sense to transplant these statements? He asks the MB in a letter:

> *The native people of Irian are not well served by a church that carries a "white stamp." For example, let the Belgic Confession of Faith be what it is, namely a Belgic confession and definitely not an Indonesian confession. You would not wish to apply article 36 as it now stands in Indonesia, would you?*

He warns them against literally transplanting doctrines from our culture to theirs. Oh, he acknowledges the value of the Confession Statements. But in a letter he warns not to ascribe too much authority to the confession.

> *Let us not turn these statements into demigods and definitely not into idols. God's people are not recognized in confessions or liturgies as such, for they can leave us stone-cold, but in being led by the Holy Spirit. This is the glorious Spirit of Pentecost, Who now dwells in the hearts of God's children.*

Rev. Kuijt further writes to the MB:

> *We would make our Reformed forefathers happy to see that in the virgin mission territories we link back to the power of the Spirit of Pentecost as experienced by the first church of the New Testament. This power of Pentecost caused the first church to continue steadfastly in the apostles' doctrine and fellowship, and in breaking of bread, and in prayers. This is something our people in Irian can understand.*

The Scripture knows of no Classis, Provincial Synod or General Synod. Scripture only speaks of local churches and if necessary meetings to resolve differences that have arisen. Confessions and forms have torn God's people apart because everyone has their own interpretation. Kuijt would like to draw the borders more generously. On the mission field he has worked together with colleagues of various denominations.

> *I personally feel at home with all those in whom the Spirit dwells, no matter what church this person may belong to, even if they call themselves Remonstrant.*

Despite his hesitation to tie the young church down to a strong connection with the Three Forms of Unity to which the Dutch churches of the Reformation adhere to, Rev. Kuijt definitely appreciates the instruction given by his colleague. He knows that his call is in reaching the unreached and in bringing them the Gospel. He rejoices when the students complete their three-year program. But now what?

In letters to the MB, the possibility has been raised to ordain these graduates as ministers of the Word and sacrament. It takes time before the MB agrees. They have quite a few questions. Do these men have a sufficient level of knowledge after completing their intermediate theological training? Is their knowledge comparable with candidates who have followed the four-year program at the Theological School in Rotterdam and who also undergo an examination concerning their state of grace and calling prior to acceptance into the Theological School? Has such an examination taken place in Irian? They realize the urgent need for more pastors but want to ensure that the pastors are equipped to minister the Word.

Following protracted correspondence between the MB and the missionaries, in consultation with representatives of *the church of Irian,* they came to a joint agreement. The students will be ordained as *gembala* or shepherd. A gembala performs the same work as a minister but unlike a *pendeta,* has not received a university education. A gembala is authorized to preach the Word and administer the sacraments. With the ordination of these men to office, another important step will have been taken towards making the church of Irian independent.

Before the students can call themselves candidates for the holy office, they must first complete the necessary examinations. Prior to this a committee examined each student with respect to his state of grace and calling to the ministry. The national church appointed three elders who will sit on this committee: Winigama Kepno, Amos Wasahe and Aderiaan Loho. Rev. P. Honkoop and Dr. Professor Moens came to represent the MB. Due to the weather, Kuijt is not able to be present but is there on the second day.

The committee examined Thomas Wandik, Sabonwarek Wandik, Enos Wandik, Onggawarlog Yare, Yen Kombo, Habel Mabel, and Yohannes Kombo. With varying degrees of confidence, they are all accepted. Yohannes Kombo is admitted to the Theological School of the ECK in Abepura.

Following the oral examinations each of the students preached a trial sermon. Rev. Kuijt wrote in his report to MB:

> *It was a long session, six sermons in a row. But we did not get tired of it. These were moving, Biblical and good Reformed sermons, although we noticed a difference in talent.*

Each of the candidates received a call from one of the congregations. When the missionaries tell them that a candidate in the Netherlands can receive as many as ten calls the future gembalas are surprised. This is incredible and is hard to understand. "Does not the Lord call you to only one place at a time?" Sabonwarek asks Rev. Kuijt. The six men accept their calls.

Rev. Kuijt and Rev. Vreugdenhil agree that they will share the ordination of the new pastors equally. Yen Kombo and Thomas Wandik are the first to be ordained. On January 26, 1982 the day preceding the ordination service team members and representatives from the various mission stations are flown into Pass Valley. Reverend H. Paul and Doctorandus G. Nieuwenhuis arrived to represent the MB. Rev. Vreugdenhil's mother and his brother-in-law also made the long flight for this occasion, as well as Rev. Mijnders, Messrs. J.L. van den Heuvel and Rijnhout. Some Yalis walked for hours to attend this special service!

Newly installed gembalas with some of the foreign guests.
L/R Enos Wandik, Thomas Wandik, Rev. C. G. Vreughdenhil, Yen Kombo,
Rev. J. Mijnders, Onggawaralog Yare, Rev. G. Kuijt, Habel Mabel,
Rev. H. Paul and Sabonwarek Wandik.

Rev. Kuijt speaks this morning from Matthew 3:1-12 about the preaching of John the Baptist. The theme of the sermon is: The duties of the Minister of the Word. Kuijt points the new gembalas to their momentous but beautiful task of proclaiming the Gospel and being a shepherd to their flock. The people listen attentively.

Following the Form for Ordination, both candidates answer clearly:

"Yes, truly with all my heart" to the questions that are asked. Subsequently they receive the laying on of hands six times in a row, while a different verse of Scripture is read out each time. Seven elders of the local churches participate, including Elder H. Looijen, from the parish of Ulunikma and from The Netherlands; Elder A. Polder from Veenendaal; Pastors Mijnders, Paul, and Vreugdenhil from Landikma. To everyone's surprise, Rev. Paul recites from memory the text of Hebrews 13:8 in the Yali language as he places his hand on the head of Thomas Wandik.

Following the ordination ceremony Rev. Paul welcomes the young pastors on behalf of the MB and the churches in the Netherlands.

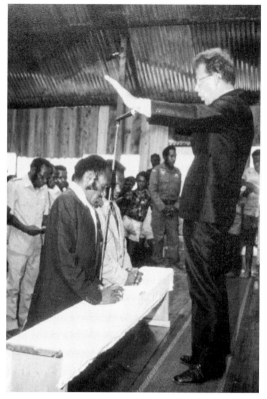

Rev. Kuijt gives a blessing for two gembalas

Later that same day, the two gembalas give their first sermon. Rev. Yen Kombo preaches about the text: "Behold I lay in Zion a chief cornerstone, elect, precious, and he that believeth on Him shall not be confounded." (1 Peter 2:6)

Next is Rev. Thomas Wandik's turn; his text is: "Being confident of this very thing, that He which has begun a good work in you will perform it until the day of Jesus Christ." (Philippians 1:6) At the conclusion of the service, Thomas pronounces the benediction over the assembly. For the first time the missionaries and guests receive the blessing from an indigenous minister. The Lord has done great things among them.

Four days later Rev. Vreugdenhil ordains three candidates: Enos Wandik, Sabonwarek Wandik, and Onggawarlog Yare. During the ordination Vreugdenhil needs an extra hand so that all three of them can be blessed simultaneously. With Kuijt's assistance the three men receive the blessing.

Kuijt is particularly touched by the fact that Sabonwarek is kneeing right in front of him. What a bond he feels with this brother! Sabonwarek, who came along with him in 1971 to open the post in Nipsan; who three years later was spared in the massacre of the workers; and in 1978 was among the first to return to Nipsan faithfully aiding Rev. Kuijt with the rebuilding and reopening of that station. Despite everything that he has experienced there, Sabonwarek has a strong bond with Nipsan, He feels sheltered under the shadow of the Almighty. This is also what he told the examination committee. When MB member Prof. Moens asked him whether he had ever been in danger, Sabonwarek answered, "No, actually, never. I am always in God's hand. They can kill my body but not my soul, which will then go to heaven. This temporary life we have will one day have to be laid down, and whether that is tomorrow or ten years from now ultimately makes no difference. I am not afraid. I am ready and therefore am never in danger."

Kuijt knows that Sabonwarek would like to stay in Nipsan to evangelize among these people until the day of his death. He has chosen Acts 1:8 as the text to pass along to his ever faithful companion: "But ye shall receive power, after that the Holy Ghost is come upon you: and ye shall be witnesses unto me both in Jerusalem, and in all Judea, and in the uttermost part of the Earth."

Following a short break, Enos Wandik is inducted separately. He preaches on 1 John 1:5: "This then is the message which we have heard of Him, and declare unto you, that God is light, and in Him is no darkness at all." Following the induction, Rev. Mijnders addresses the young gembalas on behalf of the churches in the Netherlands. Onggawarlog will preach his inaugural sermon in Bomela and Sabonwarek in Nipsan.

On Sunday February 7, 1982, Sabonwarek is introduced to the work in Nipsan. Kuijt writes in his report to the MB about this:

We had a large assembly with many of the people from the valley here. I installed Sabonwarek in his ministry and chose the following words from the Scripture: 1 Thessalonians 1: 9, where it says that the Thessalonians were converted from idolatry to serve God. A burning of idols had taken place here the day before. The Thessalonians had been converted to serve the living and true God and to await the return of his Son from heaven. May the Lord use Sabonwarek so that many will turn their backs to their idols. The burning of idols, although a good thing is not enough for eternal salvation. Conversion to God is necessary, wrought by the Holy Spirit. Then a longing is born for the coming of Christ and His Kingdom.

The installation service of the gembalas performed by Rev. Kuijt

That afternoon, Sabonwarek preaches his first sermon from Acts 10:1-16. He reads from the Indonesian Bible and preaches in the Nipsan language, after which he speaks in the Dani language. It is indeed convenient if you know different languages of the interior!

In an edifying sermon, Sabonwarek explained to those in attendance how Peter was persuaded by the Lord Himself to go to the home of a gentile, that he otherwise would have never done. Peter understood by the vision he received that he was not to despise non-Jews(gentiles). The great miracle took place while Peter was speaking to the people who had gathered around Cornelius. The Lord poured out His Spirit on those assembled there. The Jews who accompanied Peter were astonished.

"Just as in earlier times, now also the Lord wishes to give His Spirit to the gentiles, when we are united in the Name of the Lord and pray to Him as Cornelius did. The Lord noticed these prayers from heaven. The Lord observed that Cornelius prayed a great deal and gave a many alms to the poor. We also must ask the Lord for His Spirit. When the Nipsanners come to hear the Word of God and pray, the Lord will also grant His Spirit to them. If we only pray to Him with our mouths and in our hearts still hold onto idols, then the Lord will not give us His Spirit."

While speaking to the Danis, Sabonwarek stresses the following: the Lord wants us to serve Him in spiritual unity as evangelists and workers. Just as a hen gathers her chicks, Cornelius gathered his family and friends around him and the Lord blessed this. "The Lord does not want us to live in disharmony. Only when we await the Lord in fellowship with one another, will He gather us to Himself when He comes again. If we cannot live with each other now, how then will it be possible when we are with the Lord?" After singing Psalm 119:3 Yonas, one of our evangelists, closed with thanksgiving.

A few weeks later Rev. Kuijt, as moderator of Bomela, installed Gembala Onggawarlog in his ministry there. Several months later in June he inducts Habel Mabel in Langda. The reason for this delay is that Jan and Janny Louwerse who have worked for years in Langda, are on furlough at the time and want to be there for this special event.

The addition of the six gembalas considerably lightens the workload of Rev. Kuijt and Vreugdenhil. The care for the various churches can now be divided among eight pastors. But the concerns are no less especially in conjunction to the continuing strong pull of paganism.

This is definitely the case in Nipsan where, on February 6, 1982, a fetish burning takes place. War vests, skulls, stones in all sorts of sizes and shapes, shells and pig's fat are all thrown into the flames. Kuijt even recognizes a shriveled arm and hand in the fire. This is indeed an important step but Rev. Kuijt also knows that idolatry is not yet sworn off. "It is easy to make new idols," he writes to the MB.

Getting ready to burn the fetishes (idols). Note the human skull in the centre.

Burning the fetishes

More than once he expresses concern in his letters about the lack of conversion on the part of the Nipsan people. Especially sin against the seventh commandment seems impossible to wipe out. "The one case follows the other, with all the regrettable consequences." Even one of his most trusted helpers has committed adultery with a teacher. It depresses Kuijt. He recalls that Rev. Bentz commented at his farewell as a missionary from Irian: "Gerrit, I still have to meet the first converted Papua." Deep down Kuijt knows that this is not true, but right now he is not very optimistic.

On top of this he learns that the older churches in places like Abenaho and Landikma also struggle with apostasy. A few weeks after being ordained as gembala, Enos Wandik writes to Kuijt that he administered the Lord's Supper in three churches of Pass Valley but came to a sad conclusion. "Of the people here, I believe, only a small portion belongs to the true church. Many have returned to the old customs. They want to have a second wife and desire to take part in pagan traditions. Many give lip service as Christians."

What Wandik said becomes apparent a short time later. Large numbers of people trek to the sacrificial festivals in the Ilugwa and the Baliem. Despite being given warnings, the people still go there. A meeting attended by Rev. Kuijt is organized in Landikma to discuss disciplinary measures. Henk Looijen has a list of Abenaho people who frequently attend the festivals of sacrifice. Enos Wandik has a list of Landikma people who do the same.

> *We may indeed say: "Except the Lord Sabaoth had left us a small remnant, we should have been as Sodom and we should have been like Gomorrah (Isaiah 1:9; Romans 9:29)." There are entire kampongs where not a single person remains true to the Lord: chairmen of consistories, elders and deacons and members joined in. Those who did attend the rituals, brought meat back for those who stayed behind.*

After June 1984, official Synod meetings were held with the newly independent churches. J. Lock, Rev. Kuijt and Marry van Moolenbroek acted as advisors.

252

The Lord's Supper, which had seen hundreds of people attending now sadly, had only twenty-five participants, according to Hermien Tuinier and fifteen according to Enos Wandik. This is not bad as long as the people's conscience is still working but it is a sign of deep decline! I encounter little repentance and sorrow for their sins. The church had to speak out and the sinners had to be placed under censure. The sad reality is that most of those who were present at the meeting had to place themselves under ecclesiastical censure. When, following the meeting, Enos asked me when the documents for the establishment of the indigenous church had to be submitted, several thoughts went through me. Was there still a church? Is the church not the gathering of true believers in Christ i.e., those who daily experience the corruption of the flesh but still fight the good fight of faith?

Two and a half years later this milestone is indeed reached: The Gereja Jemaat Protestan di Irian Jaya, originating from the NRC mission work, becomes independent on June 25, 1984.

The work on the mission field demands a great deal from Kuijt and his family. They are concerned about the spiritual well-being of the Nipsanners but they also do what they can to improve their physical well-being. Rev. Kuijt has knowledge about medications and other medical procedures—administering injections, delivery of babies, suture wounds, pulling teeth, etc. It is true that since 1980 he has the assistance of two indigenous nursing practitioners but for the more complicated medical problems most people still come to "Doctor" Kuijt.

Mrs. Kuijt is also busy every day, caring for the people and part of the work at the station. Over the years she has acquired quite a bit of experience in diagnosing ailments and prescribing medications. She also devotes time to the care of infants, bottle feeding motherless babies at regular times in her home. She feeds malnourished adults and children. The life of a missionary's wife is demanding and at times overwhelming. She also assists her husband in whatever way she can. Both of them have to cope with the tensions that come with working in isolated areas.

Loneliness especially gnaws from time to time. Although they know that the Lord is always nearby, Kuijt and his wife experience the pain of being separated from their loved ones.

*Mother Bos and Oeni
visiting a village*

*Mother Bos makes herself at
home, especially with the
Nipsanners*

Mother Bos made this little dress

Here is the little girl wearing it

Most difficult for Mrs. Kuijt is that, for the greatest part of the year, she is separated from her children. From the age of six years old they must go to a school on the coast of Irian. In 1982 the youngest daughter, Cornelia, leaves for school as well and it becomes very quiet in the Nipsan parsonage. Mrs. Kuijt misses her five loved ones. She carries them with her in her heart and thoughts. How are they managing? When possible, they visit the younger children, Wilhelmina and Cornelia every six weeks. The older three, Klazina, Wim, and Gert, see their parents only twice a year. They attend Faith Academy, a school for missionary children in Manila, the Philippines.

Wim (in front with the pilot, so not seen here) Gert and Wilhelmina are off to school. Saying goodbye becomes more difficult each time.

The Kuijt's not only miss their children but also have moments where they wonder how their remaining parents are doing. Father Bos passed away in 1979 and Father Kuijt in the summer of 1981. They would gladly be able to peek around a corner once in a while and see them. They are very happy, when in the spring of 1981 Mother Bos spends four months with them in Nipsan. She enjoys her stay very much. In his report to the MB, Kuijt writes,

> *Mother makes herself very useful in many ways for us as well as the local people. Her hands are never idle and many pairs of pants, shorts and shirts from the people have been mended and have acquired a new look.*

For many years Mrs. Kuijt received the strength to stand by the side of her husband in everything. And when necessary she took over completely. When in the end of 1978 Kuijt departs for the reopening of Nipsan, his wife takes over the full care of the Bomela station. It is during those months that the children are home. Looking after the responsibilities of a mission station as well as her family is a heavy task but she did not complain. It needed to be done. Are not all of our labors for the extension of God's Kingdom?

After a few months, Mrs. Kuijt is relieved that nurse Marry Van Moolenbroek takes over the work at Bomela and she can now rejoin her husband at Nipsan but, deep in her heart, she feels she has reached the end of her endurance.

The work in Nipsan is not easy. The population remains reserved for a long time. Their attitude really bothers her. To some extent the people are willing to listen to her husband but to a woman, a white woman? No, that is below their dignity.

When they lived in Pass Valley, if Mrs. Kuijt took a shovel to do some work immediately someone would take over the task. Here in Nipsan if something needs to be done the men will tell her to do it herself. Ah, this is just a small matter that can be ignored. But there are other factors impacting her life which finally cause her to say to her husband, "Gerrit, I cannot keep this up." "Come on, Miep; persevere. The Nipsan people will change," was his reply.

Mrs. Kuijt wants to continue on, but in the end the whole situation becomes too much for her. In the spring of 1983, concerns about her health escalate. She is in bed with a high fever, suffers from continual headaches and complains about a sense of paralysis in her arms and legs. Miep's doctors tell her that she is physically and psychologically exhausted. It is definitely a case of burnout. They advise the couple to leave the country for an extended period of time to help her recover.

Kuijt decides to follow the doctors' recommendation to do what is best for his wife and go to the Netherlands as soon as possible. The MB still tries to persuade Kuijt by cable that while they agree to have his wife and the children go home, Kuijt must remain in Nipsan until someone can take over. This is unacceptable to Kuijt. For all these years his wife has totally given herself for the mission work and now that she is exhausted he wants to give her all his support. "This time, Miep takes priority!" he writes to the MB. Dr. Sengkerij who works in Angguruk urges the couple to leave and writes in a letter that Kuijt has to go with his wife.

The specialists of the AMC also come to the conclusion that Mrs. Kuijt is exhausted and also prescribe an extended period of rest for her.

In October 1983, the Kuijt family departs for Kandern in South Germany. In a nearby town there is the Black Forest Academy, an International Christian school for missionary children, where the two youngest children can be enrolled. In the second year of their stay Mrs. Kuijt gets counselling from Dr. Walter M. Stuart, a psychologist, who is connected to the BFA and is also their pastor and counsellor.

Rev. Kuijt stays with his family. From time to time he visits Holland for speaking engagements but for the rest of his time he is in Kandern. It grieves him that in the Netherlands there is little or no understanding for the situation in his family.

Mrs. Kuijt's recovery is much slower than the doctors had initially expected. She remains in Germany for more than a year and a half. In April 1985, the physicians determine that she has recovered sufficiently to be able to return to Irian but she should not go back into the interior. Pastor Walter believes this will be too much for her and recommends that she stays on the coast. At the end of August, 1985 Rev. Kuijt and his family return to Irian. Their tentative plan is that they will live on the coast in the small village of Sentani for one year. There Rev. Kuijt will maintain contact with the various organizations on behalf of the mission team, purchase goods for the various stations in the interior and most of all provide guidance to students who have come from the interior to Wamena for further education. When missionaries go on furlough, Kuijt can take over the station for them.

Rev. Kuijt would have gladly received the mandate to carry out evangelism in Sentani. However, the MB is afraid that this would be too much of a workload especially since there would be too few possibilities for follow-up. But Missionary Kuijt would not be a missionary if he did not grab every opportunity to pass on the Word to all those who are ignorant of it. The minute he steps into a taxi, sits in a waiting room or walks into a store, he seeks to point out to his fellowmen the necessity of knowing the one Name necessary for salvation. Once while taking a taxi, the children tried to get their father to sit in the back seat but, before they realize it, he again sat beside the driver in order to start a conversation with him and to point him to the one thing that is necessary—salvation!

Rev. and Mrs. Kuijt visiting friends in Germany

Celebrating a graduation.
L/R: Gert, Klazina, Wilhelmina, Mrs. Kuijt, Oeni, Rev. Kuijt, and
Wim are in front of the Newman Memorial Chapel.
Part of the church can be seen on the right hand side.

Almost immediately upon arrival in Sentani, one of Rev. Kuijt's acquaintances asks whether he would be willing to do some work among the migrant workers on an island in Lake Sentani. Kuijt gladly accepts. "At your request this will not be work of the NRC, and yet it will be work in God's Kingdom," he writes to the MB. He also does similar work in Dosay, a town west of Sentani.

There is no church of their denomination in Sentani. The Kuijt family worships at the Newman Memorial Chapel, an independent English-speaking church, where people of various nationalities and denominations are welcome as long as they unconditionally accept Scripture as the Word of God. Kuijt is regularly asked to preach. He does so freely and even speaks here about the Heidelberg Catechism. As long as he can bring the Word without constraint, he is not bothered by the name plate at the entrance of a church or the views of the people in the pews.

This does not mean that Rev. Kuijt is less involved in the NRC mission work but it is different. At this time the most easterly located mission stations in the Una region are evangelizing the southern lowlands. For this reason Kuijt, from his base in Sentani is still fully involved with the construction of small air-strips in Seradcla, Samboka, and Awimbon, as well as evangelizing. He notices that the work has entered a new phase and that in many respects the *Gereja Jemaat Protestan di Irian Jaya* (GJPI) takes its own initiatives. The young mission church has itself become a missionary church. Kuijt still guides the young pioneer church workers on a regular basis.

Boarding school in Wamena named after Pendeta *(Reverend) G. Kuijt*

There are quite a few young people from the interior who study in Wamena in the Baliem Valley and on the coast. Rev. Kuijt receives the assignment to carry out pastoral work among them and to arrange church services with them. In the beginning it does not work out too well. The young people enjoy their freedom. When he conducts a service, the attendance is meager. In their spare time they prefer to go into the city. And why not! Who pays attention to them? Tribal control is gone.

A number of years earlier a boarding school for boys was built in Wamena. Nearly one hundred students from the interior live here. The dorm is named: *"Asrama Pendeta G. Kuijt."* Rev Kuijt makes efforts to establish a similar facility on the coast.

Finally in 1989, after many months of difficult negotiations concerning a piece of land on the coast, a boarding school is opened complete with a simple auditorium which can also serve as a church hall. Kuijt makes every effort to bring all of the GJPI students on the coast together on Sundays. Gradually this evolves into the church of Abepura, one of the largest congregations of the GJPI with its own minister and an impressive brick church building. Rev. Kuijt again shows his pioneer spirit. From time to time he visits the large camps of migrant workers and their families along the coast where thousands of Javanese have settled.

Coastal students seeking Rev. Kuijt's advice

The Sentani shopkeeper Wimpie, a Chinese with a Buddhist background, is regularly visited and has lengthy discussions with Pendeta Belanda. One day when Kuijt gave a fellow missionary a ride in the mission van, he left the main road. "Where are you taking me now, Gerrit?" "Oh, I just need to stop off at this mission post. There is a priest with a great deal of interest in mysticism." While saying so, he took a book from the dashboard by Geesje Pamans. "I do not think it would harm him to read this book." This is the real Kuijt!

Rev. Kuijt writes the following in a letter to the MB in August, 1988:

My health is a cause for real concern. According to Miep my back has shortened by another two centimeters. It does sound somewhat unbelievable! As long as the inward man may be renewed from day to day, (although I have some concerns along these lines as well) then the exterior is of less importance. Like it says in 2 Corinthians Chapter 5 verse 4b "I long to be clothed rather than unclothed, with an eye of faith on the coming of Christ." Paul also had this longing, still having to pass through the Jordan of death.

This is not the first time that Kuijt has mentioned problems with his health to the brothers in the Netherlands. In the summer of 1986 he was treated in the Netherlands for back pain. However, it helped very little, and upon his return to Irian the pain increases. A few months later, specialists in Irian examine him again as the pain is really hindering his activities. "There is nothing we can do, Pastor," is their conclusion. They carefully suggested that he seeks lighter work in a place with a milder climate. "This definitely would benefit your overall health."

However, Kuijt is not yet ready to make this quantum step. He does feel though that the time has come for him to slowly but surely withdraw from the work; not only as his own health declines but also the health of his wife. In the fall of 1987 she has four malaria attacks within a period of four months, plus a viral infection, which takes her a long time to recover. She is constantly tired and as a result she feels disheartened.

What should they do? Kuijt and his wife talk about this predicament. They would love to remain on the mission field with the Papuans, the people who are so dear to them and with whom they have such a strong bond. But they know that the time is approaching that they will have to bid farewell to the people and the work. Both of them feel that their health is deteriorating.

But physical discomfort is not the only consideration in deciding to move on. Their concern for their children also plays a role. At this time Klazina is working in the USA and Wim is studying in the USA, while Gert has been in the Netherlands since 1988. Their two younger daughters, Wilhelmina and Cornelia, still attend Junior High school in Irian but, before long, decisions about their future education will have to be made. It would be nice if the family could spend a few years together. The missionary and his wife contemplate settling in the United States or Canada.

Indonesian Citizenship for Gerrit Kuijt —a rare honour!

In the early spring of 1989, two physicians in Irian, Vriend and Sengkerij, come to the conclusion that Rev. Kuijt needs to be examined again by specialists in the Netherlands. A trip to the Netherlands, via America, is planned for the couple for the end of May. While they are boarding the plane Rev. Kuijt feels himself becoming unwell. "I felt confronted with death," Kuijt writes a day later to the MB. A physician examines him but cannot find anything and prescribed a few weeks of rest.

The physicians in the Netherlands quickly come to the conclusion that Rev. Kuijt's back is worn out to such an extent that he can no longer perform his duties. The examining physician declares him to be sixty percent disabled. "To serve a congregation on a part-time basis is still feasible, but work on the mission field is too labor intensive."

The MB offers him full emeritus status, with the mission covering his pension until he reaches the age of 65. At that time he will be supported by the retirement fund. Rev. Kuijt accepts this offer. He formally becomes an emeritus minister in 1991 but prior to that time he must say goodbye to 'his people' in Irian. At various mission posts, gatherings are arranged and the devotion of the people to this couple is clearly demonstrated.

> *The farewell is at times difficult, but I leave the churches behind with a confident heart. Has not Christ Himself engraved the names of His children in the palms of both of His hands? There they will be safe.*

Saying farewell - Engama, Kokpan's father

The NRC missionaries also say their farewell to the Kuijt couple. Beside the many speeches and blessings there is also a little entertainment. A dialogue is written by Bart and Kees. They speak about Missionary Gerrit Kuijt, but keep asking themselves whether they are really speaking about the same Gerrit. Many aspects from the life of the missionary are placed in the spotlight, but finally Bart and Kees come to the conclusion that they are indeed speaking of the same person:

Bart: It is still a puzzle to me, my friend, whether we are really speaking of the same Gerrit.

Kees: Well, let's give it one more try! My Gerrit is a very bold man.

Bart: So is mine.

Kees: My Gerrit is very jovial with people.

Bart: So is mine!

Kees: My Gerrit has friends all over the world.

Bart: So does mine, but besides, here and there he also has a few …

Kees: My Gerrit sometimes finds it very difficult to say 'no'.

Bart: Mine too, but when he does, then …

Kees: Bart, I think this discussion has brought us closer together. I truly believe that your Gerrit and mine are one and the same person.

Bart: Yes, my friend, my initial doubt was removed towards the end of our conversation.

Kees: But let us then conclude that we are talking about a very multifaceted human being.

Bart: A special human being.

Kees: A broadly oriented human being, Bart.

Bart: An ecumenical human being, Kees.

Kees: Above all a Reformed human being, Bart.

Bart: But also an Evangelical human being, Kees.

Kees: Also a frugal human being, Bart,

Bart: But also a generous man, Kees.

Kees: Not a disagreeable man, Bart.

Bart: But neither a yes-man, Kees.

Kees: A human being with a broad perspective, Bart.

Bart: Indeed, not narrow-minded at all, Kees.

Kees: A remarkable man, Bart.

Bart: That he is.

Kees: Yes, that's our Gerrit.

The American helicopter pilot Mike Meeuwse and his family also say their goodbyes at the same time as the Kuijt family.

Goodbye

Chapter 16

Once a Missionary, Always a Missionary

"Miep, I cannot stop thinking about the enormous spiritual need of people. I feel like a bird in a gilded cage. I cannot remain idle knowing that so many people do not know the way of salvation."

Kuijt may be retired, but the needs of many nations weigh heavily on him. "I know it is my calling to proclaim the Gospel," he reminds his wife and children. Reading, and visiting family and friends can be very pleasant, but to him nothing compares to conveying the way of life. Wherever an opportunity arises to speak of his King, he will not remain silent.

Rev. and Mrs. Kuijt had agreed that upon retirement they would remain on the mission field. However, when the time came, this was no longer an option. But where would they go? Should they return to the Netherlands to be close to Mother Bos, relatives and friends? That has its appeal but would the children feel at home there? They have spent their childhood in Irian. At the age of fourteen the three older ones attended Faith Academy, a Christian International school in the Philippines with an American Curriculum and operated by American missionaries. By returning to the Netherlands, the younger children would have to learn Dutch. That would be quite a sacrifice on their part.

For the older children the situation is different: Klazina completed her training as a physiotherapist in the Netherlands and is working in the USA. Wim is studying aeronautical engineering in the United States and Gert is studying medicine at the Erasmus University in Rotterdam.

For the sake of the two younger ones, who have not yet determined the direction they will go, the Kuijts eventually decide to settle in Chilliwack, British Columbia, Canada. There is an NRC church with its own school and as Kuijt points out, "Miep, it is located between Irian and the Netherlands."

The Kuijt family together in Los Angeles, in front of the home of Elder Van der Weyde, who always warmly received the Kuijt family.
L/R Wilhelmina, Gert, Mrs. Kuijt, Oeni, Wim, Rev. Kuijt and Klazina

The NRC of Chilliwack is relatively young. It was founded in1952 by immigrants from the Netherlands. By 1990 there are nearly one thousand members. Just before Kuijt informs the MB that they wish to move to Chilliwack, Rev. A. W. Verhoef, an aging pastor, accepts a call to Beekbergen in the Netherlands thereby leaving the church vacant.

The news that Rev. Kuijt wishes to move to Canada rapidly reaches the consistory in Chilliwack. They are eager to have Kuijt as a part-time pastor. He can hold services and perform various ministerial duties. They advise Kuijt by telephone that he definitely is very welcome.

Rev. Kuijt is pleased with the friendly invitation from the brothers in Chilliwack. He does not have to worry about being without work when he retires. When he meets with the MB on August 3, 1989, he enthusiastically talks about this contact with Chilliwack. They leave the decision up to him. If he chooses to retire now, the MB will support the former missionary until he turns 65. Thereafter the pension fund will provide his support. If, however, Rev. Kuijt prefers to pastor a small congregation, the MB will top up his salary.

Kuijt's initial reaction is to reject any pension. "I will serve the Chilliwack congregation with all the strength that I still have and they will

267

look after my needs. Only when I am no longer able to work will I call upon the pension fund." The president of the MB, Rev. D. Hakkenberg, attempts to temper Kuijt's fiery spirit in a fatherly fashion, "Dear brother Kuijt that would not be wise. Chilliwack is a large congregation and you have already given your life's strength to the mission work. The care of such a large church will be too much for you. Let Chilliwack know that you intend to settle down among them as a retired missionary pastor. They will ask you to preach for them. They are bound to do this often. But then you remain independent of them and they remain independent of you. Then they can just go on to call a minster. Should they get a new pastor then there is still much work to be done in our Master's vineyard."

Rev. Kuijt: "I am and will remain a Missionary"

Kuijt contemplates the well-intended advice of his friend and fellow minister. He sees the wisdom of this advice, but to retire with pension goes too far for him. He wishes to be reimbursed for his work only.

A final decision is made that Kuijt will assist in the Chilliwack congregation. He will preach on twenty-five Sundays per year, for which Chilliwack will pay him a stipend: meanwhile, the congregation will continue to look for a full-time minister. Two members of the MB, Rev. L. Blok and G. Nieuwenhuis discuss this with the Consistory of Chilliwack in October 1989. The missionary minister officially retires in 1991, but since he still has some furlough due, he leaves Irian-Jaya the year before.

268

Rev. and Mrs. Kuijt on one of their visits to New Zealand,
where he served the church and the school

After settling in Canada in 1990, Rev. Kuijt only serves the Chilliwack congregation for a few months. In the spring of 1991 Rev. H. Hofman of Sioux Center, Iowa, in the United States accepts the call to this congregation.

Following the arrival of Rev. Hofman, Kuijt still has enough work to do. He preaches regularly, especially in Lynden, a neighbouring congregation in Washington and becomes attached to the people and the people to him. Yet Kuijt does not feel totally satisfied. "There remains so much fallow ground."

Together with some members of the Chilliwack church he starts a prison ministry. "The Lord Jesus also concerned himself with the lot of the undesirables. Then His followers should not forget them either" is his philosophy. When at home, he continues to visit the inmates and motivates the NRC members to go on with this work while he is absent.

Thus there is always plenty of work. But deep within his heart he remains preoccupied with the needs in Asia, the continent where he worked for so many years. He keeps in touch with the work in Irian Jaya through letters, reports, and telephone calls. He rejoices that the work is being carried on.

In 1987 he visited the island of Bali for the first time, when the family traveled through Indonesia to celebrate their twenty-fifth wedding anniversary. The primary purpose of the trip was to enjoy the splendid beauty of nature and culture. Kuijt is aware of the extent to which the Balinese population practices Hinduism. The Balinese variant of Hinduism, *"Agama Hindu Bali"* is a blend of pre-Hindu, Buddhist, and Hindu elements. A large number of gods, deified ancestors, and demons are venerated. Temples are found everywhere. Every property has its own house temple. Everywhere Kuijt goes he sees people sacrificing to Hindu gods. Even the taxi driver has on his dashboard a small sacrifice. In every corner and yard is a small altar. While driving through the city, cars have to brake repeatedly since dogs feast on the offerings placed there in the morning. On the streets women walk with baskets full of gifts to offer up at one of the many temples.

After this initial trip to Bali, there follows a second trip in 1990. In 1992 he makes another trip to the island with some friends. A taxi driver puts them in touch with the pastors of the Christian churches of Bali.

"Gerrit, you really need a new suit. Now that we are in the Netherlands, we should take care of this," suggests Mrs. Kuijt to her husband in June of 1993. The missionary nods. Although buying clothes is not his hobby, it cannot always be avoided. "Why, do we not check out Mol's clothing store in the city of Krabbendijke," Mrs. Kuijt proposes. She agrees that it will be quite a drive from The Hague where they are staying. But through Mother Bos, Mr. Mol is a distant family member.

So they drive toward the Province of Zeeland. Along the way Mrs. Kuijt wonders whether it is not a bit foolish to go so far just to buy a black suit. "Gerrit, what are we actually doing?" she asks her husband. "Well, you did want to go to Krabbendijke, now we better keep going."

A suit is quickly bought. But it takes a long time before they drive back to The Hague. While in the store, they start a conversation with the owner, Ab Mol, a son of Rev. J. Mol, who also just retired, like Rev. Kuijt. Ab Mol, an elder in the church of Krabbendijke, recounts that as a young boy he thought to have received a promise from the Lord that one day he would do mission work with Rev. Kuijt. Of course, this is now no longer possible as Kuijt has retired and Mol operates a clothing store. Kuijt listens to Ab Mol's story with amazement. Has he just found the right man for the work in Bali? Throughout his life he has spoken frequently with people who express a desire to do mission work. Often it turned out to be nothing more than a morning mist or an early dew. But he feels that for this man the desire goes deeper.

Kuijt tells Mol of his longing to work in Bali and of the barriers he has encountered.

> *The MB sees no possibilities to take this on. I have some friends who are willing to support this work financially, but we need people who are willing to go to Bali. Personally I cannot settle permanently on the island. My health and my family situation prevent this.*

Rev. Kuijt with Bapa Enos , parents and family in Bali

The account of Rev. Kuijt touches Mol deeply. Would it then still be possible for him to work together with this veteran missionary? He asks Rev. Kuijt for advice. The latter suggests that he first asks the Lord whether it is indeed his purpose that he devotes himself to work on the Island of Bali.

> *You should never start a work if you do not know for sure that the Lord will go with you. It is not an adventure with an uncertain ending. You should only go if you have received the assignment*

directly from the Lord. Then the outcome is not in doubt and the end results will be to God's honor.

In the months that follow, Mol gains the conviction that he must take on a work in Bali together with Kuijt. He immerses himself in the study of the Indonesian language and culture. He also searches out organizations that are willing to support their work.

For many years Mol has kept in touch with J. Bor, director of SDOK (*Stichting de Ondergrondse Kerk*—The Foundation for the Underground Church). He visits him and talks about his desire to do work in Bali in combination with Kuijt. Carefully he asks whether SDOK would be in a position to give some support to this work. Mr. Bor and his board hesitate. They are set up as a support organization for churches and Christians suffering under communism. The kind of work that Kuijt and Mol would like to do is not part of the foundation's mandate. At the same time the people of SDOK cannot distance themselves from the need of which Mol speaks and the scope that exists in Bali for the proclamation of the Gospel.

Following extensive deliberation, SDOK decides to investigate the possibility of work in Bali. With this assignment Kuijt and Mol visit the island for two months in the fall of 1994. In a report on this orientation visit, Kuijt writes that ways opened miraculously.

> *The taxi driver Madé drove us again. He informed us about a house for rent in Sanur. We saw this house and concluded that it was very suitable as a home and office. On the same compound a second home is going to become available later on this year and a third is a little dwelling that could be used for storage, and, if necessary, as a guest suite. This is where we could establish a centre. We agreed that we would rent these homes.*

Rev. Kuijt and his traveling companion establish contact with representatives of a few Protestant churches with whom they could be affiliated. They are the *Gereja Protestan di Bali* and the *Gereja Kemah Injil Indonesia*. Also encouraging are the initial contacts with the local Baptist churches.

When the two have completed the analysis of the situation after six weeks, Director J. Bor along with two members of the SDOK Board arrive. They are soon convinced of the possibility for a project there. Their decision is made: SDOK will support their work

Representatives of the Balinese churches form a *yayasan*

(foundation). The purpose of this organization is: "To provide social and other needs for the inhabitants." It is not the intention to establish a new church. Anyone who is interested can join any of the existing churches.

The Board of the Yayasan appoints a local Pendeta as director. The board also appoints Rev. Kuijt to be supervisor and A. Mol as consultant.

Rev. Kuijt, J. Bor and J. Sommer having a meeting.

Laying the first stone for a church

By the end of November 1994, plans have been completed and premises rented. There is a foundation with a director; there are good connections with local churches; and financial support. With thankful hearts, Rev. Kuijt and brother Mol travel homeward. Mol hopes to move to Bali in the spring of 1995 and Kuijt and Miep want to move to Bali in November of that year. The agreement is that they will not join SDOK, but will be reimbursed for costs actually incurred.

Upon their return Mol arranges an information session in his home town. Rev. Kuijt shares his experiences with churches wherever he speaks in the United States and Canada.

But among the members of the NRC churches there arises some confusion—is this a new field? Others dispute this, because in that case SDOK would not be involved. In December this organization publishes its first issue of Bali news. News items in the media soon make it clear that the new work does not come under the auspices of the NRC but the SDOK. This does not mean that there is no support from NRC members. Rev. Kuijt has great credibility within the NRC churches and others.

Balinese co-workers planning a child sponsor program

However, the plan to move from Canada to Bali does not materialize. Both Rev. and Mrs. Kuijt realize that this would mean another upheaval in their family life. Two of their children, Klazina and Gert, now live in the Netherlands. If father and mother Kuijt would depart for Bali, they would have to leave the other three children behind in Canada. This is not an option! Chilliwack remains home for the family. Kuijt travels to Bali from time to time over the next four years. The first time he stays there for nearly half a year. This is too long. His wife urges him to make shorter trips, perhaps three to four months at a time. Several times she goes along with him, other times she stays home with their children.

In 1997 Rev. Kuijt tells his wife, "Miep, I am not feeling well, something is wrong with my lungs." He decides to visit the family doctor, who examines him and sends him on to get some x-rays taken. These show some scarring on his lungs. Kuijt wonders whether the doctor saw old scars from his earlier bouts with tuberculosis or is this something new. The minister has no pain in his lungs; however, he has severe pain in his back. On a daily basis he needs to take strong pain medication.

Rev. Kuijt giving a presentation

Rev. Kuijt carries on with his work. At the end of 1997, he makes another trip to visit his friends on Bali. This time he catches a severe cold, which he cannot get rid of. When his wife sees him upon his return, she is shocked about his appearance.

Again he visits the doctor, who sends him on to a specialist for his back problems. Could his health problems be related to his back? But this is not the case. Next he needs to see a lung specialist, who comes to the conclusion that Kuijt probably has lung fibrosis. With this relatively rare illness the lungs become scarred so that eventually they can no longer transfer oxygen to the blood vessels. The specialist tells his patient that there is little chance of recovery. There are several medications which can suppress the symptoms, but the problem will persist.

This news makes plans for the future rather uncertain. The following spring he and his wife visit Holland. There they ask a specialist for a second opinion. The latter gives the reassuring message that they are dealing with a dormant form of lung fibrosis. Somewhat relieved, they return to Canada, but it soon appears that the specialist was mistaken: the condition intensifies.

The Canadian specialist recommends a biopsy to identify whether it is indeed lung fibrosis or whether it relates to a tropical disease. Initially Rev. Kuijt is not keen to undergo this procedure. The lung specialist, however, says that it is necessary. "When they try to treat the fibrosis and the medicine does not work, they are again faced with the original question. What is it? Is it the medicine or is it a tropical disease?" The missionary agrees and in September 1998 the test confirms it is definitively not related to the tropics but lung fibrosis. By the end of 1998, Rev. Kuijt walks like an old man and shuffles step by step. He lacks the strength to adequately lift his feet. He now requires oxygen. What a difference! He can walk normally again.

When the minister begins the medications, it appears as though progress is made. He writes:

> *What joy fills our hearts! I thank the Lord from the bottom of my heart that the medications work. I may belong to the very small group of people who obtain good results.*

But his joy does not last long.

Rev. Kuijt has friends all over the world. In Calgary, Alberta where the minister spends three Sundays each year, good relationships have been formed, on a personal and spiritual level. Coby Heikoop, granddaughter of Rev. M. Heikoop, cannot passively observe Rev. Kuijt's decline in health. His illness is progressing along with increased suffering from intense pain in his back. The oxygen dosage needs to be increased until the highest setting possible is reached. Then he is given one hundred percent pure oxygen from a tank.

Deep wrinkles form in the minister's face and he walks with a more pronounced stoop and rapidly ages. Coby has a friend, Dr. H. Sawada, who is a physiotherapist and has also studied medicine. This man is known for his many capabilities. Coby is anxious for Rev. Kuijt to be treated by him. The therapist, however, does not expect to be able to do anything for the patient. But Coby persists and the therapist promises to stop in at the Kuijt's home when passing through Chilliwack. The examination that he performs, confirms his earlier prognosis. No, he will not be able to ease this lung condition, but he can try to relieve the back pains. The minister will have to come to Calgary for treatment. Mrs. Kuijt does not believe this is feasible, because it would be an all-day drive, for the largest part through the Rocky Mountains, and throughout the journey she would have to drive while monitoring her husband's oxygen level. But the Lord provides a way out.

Friends Arie and Jeanette Drogendijk offer to drive them to Calgary and back to Chilliwack after the treatments. Within their own family they have seen what it means when someone's lungs deteriorate. During their time spent together, Rev. Kuijt would sometimes ask questions. "What will the future be like?" "How, will this illness progress?" The answers are given carefully, tactfully, but also always honestly. Humanly speaking, the final stretch of his life's journey will become increasingly difficult.

To Kuijt's utter amazement, after ten intense treatments by the physiotherapist, he can leave the painkillers untouched on his bedside table. He barely needs them anymore. The pain would never return as intensively as before. With deep gratitude they return to Chilliwack.

To make his life a bit more manageable, a long tube is connected to his oxygen tank giving him more mobility in his home. "Fortunately, I am not shackled to a chair or a bed," he optimistically tells one of his friends.

He is not a person to sit in despair. In the initial phase of his illness he is quite convinced that if he keeps exercising, he will remain relatively healthy. To maintain his lung capacity, he goes for walks. He asks his wife to follow him by car, so she can take him home in case he cannot make it. With amazement and concern Mrs. Kuijt follows him with his car on that first walk. Her husband walks one, two, three kilometres. But Kuijt does not stop. A little further! Then he is exhausted. Totally out of breath he falls down on the seat beside his wife in the car. "This cannot be good Gerrit." she says. As quickly as possible the portable oxygen is reconnected.

The walks soon come to an end. He has to take a step back. Yet he wants to remain mobile as long as possible. He is advised to participate in a rehabilitation program. Even though he knows that the exercises ultimately cannot help him, he is encouraged to keep coming. The interaction with other patients motivates him and he enjoys being out of the house.

The wedding of their daughter Cornelia takes place in December 1998. How great it would be if her father could still officiate. But his condition does not allow this. From the beginning of November he is on pure oxygen. Until the last moment it remains doubtful that he will even be able to attend the service. But the ailing minister is also keen to conduct his daughter's wedding ceremony. He begs the Lord for strength. But will it be possible?

When the day of the wedding arrives, it is questionable whether her father will even be able to escort his daughter down the aisle of the church. At 12:00 noon, he leans on the bathroom vanity. "It will not work, Miep. It really will not work. I can't do it."

Photos of the couple and families are taken and father Kuijt then is required to rest. At three o'clock, he walks down the aisle with his daughter on his arm without any oxygen. It is not a long service and the Lord sustains His ailing servant. Rev. Kuijt is able to perform the marriage of his beloved "Oeneke" to Nico Kattenberg.

It is the end of 1999 when Len van Wingerdan and his family return to the U.S.A. For many years this young man from Lynden, Washington, served on the mission field. He was a helicopter pilot and made numerous flights for the NRC mission. But his life took an abrupt turn when specialists in Jakarta discovered a tumour in his brain. Surgery in the U.S. was only partly successful and Len spiraled into a coma. Lovingly he was cared for during the final months of his life in Lynden. He passed away on June 1, 2000. Who would have thought that the young MAF pilot Len van Wingerden would pass away before Rev. Kuijt.

Rev. Kuijt can hardly believe it. He knew the young man so well and regularly visited with his parents in Lynden. What a shock for his wife Jany, for their small children, for Len's parents and his family.

Rev. Kuijt is keen to attend the funeral but his health does not permit it. When he speaks with father van Wingerden by telephone, the latter suggests that Rev. Kuijt attends the condolences. If he arrives early, it will not yet be busy. Just before the end of the condolences Rev. Kuijt arrives and is brought into the room in a wheel chair. He lacks the strength to walk on his own. When the condolences have been concluded with Scripture reading and prayer, everyone remains seated. Father Van Wingerden asks Rev. Kuijt to say a few words. The minister indicates that he has the desire but is not sure if he has the ability to do so. Then he gets up out of the wheelchair and speaks heartfelt words to the bereaved family. It is not a long speech, but very emotional. To everyone's amazement, he then walks behind his wheelchair to the door.

Rev. Kuijt keeps driving as long as possible even though he is on oxygen. When he has to retake his driver's test, his daughter, Klazina, accompanies him. Miep was not certain he would make it, but Rev. Kuijt passes the test with flying colors.

Even though he passed his driving test, Rev. Kuijt gradually has to give up many of his everyday activities. His wife notices that it costs him too much exertion to dress himself. "Will I help you," she offers. "Absolutely not," Rev. Kuijt responds. Yet Mrs. Kuijt persuades him. "Gerrit, let me help you. Then you can use the energy for something else."

Dr. N. Hilliard, the family doctor, provides whatever assistance he can. But he sees his patient deteriorate and can do nothing to change the situation.

Rev. Kuijt does not complain about his illness. He does not easily convey his inner feelings during this time of trial. On one occasion, he says to Rev. P. Van Ruitenburg: "At times you would just like to cast it off." Van Ruitenburg looks at him questioningly, "What do you mean?" "Well, this illness," replies Kuijt.

Some people have the idea that Rev. Kuijt refuses to acknowledge the seriousness of the situation. But Miep knows better: he definitely realizes the severity of his illness. For example, one time he rather abruptly says, "Miep, if I were you, I would stay in this house." But Rev. Kuijt does not like to talk a great deal about his illness. Miep knows that he does not want to be forced to speak about it. Her husband needs all the courage he has to survive each day.

When he has visitors he is interested in all kinds of subjects. "To talk about my illness does not help," is Rev. Kuijt's motto. On the other hand he does not keep it a secret either and is very much aware of his condition. With his wife and a few intimate friends he speaks from time to time about the approaching end. Precisely during the final phase of his life, Rev. Kuijt learns—anew—what it means to be a poor sinner. "Soon I will stand before the Lord with empty hands", he says. "Then I really cannot say: Lord, I have opened so many stations, built so many landing strips, and planted so many churches." He realizes that death is the king of terror. But there are also times that he may look forward to the day when he will see his Saviour and be with Him for eternity.

Last portrait of the Kuijt family

In mid-August 2000, Rev. Kuijt is admitted to the hospital. His condition deteriorates. The end is approaching. On Saturday evening, August 19th, Rev. Kuijt receives a visit from a fellow pastor and the latter tells him and the family who are there that the end is near. The missionary turns to his wife and says: "Well, you heard it." After the pastor leaves, Mrs. Kuijt asks carefully: "Gerrit, what should it say on your tombstone?"

"Missionary," answers Rev. Kuijt unequivocally. "Yes, but you are also a minister," she replies. *"Okay, verkondiger van het Heilige Woord.* (proclaimer of the holy Word)," her husband answers in Dutch. Miep wonders how to describe this in English. She decides for herself it will be "Missionary-Minister to Irian Jaya."

The hour of death approaches faster than anyone has expected. Not all of the children are present. Klazina has to come from Uganda and cannot get a flight. For Gert it is also impossible to be there in time. This does not prevent father Kuijt from having a personal word for each of his children. Wim also receives a personal promise. These are emotional moments. Miep, son Wim, daughters Wilhelmina and Oeneke, and Wilhelmina's husband Doug, sing hymns at his bedside.

On the Lord's Day, Sunday, the 20th of August, 2000, Gerrit Kuijt—Missionary Minister—breathes his last breath here on Earth. He has won the battle and does not need to continue on. On Earth he dare not rest; this inner urge to carry on is now silent.

Rest remains for God's people.

Chapter 17

Rest for the People of God . . .

On Saturday, August 26, 2000, in the sanctuary of the Bethel Netherlands Reformed Congregation, members from Chilliwack, Lynden and others gather to mourn and pay their last respects to Rev. G. Kuijt. The funeral service for him is held prior to the internment.

Missionary Minister

In the front pews are his wife Miep Kuijt, Klazina and Gert Pap from Uganda, Willem from Alberta, Gerrit and Christel and baby son Willem from Belgium, Wilhelmina and Doug Luteyn and son Bradley from Chilliwack, and Cornelia and Nico Kattenberg from Guatemala.

People from abroad are also present. Nurse Marry van Moolenbroek traveled from Irian Jaya. For years she enjoyed close ties with the Kuijt family. She is one of the few with whom the missionary could share his heart. Mrs. Kuijt hoped that Marry would bring along Sabonwarek. To everyone's regret—not the least of the GJPI—these mission churches are not represented. The GJPI sends a written condolence in which they convey that it will be difficult to forget the name of Rev. Kuijt.

Those who mention Gerrit Kuijt also mean the GJPI and those who mention the GJPI, also mean Gerrit Kuijt. With love we remember the efforts of Gerrit Kuijt. When we heard the announcement of his passing, we indeed felt deep sorrow due to the loss of our spiritual father. Oh, father! We wish that we could see your earthly body. We would love to linger for a moment beside you! How we would have loved to have carried your remains to its final resting place! However, it is so sad and cannot be fulfilled. We can only, by means of this letter, declare that all of us, as members of the GJPI, express our very deep sorrow over the death of our beloved father, Gerrit Kuijt. May the Lord God receive him at His side after all he has done with devotion during his life here on earth. For the family that he leaves behind, his wife and children, we pray to the Lord that his Spirit may comfort them and provide them the power and perseverance of faith throughout the remainder of their lives.

Finally, Gerrit Kuijt, farewell; appear without terror before the Creator. One more thing which is for sure; we will meet again in the New Jerusalem.

Amen.

Present are Rev. H. Paul and A. Elshout who represent the MB in the Netherlands; and elder Nico Bertram who represents the NRC church of Carterton. This church was instituted by Rev. Kuijt and he served in it on several occasions. On behalf of the Bos family, brother Kees has come from the Netherlands.

The funeral service is officiated by the local pastor, Rev. Van Ruitenburg. He begins by reading the death announcement which quotes Romans 15:20: "Yea, so I have strived to preach the Gospel, not where Christ was named lest I should build upon another man's foundation." After reading Hebrews 4:4-16, Rev. Van Ruitenburg calls attention to verse 9: "There remaineth therefore a rest to the people of God." The minister points out that this passage focuses on various types of rest:

"God rested from his work after the creation. Every Sunday speaks of this rest. Christ rested, once He had completed his work on earth. But also God's children enter into this rest. We can say that now our brother is resting from all his labour.

"This well-known chapter, however, also tells us that we must seek to enter into that rest. Those who do not strive to enter, who do not labour spiritually, will never find this heavenly rest. Here below we are called to fight the good fight of faith. God's Church on Earth is a Church militant and fights a holy war, without which there can be no victory. The life of the Church consists of the fight against sin, unbelief, Satan and the evil world. But in God's time there will be rest for His Church.

"Brother Kuijt received the privilege and the grace to labour faithfully for many years. In his many labours we see also something of the work and the strife of God's Church on Earth," says Rev. Van Ruitenburg. He goes on to highlight a number of aspects of Rev. Kuijt's work.

"Traveler: Rev. Kuijt traveled a great deal in his lifetime: on foot, by car, by train, by plane. He traveled to new areas. He continually met new people and preached in many different places. He was frequently en route, just as God's Church on Earth is also spiritually en route. Together with the saints in heaven, he may now completely rest in God and Christ. There remains therefore, a rest for the people of God!

"Speaker: In his lifetime, Rev. Kuijt spoke with people of many diverse backgrounds. He was continually looking out for those who had not yet been reached by the Gospel. It was the desire of his heart to proclaim God's Name, because He is so worthy to be praised. He was blessed with the ability to quickly understand new languages, customs, and cultures. Our brother may now rest from his missionary labors and eternally and tirelessly speak in favour of his King. In the meantime the work on earth is carried on. The great Missionary, the Lord Jesus Christ, has not yet finished this assignment. The same Lord God also speaks to us in this funeral service.

"Builder: Our brother was a pioneer-missionary. He was an experienced builder. He built homes, churches, small schools, and so forth. But he also was a builder in the spiritual sense, and now he may rest in a house not built with hands, but in dwellings prepared for him and all of God's Church. He has entered into the eternal Sabbath rest.

"He prayed: Rev. Kuijt was a man of prayer. He prayed for his wife, children, and grandchildren, for me and my ministry here in Chilliwack and also for the pastors and people in Papua. He prayed for his fellow mission workers and mission work around the world. Now he also rests from this labour. Now he prays no more. Yet his prayers remain before God's throne of grace and the Lord hears the prayer of the righteous. In addition: the great High Priest continues to pray. The Lord Jesus Christ prays at the right hand of His Father and through Him the work will thankfully continue.

"Singer: Our brother loved music. Due to his declining health, singing became increasingly difficult for him. Now he no longer needs to strain to sing along or to persuade others to sing a psalm. Now he can sing again to his heart's content, sing with beauty, sing with perfection. As part of the Church in heaven, he may now open his mouth to God's honour, and in this way proclaim the praise of the Lord tenderly and devoutly. No note will be out of tune.

"Husband: Rev. Kuijt was wholly united with his beloved wife. His interaction with her reflected both respect and care. Now together with the triumphant Church, he may rejoice in the wedding of the Lamb. He may find fulfilment in God. Now he may taste perfect communion with the Triune God. Mrs. Kuijt, may the Lord grant you vigour and strength, and fulfill all your needs as a Husband of widows. Your husband has entered his rest and we continue to battle.

"Father: Brother Kuijt greatly loved his children and did a great deal to show this. He discussed with me his shortcomings in this regard; shortcomings felt by every parent. He bore the burden of the souls of his children. He may now rest from this labour and experience total peace in the presence of the perfect Father. His prayers for you, children and grandchildren, remain before God's throne.

Children, your father is no longer with us; but the God of your father continues to be here. May He extend His Fatherly care over you.

"Griever: Our brother also knew times of discouragement. He experienced trials and temptations, including when physical weakness hindered him. He may now rest from all these cares. He can now freely breathe again in heaven. He is no longer short of oxygen. He is now free from sin, free from impediments, free from imperfections, indeed, free from a sinful self. He now has perfect rest in God.

"There remains a rest for the people of God. The text does not speak of a rest for ministers, missionaries or office bearers, but only for the people of God. Our brother knew this very well. He also knew that his missionary work was no ground for salvation. We must come to God as sinners who seek salvation in Jesus Christ. There is a rest for the people of God only because of the work of Jesus Christ.

"Today we may thank the Lord for what he gave us in brother Kuijt. The Lord granted him special love and zeal for gentiles. He was specially endowed and equipped by the Lord for his work as a missionary. May the seed sown by him as a father, pastor, missionary, and friend be richly blessed by the Lord and bear much fruit in his family, the various tribes he worked among and in our congregations of Chilliwack, Lynden and other churches where he brought the message, and to anyone he spoke with.

"Now our friend may experience what true joy is. It is beholding God, drinking from the fountain of His salvation, and being satisfied with His image. May I encourage all of you to seek this true joy. May the Lord richly bless Rev. Kuijt's labours to the honour of his glorious Name and the coming of His Kingdom."

Rev. Van Ruitenburg closes the service with thanksgiving. Then Rev. H. Paul, the former secretary of the MB for West-Irian, speaks a few words to the family and all those present. As he addresses everyone in Dutch, the mission administrator, Mr. A. Elshout, translates his words into English. On behalf of the congregations in the Netherlands, fellow pastors, and especially the MB, he conveys their sympathy and their heartfelt condolences in the great sorrow and the loss that has struck the Kuijt family.

"Rev. Kuijt had a special place in our congregations. To many he was 'The Missionary.' He was a cordial brother and a warm friend. He steadfastly considered the mission field as the place that the Lord had specially assigned to him. The Lord called him to this work when he was still quite young. Through trials, the Lord fulfilled his promises to him. He did this in ways that made us admire the work of the Lord. What a miracle it is that the Lord calls people and not angels to proclaim His Word. His Gospel must be proclaimed throughout the world. The entire world must hear of God's wonders in Christ for lost sinners. For this reason the Lord called your husband and father and endowed him so excellently for his task. On the one hand knowing the terror of the Lord and on the other hand being persuaded by the love of Christ, he could do nothing but proclaim the Name of Christ to others. He loved both his fellow creatures and his Master. For this reason he sought to win souls for the Lord.

"Your husband and father was instrumental with the Lord's blessing in the commencement of our mission work. His visits to the congregations in the Netherlands contributed in an important way to the nurturing of love for mission work. This love was also expressed in growing involvement and increasing generosity. Fortunately, others subsequently followed in his footsteps and could be sent out to the mission field. In this way the work could be continued and extended.

"Dear family, we hope that you may retain more than you have lost. With the God of your husband and your father, you can carry on. With Him you can go through this life and also pass from this life into eternity. I have personally witnessed that the work of your husband and father in Irian Jaya has been richly blessed. I was privileged to be present at the occasion of the ordination of the first gembalas. At that occasion I could speak on Zechariah 4:6; "Not by might, nor by power, but by my spirit, saith the Lord of hosts." May these words also comfort us today. The Lord and his Word remain to all eternity. With gratitude we may commemorate all that the Lord gave us in your husband and father. We may comfort ourselves in the knowledge that all his work has not been in vain in the Lord."

Looking for that blessed hope and glorious appearing
of the great God and our Saviour Jesus Christ (Titus 2:13)

The trip to the cemetery followed. A few months before his death, Rev. Kuijt and his wife together selected the place where he is now laid to rest. His grave is situated on a hill that forms part of the Coastal Mountains, a place that is reminiscent of the mountains of Irian Jaya.

At the cemetery, Rev. Van Ruitenburg reads the first eight verses of Revelation 19. He points out to those who are gathered at the grave site that it is the work of the saints in heaven to glorify God:

"This is now the wonderful work of our beloved brother. Let us be glad and rejoice, and give honour to Him; for the marriage of the Lamb is come. This now is the rich inheritance of our brother.

"Let us follow the example of our brother, Kuijt. When at the conclusion of the funeral service I was standing in the hallway of the church and saw all of you pass by, I was thinking of how many people are connected with brother Kuijt. Across the entire world there are people with whom he had ties and who loved him. He was an open, honest, and congenial man. His labour has been a blessing for many.

"Today we mourn, but we are also glad. It is a sad day, but it is also a day of hope and gladness. Rev. Kuijt has received the desire of his heart to be with his Lord forever. It was his desire that all of you would love and follow the Master too.

"Mrs. Kuijt, you have lost a beloved husband and friend. This is a difficult path for you. I hope and pray that you may find strength and comfort in the Lord and in his Word. May you also be a part of the heavenly Bride who is adorned for her heavenly Bridegroom!

"Children, your dad loved you so dearly. Perhaps he did not always express this in as many words as he wanted. But he prayed a great deal for you. It is my heartfelt desire that you may find comfort in the Lord. Indeed, I hope that you will find not only comfort, but the Lord Himself."

Next Elder N. Bertram spoke on behalf of the congregation of Carterton, New Zealand. He recalls the contributions that Rev. Kuijt made in establishing this congregation.

"Also in New Zealand the work of Rev. Kuijt was blessed. Today we say farewell to a King's Son. In Daniel 12:3 we read, 'And they that are wise shall shine as the brightness of the firmament; and they that turn many to righteousness as the stars forever and ever.' Rev. Kuijt had a childlike faith and trust in his God. When there were concerns, he always kept his eye on the Lord, who could resolve all problems. Mrs. Kuijt and family—May the Lord bless you and look after you."

Finally, Wim Kuijt speaks on behalf of the family. He thanks everyone who is present. He thanks those who stood by Dad so faithfully during his illness, especially Rev. van Ruitenburg, who visited his father regularly.

He concludes by saying, "Above all, thanks are due to the Lord for His Fatherly care. How would we have managed without His help?"

Reflections on our Father

Klazina Kuijt-Pap, Papua, Indonesia

Papua has changed a lot since we were children living in the jungles of New Guinea. In most places, life isn't as primitive. Roads make getting supplies easier; cell phones and the internet make communication possible. But along with these conveniences, come negative influences. Fifty years ago, the Papuans had a strict moral code which is now being eroded by the influences of modern society.

But missionaries like my parents brought the people of Papua the *Good News* about Jesus, the One who delivered them from the evil spirits that haunted them and from their bondage to sin and so there is hope.

I have always been proud of the work my parents did, even though it came at a high cost. My mom taught me through her actions to persevere, in spite of great difficulties. My dad taught me that obeying God and being sensitive to His will was more important than pleasing people.

People often misinterpreted his persistence and single mindedness with being obstinate or disrespectful, but he was neither. He just had an incredible burden and *urgency* to pass on the Good News of salvation through Jesus Christ to other lost souls. When he felt he had been unjustly accused, he did not defend himself; he would just calmly say, "I don't have to fight this. God will fight for me."

My dad truly sacrificed all because Christ sacrificed all for him, to the point of dying on the cross (Romans 5:6-8). Because of my dad's love for God and his complete devotion to following Him, my dad was able to sacrifice time spent with his family, his health and, ultimately, his life.

This *chapter* in my Dad's life is over and he is now rejoicing with the saints in Heaven. But the *book* isn't finished. There is still work to be done—in Papua and all over the world!

My prayer is that "God will use this book to inspire many to go out and obey the great commission."

May God's name be glorified through the life my dad lived!

Willem Kuijt, Alberta Canada

My dad was human like everyone else, but when I reflect on his life and dedication to the Lord, I think of Paul. At the end of my Dad's life, short of breath, and barely able to walk, my dad was still bearing witness of the Lord.

Being on the mission field put us in plenty of situations that were less than ideal. We went to boarding school, lived among cannibals, and even ran for our lives in Nipsan. We all know God's plan through His Son Jesus Christ. If we ask ourselves "is it right (from a human point of view) that He was tortured and put to death?" we have to say "no" as He was innocent, without sin, yet He still bore the cross so we can be saved.

When I think of the connection that I have with my children, I can't imagine what God felt like to see His Son suffer. So looking back and remembering the hard times, I realize that it was a small price to pay for the furtherance of the Gospel and that Stone-age people will now be in heaven because of God's leading hand in sending my parents to the mission field.

Gert Kuijt, Belgium

What I remember most about my father is that he was a fun person to be with. When reading to us as small children it was easy to get caught up in his telling of the story. If it was a funny story, it was fun to get swept along with his laughter. These memories still bring a smile to my face!

He was also a source of stability in times of trouble. When we were young and we kids all came home from school infected with hepatitis, he sought diversion by daily teaching us how to play chess. He taught us so well in fact, that after a time he was no longer able to win, which took some getting used to. But he was also stable when trouble loomed in the form of personal danger. He always remained calm and collected, giving rest and peace to those around him.

Near the end of his life, when disease no longer allowed him to travel, I have fond memories of many long talks over brunch at Clark's in

Chilliwack, B.C. By the time we were ready to leave, we had pretty much tried everything that was on the menu and had discussed many of the great themes of life.

There is a time for coming and a time for going, as in all things under heaven. Apparently it was my father's time to go. For us that is too bad, for he is sorely missed.

Wilhelmina Lutyen, BC, Canada

"How then shall they call on Him in whom they have not believed? And how shall they believe in Him of whom they have not heard? And how shall they hear without a preacher?" (Romans 10:14)

My parents were an example of true pioneer missionaries, who followed the call of Christ to bring the Gospel to the unreached tribes of Papua. They trekked into unknown territories, where no white man had ever been, to a people living in complete darkness, and brought them a message of hope and deliverance. These people were hostile, Stone-aged cannibals, but now they know the glorious news of the Gospel. It was a privilege to be a witness of such a transformation.

My dad was a true example of love for Christ and love for the lost sinner. He received extraordinary courage during times of great danger and showed us perseverance during the times of hardship and loneliness. He was a testimony of boldness for the Gospel of Christ and he was filled with an unashamed devotion to Christ. He carried with him a burden to see the lost saved and always reminded us that our mission field was wherever God placed us, not just the jungles of Papua.

Thank you, dad, for teaching us through your example.

Love you always.

Lia Kattenberg, Guatemala

"Looking for the blessed hope and glorious appearing of our great God and Savior Jesus Christ." (Titus 2:13)

Growing up with missionary parents among the cannibals in Papua gives me the most interesting stories to tell. Sometimes I feel like I'm making it all up it as it sounds so unreal to the average person. My parents did EXTREME mission work: trekking into unknown, hostile territories to Stone-age people who had never seen white people before, let alone heard about God. For us kids these people were normal, life there was our reality. But looking back, it was clearly the love of God that sent my dad and mom there to proclaim the Good News, to pierce the darkness with the marvelous light. These people were steeped in evil traditions and were in bondage to the forces of darkness but now "they have defeated the accuser by the blood of the Lamb and by their testimony." (Rev.12:11)

Being a missionary myself now, I often pray that God would give me just a little bit of what Dad had for other people: a burning desire to see them saved, an eagerness to share the hope that lies within us.

Dad finished the race and he ran well, "Those who lead many to righteousness will shine like the stars forever." (Daniel 12:3) Dad lived out his faith, leaving us a rich legacy to follow so "Let us hold fast the profession of our faith without wavering for He is faithful that promised." (Hebrews 10:23)

I love you Dad.

Reflections on our Mother

The stories in this book would not have had the same ending and our lives would not have been as blessed without the loving heart and caring nature of our mother, Miep Kuijt-Bos. On behalf of my three siblings, Klazina, Wim, and Gert, we write this—a tribute to our mother.

Our mother has always been an inspiration to us.

Who would leave the comforts of home to live in a far-away land for a calling not even her own? Our mother did. She followed her Lord by following her husband, which she DID feel was her calling.

The work of a missionary's wife often goes unnoticed and unacknowledged, but our dad was well aware of the sacrifices she had made. The day before he died, my dad said goodbye to all of us but the first person he addressed in his goodbyes was our mother, his wife, 'Miep, my faithful companion ...' There was a HIGH price to pay in being a faithful companion.

Our mother missed the loving extended family she grew up in. She was absent for her two brothers' weddings, her parent's 40th wedding anniversary celebration, and all the birthdays and celebrations and family gatherings in between. Thankfully she was called home shortly before her father died. They shared a very strong bond; living half-way around the world, she did miss him and his wise counsel.

She also missed big chunks of her childrens' lives. In order for us to receive an education, we had to go to boarding school. We know the goodbyes at the beginning of each school semester left a gaping hole in her heart. She thought she hid it from us but to this day, I can still see and feel the emotion well up in her as she kissed us goodbye. She would not see the younger children for three months or more, the older children for at least six months—far too long for a mother to be away from her children.

Naturally we are all now living all over the world—Klazina in

Indonesia, Wim in Alberta, Gert in Belgium, Lia in Guatemala—and only Wilhelmina lives close by. We are all grown up and have our own children. Yet still, when we have to say goodbye, it brings back many sad memories for mom. We think we can safely say that she hates goodbyes!!

Mom, the day will come when we won't ever have to say goodbye again, there will be no more separation, no more tears and no more sorrows. We look forward to that day, but for NOW, we are so blessed to have you. We love you and admire you. Your creator God, your Maker is now your husband. We wait with anticipation to see where He will lead you next.

Lia Kattenberg and Wilhelmina Luteyn for all of us kids.

And How Are They Now?

The following notes are taken from the February 2012 issue of *Pap's Post*, a newsletter that was produced by Klasina, who now lives in Papua with her husband, Gerrit, and their five children, Benjamin, Sarah-Anne, Josiah, Jonathan and Matthias.

"But we have this treasure in earthen vessels, that the excellence of the power may be of God and not of us. We are hard pressed on every side, yet not crushed; we are perplexed, but not in despair; persecuted, but not forsaken, struck down, but not destroyed – always carrying about in the body the dying of the Lord Jesus, that the life of Jesus also may be manifested in our body."
(2 Corinthians 4:7-10)

THANK YOU to those who faithfully pray for us. Again, I cannot tell you how much that means to us, knowing that God has not forsaken us and that He brings us to your minds!

After very stressful days leading up to Christmas, our family spent a week in Abenago, the valley I grew up in, and we all had a very good time; even the kids! (I wasn't sure how they'd react to people in the interior: yet another new experience for them!)

Christmas in Pass Valley

Before the semester ended, the dorm closed. Because of this I flew out to Sentani to look after Sarah-anne and Jonathan. The youngest 3 were in Gerrit and Rose's capable hands. (Rose is the wife of Dennis, the other MAF pilot.) The kids love her so they didn't mind that Mom wasn't with them. It felt very strange to be split into 2 family units! There was a wonderful new MAF couple that offered to take our oldest 2 into their home. I helped get them settled and flew home, in time to get ready for our trip interior. The family was united once again Dec 23rd in Wamena, from where we flew to Abenaho, or Pass Valley in pilot-terms. I'll let the pictures speak for themselves. All I can say is that it was an amazing experience, one the kids will also not forget. As a matter of fact, they want to go back for another visit!

Emotional Reunion with Pastor Thomas

This man hid behind a waterfall to avoid being killed for the sake of the Gospel until night time, before fleeing for his life.

These precious men and women know what it means to suffer for the sake of the Gospel. Most of them helped my parents bring the Gospel to new areas, after they themselves believed and were saved. They HAD to share the Good News to other tribes! But in the process, they experienced tragedies that most of us know nothing about; massacres where their loved ones were killed and eaten by cannibals.

This lady was left for dead after being shot by 5 arrows for the sake of the Gospel. She was covered with grass to be picked up later and cooked, but she wasn't dead. She survived by hiding in the jungle 1 week until an MAF plane came to survey the area. Her husband, however, didn't make it.

Sabonwarek, in the middle, was my father's right hand helper. He was an orphan when my parents first came and he adopted them as his parents! He followed my dad wherever he went. Jan, the man next to me was a carpenter. He helped my mom build the houses we lived in. His son, far left, studied in Bandung and Jakarta and now has a masters degree in Theology; a wonderful leader and mentor for his tribe!

How does this relate to MAF?

I hope the pictures give you an idea of what our Christmas was like. You may be wondering what this has to do with MAF. Well, without MAF, these people would still be living in Darkness spiritually, because without MAF, my parents couldn't have gone into this remote area where no white man had ever trod. Pastor Thomas (front page and 2nd left on the next page) is praying that our family will one day come back to live in Pass Valley. He says that because of his prayers we have moved from Uganda to Papua. It's easy for God to bring us even closer, back to the valley where I was born!

Acknowledgements

First of all a word of thanks to:

Mr. A Bel, who represents the publishing company, *Den Hertog*, kindly provided the photos from the original book and gave permission for the English version.

W. B. Kranendonk and A.F. van Toor who wrote the original book, *Al 't heidendom zijn lof getuigen*, and who also gave their permission for this second edition.

My thanks as well to the following people who assisted with the book:

Gerrit Bilkes: translation

Rev. L. W. Bilkes: translation

Judy den Hertog: translation

Coby Heikoop: translation

Elizabeth Collins Oman: Editor (who went the extra mile to help us!)

Ron Steffin: slides to pictures

Martinus McEachern: assisted where necessary

Leigh Greyn: assisted where necessary

Special thanks to Coby Heikoop for her much needed, and much appreciated, encouragement and support.

Also, thanks to Pastor Michael Pickett for his help in getting this book published.

There are, as always, many others who contributed with their acts of kindness, their prayers, and their support over the years. I am in gratitude to you all.

To the people of Papua, part of Indonesia, who changed my families and my Life forever—Thank You.

Above all I thank the Lord for His many mercies. "How could we have managed without His help!"

Miep Kuijt-Bos